NEW YORK

OFF THE BEATEN PATH®

OFF THE BEATEN PATH® SERIES

TENTH EDITION

NEW YORK

OFF THE BEATEN PATH®

DISCOVER YOUR FUN

REVISED AND UPDATED
BY RANDI MINETOR

Globe
Pequot
Guilford, Connecticut

All the information in this guidebook is subject to change. We recommend that you call ahead to obtain current information before traveling.

Globe Pequot

An imprint of The Rowman & Littlefield Publishing Group, Inc.
4501 Forbes Blvd., Ste. 200
Lanham, MD 20706
www.rowman.com

Distributed by NATIONAL BOOK NETWORK

British Library Cataloguing in Publication Information available

Library of Congress Cataloging-in-Publication Data available

ISBN 978-1-4930-5357-5 (paper : alk. paper)
ISBN 978-1-4930-5358-2 (electronic)

∞™ The paper used in this publication meets the minimum requirements of American National Standard for Information Sciences—Permanence of Paper for Printed Library Materials, ANSI/NISO Z39.48-1992.

Contents

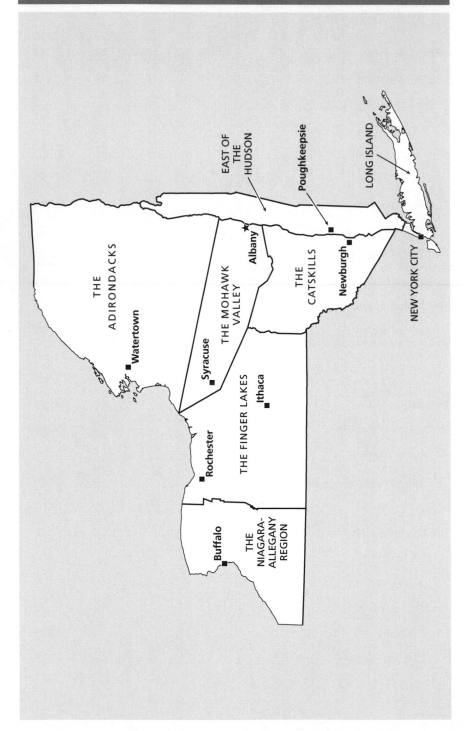

THE ADIRONDACKS

Watertown

THE MOHAWK VALLEY

Syracuse

Albany

EAST OF THE HUDSON

THE CATSKILLS

Poughkeepsie

Newburgh

LONG ISLAND

NEW YORK CITY

THE FINGER LAKES

Ithaca

Rochester

THE NIAGARA-ALLEGANY REGION

Buffalo

About the Author

A lifelong Rochester resident, Randi Minetor has written more than a dozen books about hiking, driving, and exploring New York State, including the best-selling first and second editions of *Hiking Waterfalls in New York* in collaboration with her husband, photographer Nic Minetor. Together, the Minetors created the books *Hiking through History New York*, *Scenic Driving New York*, *Hiking the Lower Hudson River Valley*, and five *Best Easy Day Hikes* books on Rochester, Buffalo, Syracuse, Albany, and the Hudson Valley. They also collaborated on two editions of *The New York Immigrant Experience* in the Historical Tours series. Randi writes extensively about America's national parks, birding, and other nature topics, and she is delighted to have the opportunity to update, revise, and refresh *New York Off the Beaten Path*.

Introduction

"New York, New York, it's a wonderful town," wrote Betty Comden and Adolph Green in 1944 for the musical *On the Town*, and while the lyric spoke specifically of New York City, the state easily became subsumed with the nation's largest metropolis. We who live anywhere in the state find ourselves explaining that our home involves much more than crowded streets and skyscrapers. As grand and exciting as is the city that never sleeps (another famous lyric), beyond Times Square and Fifth Avenue, a cornucopia of fascinating sites awaits any traveler willing to go farther than its boundaries.

Inhabited first by Native Americans, many of them of the Six Nations of the Iroquois Confederacy, the territory that became New York State began with Dutch settlers in the 1600s, moved to the British before the century ended, and then became one of the focal points of the Revolutionary War. With the war behind it, New York's economic and agricultural expansion accelerated with innovations including the Erie Canal, a number of short-run railroads, and distribution to the west of its many natural resources, from lumber to garnets. Captains of industry found their fortunes here, inventors changed the way people lived and worked, and millions of immigrants arrived and spread throughout the state, building its canals, dams, roads, and bridges, farming its vast acreage of fertile soils, and creating more cities along its rivers and lakes.

The state, however, provides value beyond its many industries and crops. Nothing rivals the Adirondack Mountains when they burst into vibrant shades of crimson, yellow, and orange in fall, or the sparkle of the Finger Lakes under the summer sun. New York's wine country produces vintages that take top prizes in national and global competition, with Long Island's North Shore and the Finger Lakes region capturing the highest praise. The stunning scenery in the Catskill Mountains and the Hudson River Valley inspired a uniquely American

NEW YORK REGIONAL TRAVEL INFORMATION

New York State Office of Parks, Recreation, and Historic Preservation
(518) 474–0456
parks.ny.gov

Empire Pass, a one-time annual charge, allows unlimited vehicle entrance to all state parks: parks.ny.gov/admission/empire-passport/.

New York State Division of Tourism
(800) CALL–NYS
(outside United States: 518–474–4116)
iloveny.com

artistic style known as the Hudson River School, painting landscapes that lucky tourists can continue to visit today. Writers including James Fenimore Cooper, Washington Irving, and Edna St. Vincent Millay found their muse among the hills and forests of upstate New York, and Gustav Stickley and Elbert Hubbard created a new style of furniture making and home decoration that lives on in homes throughout the nation.

New York remains rich, as are few other states, with the homes, libraries, and workshops of distinguished people; with the remnants of historic canals; with museums chronicling pursuits as divergent as horse racing and winemaking; and with the stories of people who changed the course of history. In a place where people have done just about everything, here are reminders of just about everything they've done. Best of all, New Yorkers through the years have had the good sense to restore landscapes once harvested almost to death, and in some cases, to preserve nature in its untouched state for all generations to enjoy.

Whether you live in New York State and are looking for your next day trip, or you plan to explore New York as a tourist, this book will help you find places you didn't know existed. Some provide the solid, comfortable history you expect from old mansions and town museums, while others will surprise the heck out of you—and even make you laugh with pleasure. In between, you will have the opportunity to sample the best of New York's bounty, from goat's milk fudge to Buffalo chicken wings.

Make the most of your time in New York by getting away from the busy streets and highways, and explore what lies just beyond, on the roads fewer people travel. There's so much more to see when you get off the beaten path.

Transportation
MAJOR AIRPORTS

Albany International Airport (oldest municipal airport in the country)
Buffalo Niagara International Airport
Frederick Douglass Greater Rochester International Airport
John F. Kennedy International Airport (New York City)
La Guardia Airport (New York City)
Newark Liberty International Airport (Newark, New Jersey)
Syracuse Hancock International Airport

TRAINS

AMTRAK, amtrak.com
Metro-North, (212) 532–4900; service between Grand Central Station, New Haven, Long Island, and the Hudson Valley; web.mta.info/mnr

Fast Facts

- With an area of 54,556 square miles, New York ranks twenty-seventh in size among the fifty states.

- The state's total population was about 19,450,000 at the end of 2020, ranking it fourth most populated in the nation.

- The state has five mountain ranges: Appalachian, Adirondack, Catskill, Shawangunk, and Taconic.

- New York has more than 70,000 miles of rivers and streams, 127 miles of Atlantic Ocean coastline, and, including lake, bay, and oceanfront, 9,767 miles of shoreline.

- The state flower is the rose.

- The state bird is the eastern bluebird.

- The state freshwater fish is the brook trout; the saltwater fish is the striped bass.

- The state tree is the sugar maple.

- The state motto is "Excelsior," and the state song is, of course, "I Love New York."

- The average low temperature in the coldest months is 26°F.

- The average high temperature in the hottest months is 84°F.

BUSES

New York Trailways, trailways.com
Greyhound, greyhound.com

FERRIES

New York Waterway Ferry System, nywaterway.com
Staten Island Ferry, siferry.com

Major Newspapers

Buffalo News (Buffalo)
Daily News (New York City)
Long Island Newsday (Long Island)
New York Post (New York City)
New York Times (New York City)
Plattsburgh Press-Republican (Plattsburgh)

Rochester Democrat and Chronicle (Rochester)
Syracuse Post-Standard (Syracuse)
Times Union (Albany)
Wall Street Journal (national)

East of the Hudson

Named for the English navigator who first explored its waters in 1609, the Hudson River has been the lifeline of New York from its earliest days as a royal colony to its emergence as a world center of commerce and culture.

These days, of course, railroads and highways handle the bulk of commercial traffic, and the river is less of a thoroughfare and more of an escape for pleasure boaters, a way to savor the enduring beauty of the Hudson Valley. It's not hard to see how this majestic landscape inspired the artists of the Hudson River School of painting, who portrayed a vision of the pristine American landscape as the new Garden of Eden. In addition to artists like Jasper Cropsey and Frederic Church, the area east of the Hudson has plenty of famous names to drop—Roosevelt, Vanderbilt, and Rockefeller among them.

Over the years, many of the writers, artists, inventors, political leaders, and business tycoons who shaped this state—and the nation—have called this area home. The grand and historic country estates they left behind make a drive along the scenic Taconic Parkway a weekender's delight.

This chapter starts in the crowded bedroom communities of Westchester County. From there, like Friday-night weekenders, we'll travel north.

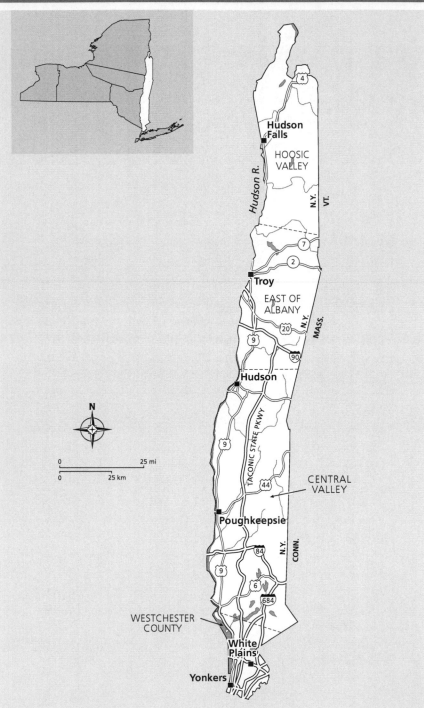

Hudson Falls

HOOSIC
VALLEY

Hudson R.

N.Y.

VT.

7

2

Troy

EAST OF
ALBANY

N.Y.

MASS.

20

9

90

Hudson

TACONIC STATE PKWY

9

44

CENTRAL
VALLEY

Poughkeepsie

N.Y.

CONN.

84

9

6

684

WESTCHESTER
COUNTY

White
Plains

Yonkers

N

0   25 mi
0   25 km

Westchester County

Just beyond the New York City limits, in Yonkers, the ***Hudson River Museum*** occupies the magnificent 1876 Glenview Mansion. As the preeminent cultural institution of Westchester County and the lower Hudson Valley, the museum's resources reflect the natural, social, and artistic history of the area.

A visit to the Hudson River Museum (HRM) includes a walk through the four meticulously restored rooms on the first floor of the mansion itself. You'll hardly find a better introduction to the Aesthetic Movement in residential design, perfected by Charles Locke Eastlake and marked by precise geometric carving and ornamentation—from floors inlaid with contrasting wood to straight lines and decorative tiles that echo a medieval influence.

Aside from the furnishings and personal objects that relate to the period when the Trevor family lived in the mansion, the museum's collections have grown to include impressive holdings of Hudson River landscape paintings, including works by Jasper Cropsey and Albert Bierstadt.

The HRM offers as many as thirty special art, science, and history exhibitions each year, centered on the work of American artists of the nineteenth and twentieth centuries. Summer concerts in the outdoor amphitheater and a Victorian Holiday celebration each December round out the calendar of events and entertainment. In contrast to the period settings and historical emphases of the older parts of the museum, the state-of-the-art Andrus Planetarium features the Definiti 4K Hybrid System, with Ohira-Tech Megastar II computer-controlled optical star projector. The system projects the millions of individual stars of the Milky Way with gasp-inducing realism.

The Hudson River Museum (511 Warburton Ave., Yonkers; 914–963–4550; hrm.org) is open Wed through Sun, noon to 5 p.m.; Fri until 8 p.m. Admission to the museum galleries is $8 for adults, $5 for senior citizens, and $4 for

AUTHOR'S FAVORITES EAST OF THE HUDSON

Croton Gorge Park	Roosevelt Farm and Forest
Culinary Institute of America	Top Cottage
Locust Grove	Val-Kill Cottage
Olana State Historic Site	Walkway over the Hudson
Old Croton Aqueduct Trail	

children 3 to 18. Admission to the planetarium is $5 for adults, $4 for senior citizens, and $3 for children 3 to 18.

Hundreds of years before Glenview Mansion was built, the Philipse family assembled a Westchester estate that makes Glenview's twenty-seven acres seem puny by comparison. Frederick Philipse I came to what was then New Amsterdam in the 1650s and began using his sharp trader's instincts. By the 1690s his lands had grown into a huge estate, including a 52,500-acre tract that encompassed one-third of what is now Westchester County.

In 1716 Philipse's grandson Frederick Philipse II assumed the title of Lord of the Manor of Philipsborough, greatly enlarged the cottage built by his grandfather, and used Philipse Manor Hall as a summer residence. Col. Frederick Philipse (III) rebuilt and further enlarged the Georgian manor house, planted elaborate gardens, and imported the finest furnishings for the hall. His tenure as Lord of the Manor ended when he decided to side with the Tory cause at the beginning of the American Revolution.

Confiscated along with the rest of its owner's properties after the war, **Philipse Manor Hall** was auctioned by the State of New York and passed through the hands of a succession of owners until 1908, when the state bought the property back. The state has since maintained the mansion as a museum of history, art, and architecture. Home to the finest papier-mâché rococo ceiling in the United States, inside and out it remains one of the most perfectly preserved examples of Georgian style in the Northeast.

Philipse Manor Hall State Historic Site (29 Warburton Ave., PO Box 496, Yonkers; 914–965–4027; parks.ny.gov/historic-sites/37/details.aspx) is open Apr through Oct, Tues through Sat, noon to 4:30 p.m.; Nov through Mar, Tues through Sat, noon to 3:30 p.m. Admission is $5 for adults, $3 for students and seniors, and free for children under 12. Group tours are available by appointment.

The Real "FDR Drive"

The **Taconic Parkway** offers motorists the most scenic of several routes along the east side of the Hudson River. Begun in 1927, the road was planned as an offshoot of the Bronx Parkway, but even before ground was broken, officials began planning a major extension. In 1924 they formed the Taconic State Park Commission, and its commissioner, Franklin D. Roosevelt, pushed to lengthen the parkway north as far as Albany. It didn't get quite that far—in 1963 the Taconic eventually reached its northernmost point at the intersection with Interstate 90 in Chatham. It was FDR, however, who insisted on the road's scenic path through some of the most majestic portions of his beloved Hudson Valley. He even prescribed the rustic, thickly mortared stone bridges that help make the Taconic such a handsome rural thoroughfare.

Happy Holidays East of the Hudson

The holiday season is a perfect time to explore the great houses of the region, decked out in festive finery throughout the month of December. Sunnyside, Philipsburg, Lyndhurst, Boscobel, Van Cortlandt Manor, and others offer such events as candlelight tours, bonfires, carols, storytelling, and dancing. Check hudsonvalley.org/calendar and the individual websites of the manor houses for information on specific events.

Fans of the nineteenth-century New York–born Hudson River School painter and architect Jasper F. Cropsey will want to make appointments to visit **Ever Rest**, his Gothic home and studio, and the **Newington Cropsey Foundation Gallery of Art** (newingtoncropsey.com). Ever Rest is preserved as it appeared when the artist and his wife, Maria, lived here in their twilight years, and now exhibits his paintings, watercolors, and sketches. The handsome Gallery of Art, with its octagonal gallery built to resemble "Aladdin," Cropsey's studio in Warwick, New York, houses the world's largest collection of the artist's works.

They're both in **Hastings-on-Hudson**: His home and studio (49 Washington Ave.; 914–478–7990) is open weekdays, 10 a.m. to 1 p.m. by appointment only. The gallery (25 Cropsey Ln.; 914–478–7990) offers forty-five-minute tours by appointment only (at least a week in advance) from Feb through July, and Sept through Nov, weekdays from 1 to 4 p.m.

In 1838, the great Gothic Revival architect Alexander Jackson Davis designed **Lyndhurst** for former New York City mayor William Paulding. Now overlooking the broad expanse of the Mario Cuomo Bridge from the east, this beautiful stone mansion and its landscaped grounds represented the full American flowering of the neo-Gothic aesthetic that had swept through England since the closing years of the eighteenth century.

Lyndhurst remained in the Paulding family until 1864, when it was purchased by wealthy New York merchant George Merritt. Merritt had Davis enlarge the house and add its landmark stone tower, a large greenhouse, and several outbuildings. He also laid out the romantic English-style gardens to complement the Gothic architecture of the main house.

One of the most notorious of America's railroad robber barons, Jason "Jay" Gould, acquired Lyndhurst in 1880 and maintained it as a country estate. When he died in 1892, Lyndhurst became the property of his oldest daughter, Helen, who left it in turn to her younger sister Anna, duchess of the French property Talleyrand-Périgord, in 1938. The duchess died in 1961, leaving instructions that the estate become the property of the National Trust for Historic Preservation.

Lyndhurst (635 South Broadway., Rte. 9 just south of the Mario Cuomo Bridge, Tarrytown; 914–631–4481; lyndhurst.org) is open daily, mid-Apr through Dec, 9 a.m. to 5 p.m. Closed Thanksgiving, Christmas, and New Year's. Guided tours and self-guided audio tours are available. Grounds are open daily, 9 a.m. to 5 p.m. for visitation and landscape tours. Admission is $10 for adults, $4 for children 12 to 17, and free for children under 12 with a paying adult. For tickets, call (888) 718–4253.

While you're in the neighborhood, plan to spend a night or two at the **Bedford Post Inn** (945 Old Post Rd., Bedford; 914–234–7800; bedfordpost dining.com). Area residents Russell Hernandez and Richard Gere recently rescued and restored this historic eight-room luxury inn, in which most rooms

ANNUAL EVENTS EAST OF THE HUDSON

JANUARY

Hudson Valley Wingfest
Poughkeepsie
baptickets.com

FEBRUARY

Hudson Jazz Festival
Hudson
(518) 822–1438
hudsonhall.org

MARCH

Annual Hudson Valley Philharmonic String Competition
Vassar College
Poughkeepsie
(845) 473–5288
app.getacceptd.com/hvp

Spring Farm Days
Harlem Valley Farm and Food Alliance
Remsburger Maple Farm and Apiary
Dover
harlemvalleyfarmandfoodalliance.com/

Hudson Valley Restaurant Week
hudsonvalleyrestaurantweek.com

APRIL

Annual Movable Feast
Hudson Opera House
Hudson
(518) 822–1438
hudsonoperahouse.org

John Flowers Old-Fashioned Easter Egg Hunt
Poughkeepsie
(845) 462–1863
dutchesstourism.com/

JUNE

Caramoor International Music Festival
Katonah
(914) 232–1252
caramoor.org

Clearwater Festival
Croton Point
(800) 677–5667
clearwaterfestival.org

Hudson Valley Shakespeare Festival
through Aug
Boscobel Restoration
(845) 265–7858 or
(845) 265–9575 (for tickets)
hvshakespeare.org

have their own working fireplace, and some have terraces as well. The endlessly romantic little inn features three brand-new restaurants: the Barn, a casual bistro with French influences; the Terrace, an outdoor eatery set in the inn's bountiful and fragrant gardens, featuring a full menu prepared in the inn's wood-burning kitchen and a "patio-focused" drink menu; and the upscale, candlelit Farmhouse, with the choice of a prix-fixe menu or a constantly changing tasting experience, depending on what's fresh from Hudson Valley farms. There's also a yoga studio, if you wish to reach true tranquility in the midst of all this comfort.

One of Tarrytown's best-known residents was Washington Irving, author of *Rip Van Winkle*, *The Legend of Sleepy Hollow*, and *Diedrich Knickerbocker's*

Rhinebeck Crafts Festival
Dutchess County Fairgrounds
Rhinebeck
(845) 331–7900
artrider.com/rhinebeck-crafts-festival

JULY
Falcon Ridge Folk Festival
Hillsdale
(860) 364–2138
falconridgefolk.com

River Fest Ramble
Troy
(518) 273–0552
downtowntroy.org/troy-river-fest#ramble

AUGUST
Bard Music Festival
Annandale-on-Hudson
(845) 758–7900
fishercenter.bard.edu/bmf/

SEPTEMBER
Battle of Saratoga Encampment
Saratoga National Historical Park
Stillwater
(518) 670–2985
nps.gov/sara

Hudson Valley Wine & Food Fest
Dutchess County Fairgrounds
Rhinebeck
hudsonvalleywinefest.com

OCTOBER
Halloween in Sleepy Hollow
Sleepy Hollow
visitsleepyhollow.com/
halloween-in-sleepy-hollow/

Rhinebeck Antiques Fair
Dutchess County Fairgrounds
Rhinebeck
(845) 876–4001
www.barnstar.com

NOVEMBER
Holiday Craft Fair
Dutchess Community College
Poughkeepsie
www.sunydutchess.edu/alumni_
foundation/foundationevents/
annualcraftfair.html

DECEMBER
Westchester's Winter Wonderland
Valhalla
wwinterwonderland.com

History of New York. Irving described his home, **Sunnyside**, as "a little old-fashioned stone mansion, all made up of gable ends, and as full of angles and corners as an old cocked hat."

Irving lived at Sunnyside from 1836 to 1843 and again from 1846 until his death in 1859. Here he entertained such distinguished visitors as Oliver Wendell Holmes, William Makepeace Thackeray, and Louis Napoleon III. On view here is the writing desk where Irving penned *Astoria*, his account of the Pacific Northwest, as well as *The Crayon Miscellany*, *Wolfert's Roost*, and *The Life of George Washington*. In his leisure hours, Irving laid out Sunnyside's splendid flower gardens, arborways, and orchards, which flower and bear fruit to this day.

Located at West Sunnyside Lane (1 mile south of the Mario Cuomo Bridge on Route 9) in Tarrytown, Sunnyside (914–591–8763; hudsonvalley.org/historic-sites/washington-irvings-sunnyside/) is open daily, 10 a.m. to 5 p.m., except Tues and major holidays, from Apr through Oct. In Mar it is open weekends from 10 a.m. to 4 p.m. Admission is $10 for adults; $8 for seniors 65+, students 18 to 25, and children 3 to 17.

One of the most popular times to visit Sunnyside is during **Legends Weekend** in October (914–631–8200; visitsleepyhollow.com/halloween-in-sleepy-hollow/). Dramatic readings of *The Legend of Sleepy Hollow* take place at both Sunnyside and Philipsburg Manor, along with a host of family activities based on Irving's tale—magic shows, ghost stories, woodland walks, ghostly "apparitions," and even an appearance by the Headless Horseman himself.

The town of North Tarrytown, home to two wonderful old churches, was so closely identified with Irving's tale that it officially changed its name to Sleepy Hollow. The **Old Dutch Church of Sleepy Hollow** (430 N. Broadway, Sleepy Hollow; 914–631–4497; reformedchurchtarrytowns.org/old-dutch-church/), built in 1685, is still heated by a woodstove, and hence opens seasonally; Sunday services are held at 10:15 a.m. from the third week in June through the first week in Sept. Tours are given Sat and Sun from 2 to 4 p.m. from Memorial Day through Oct; Mon, Wed, and Thurs from 1 to 4 p.m. from Memorial Day through Labor Day; or by appointment.

Adjacent to the Old Dutch Church, the creator of the Headless Horseman rests in peace in the **Sleepy Hollow Cemetery** alongside the likes of Andrew Carnegie and William Rockefeller, IBM founder Thomas J. Watson, and political advisor Belle Moskowitz. This, by the way, is also the cemetery in which the punk rock band the Ramones were buried alive during the 1989 filming of their "Pet Semetary" music video. Free guided tours are given daily at 2 p.m., Memorial Day through Oct; check the schedule at sleepyhollowcemetery.org.

The tiny **Union Church of Pocantico Hills** at 555 Bedford Road in Tarrytown (914–631–2069; hudsonvalley.org/historic-sites/union-church-of-pocantico-hills/) has a magnificent collection of stained-glass windows by Henri Matisse and Marc Chagall, which were commissioned by the Rockefeller family. It's open for hourly tours Fri through Sun (except Christmas and New Year's Day), 10 a.m. through 4 p.m. Admission is $9; advance reservations are required. Church activities may preempt visiting hours.

The menu at the lovely **Crabtree's Kittle House Restaurant and Country Inn** changes daily, but the food, ambience, and service remain consistently superb. Guests can choose from locally sourced offerings like Montauk swordfish steak or breast of Hudson Valley duck a l'orange, or a pan-roasted Berkshire pork chop. For many, dessert is the high point of a meal in this 1790 mansion, with fanciful confections such as chocolate chip bread pudding with Hudson Valley bourbon sauce, or a New York–grown Macoun apple tart. *Wine Spectator* magazine awarded the restaurant its "Grand Award of Excellence" several times for having one of the most outstanding restaurant wine lists in the world—more than forty thousand bottles in its cellar, and four thousand selections from which guests can choose.

Crabtree's Kittle House Restaurant and Country Inn (11 Kittle Rd., Chappaqua; 914–666–8044; crabtreeskittlehouse.com) also has twelve guest rooms with private baths. Lunch and dinner are served Tues through Sat, and brunch on Sun from noon to 2:30 p.m., followed by dinner from 3 to 7 p.m. Reservations are highly recommended, especially on weekends.

The hospitality is far less inviting at **Sing Sing Correctional Facility** in Ossining, the operating maximum-security prison that currently holds some 1,700 prisoners. Plans are in the works to convert the original 1825 convict-built cell block into a museum, but in the meantime, you can view a replica of the creepy electric chair—the same kind that took the life of gangster Rocky Sullivan (played by James Cagney) in the 1938 hit film *Angels with Dirty Faces*—along with confiscated weapons and other artifacts at the **Ossining Urban Park Visitors Center** (Joseph G. Caputo Community Center; 95 Broadway, Ossining; 914–941–3189; www.singsingprisonmuseum.org). Open Mon through Sat, 10 a.m. to 4 p.m. Admission is free.

A stop at the ninety-seven-acre **Croton Gorge Park** offers an opportunity to stretch your legs and enjoy some amazing views of the Croton River. Here the first large masonry dam in the United States rose from 1837 to 1842, becoming a major element in bringing clean, fresh water into New York City when sanitation issues demanded a better solution. Until that time, springs and wells provided what little fresh water the massive population could access, and disease ran rampant in slum areas like Five Points in Lower Manhattan. When a cholera outbreak killed 3,500 people in a single year, city leaders finally formed a commission to address the issue. The original dam operated here until the late nineteenth century, when the demands of the growing city once again outpaced the water supply. Today you can see the new Cornell Dam, built in 1906, which creates a powerful waterfall while supporting the Croton Reservoir's thirty-four billion gallons of water.

In addition to viewing the dam from the bridge that spans the Croton River, you can explore the route the original water system took through Westchester County by walking some of the twenty-six-mile-long *Old Croton Aqueduct Trail*, which begins here at the park and ends at 173rd Street in Manhattan.

Croton Gorge Park (35 Cortlandt Rd., Cortlandt; 914–827–9568; parks .westchestergov.com/croton-gorge-park) is open daily, 8 a.m. to dusk. There is a $10 parking fee per car from Memorial Day to Labor Day.

Peekskill is home to more than seventy artists who work in a variety of media. Many of them host *Open Artist Studio Tours* the third Saturday of each month, and there's a two-hour guided art tour, which leaves from the Paramount Theater at 10:45 a.m. ($10; seniors $8.50) from May through Oct. If you're visiting between mid-June and Oct, stop at the Peekskill Farmer's Market on Bank Street. For information contact the Peekskill Arts Alliance at (914) 737–2780; peekskillartsalliance.org.

Just as the Broadway play *Hamilton* brought a forgotten Founding Father to life, so does a visit to the *John Jay Homestead* (400 Jay St., Katonah; 914–232–5651). One of the most accomplished of the men who wrote our nation's earliest laws, Jay served as one of the authors of the New York State constitution, president of the Second Continental Congress, secretary of Foreign Affairs, and a key negotiator of the Treaty of Paris, which brought the American Revolution to an end once and for all. When George Washington became president, he appointed Jay as the nation's first Chief Justice of the Supreme Court. As if these titles were not enough, he also served two terms as governor of New York, signing the Act for the Gradual Abolition of Slavery in 1801. Finally reaching retirement, he moved to his 750 acres of land near Katonah and spent his last years in this lovely farmhouse with the three youngest of his five children after losing his wife, Sarah, to illness in 1802.

You can learn much more about John Jay and his considerable influence on the shaping of the United States by taking a docent-led tour of his home, Bedford, and strolling the meticulously maintained grounds. Start at the carriage barn, which has been converted into a visitor center and features a twelve-minute video about Jay's life and times. The home is open year-round, May through Oct on Wed through Sun, with tours at 1, 3, and 4 p.m. Thematic tours are given Wed through Sat at 2 p.m., with specialty tours on Sat and Sun (check johnjayhomestead.org for times and subjects). The Carriage Barn Education & Visitor Center is open Wed through Sun, 12:30 to 4:30 p.m. Nov through Apr; docent-led tours of the house are Thurs through Sat, 1 and 3 p.m. Themed tours are given Wed through Sat at 2 p.m.; the Carriage Barn is closed for the season. All tours are $10 for adults, $7 for students and seniors, and free to members and children under 12.

Caramoor Center for Music and the Arts is yet another of New York's great houses. It was built over a decade's time from 1929 to 1939 by Walter and Lucie Bigelow Dodge Rosen, who filled it with Asian and Renaissance art and created the place that became home to the International Music Festival. Like the wealthy robber barons of yore, the Rosens purchased entire rooms from Europe's palaces and churches and had them reconstructed in their own Spanish-style villa—resulting in an arts and antiques collection that is, to say the least, eclectic. In 1945 they bequeathed the estate as a center for music and art, and it opened to the public a year later. As the festival's reputation grew, Lucie Rosen constructed a larger space, the Venetian Theater, which opened in 1958.

Twenty of the house's magnificent rooms are open to the public; docent tours last about an hour. In the opulent music room, there are chamber concerts throughout the year. On Thurs and Fri afternoons at 3 p.m., tea is served on the family's original china in the Summer Dining Room.

At Caramoor (149 Girdle Ridge Rd., Katonah; 914–232–1252; caramoor.org) guided tours are offered May through Dec, Wed through Sun, from 1 to 4 p.m. Admission is $9 for adults, free for children 16 and under.

Better Than His Pulitzer

When people talk about the romance of the rails, they seldom have commuter trains in mind. But New York's Metro-North, which hauls thousands of suburbanites into and out of Grand Central Station each day, has taken on a bit more panache since it began naming individual cars after prominent people associated with its territory along the Hudson Valley.

None of these cars is more freighted with poignant associations for Westchester commuters than the John Cheever. Cheever, a longtime resident of Ossining, was the great chronicler of postwar suburban life. His heroes and heroines poured into Grand Central from places like Shady Hill and Bullet Park, and rode back each night to seek love and redemption among their rhododendrons.

If you're walking along the Hudson at twilight and see the John Cheever roll by, raise a phantom glass (very dry, with an olive) to those phantom commuters and to the man who made their longings universal.

During a late-night walk in Tallahassee, Florida, in 1991, French pianist Hélène Grimaud had a life-changing moment. She experienced an unforgettable encounter, which she later decided was with a she-wolf, probably part dog and part wolf. In her memoir, *Wild Harmonies: A Life of Music and Wolves*, Grimaud described how the animal slid under her outstretched hand of its own volition. The touch made her feel a spark shoot through her body, she said, and she became aware of a "primeval force" calling to her.

It was then that Grimaud conceived her mission: to change the image of wolves as villainous creatures and to educate the public that wolves are essential "biodiversity engineers" that help preserve the balance among animal and plant species.

In 1999, with her then-companion, J. Henry Fair, Grimaud opened the **Wolf Conservation Center** (7 Buck Run, South Salem; 914–763–2373; nywolf .org), a twenty-nine-acre facility that houses a total of thirty-nine Mexican gray wolves and red wolves as candidates to be released into the wild, and three "ambassador wolves" that the public can see when they visit. Appointments are required for visits and must be arranged online in advance.

Muscoot Farm (51 NY 100, Katonah; 914–864–7282) is an agricultural holdout in the rapidly developing Westchester landscape. Dating to the early 1900s, the 777-acre working farm has a twenty-three-room main house, barns and outbuildings, antique equipment, a large demonstration vegetable garden, and lots of animals. Weekends are a busy time; in addition to hayrides, agricultural programs cover topics such as sheepshearing and harvesting. There's also a full roster of seasonal festivals. The farm is open daily, 10 a.m. to 4 p.m.

Central Valley

Named for a prominent nineteenth-century family, the town of Brewster in southern Putnam County is home to the **Southeast Museum**. The museum serves as an archive of the diverse enterprises that have taken root here over the years, including mining, railroading, circuses, and even the manufacture of condensed milk.

The first European settlers arrived in Brewster around 1725, and for more than one hundred years, they farmed and set up modest cottage industries. In the mid-nineteenth century, Brewster's economic horizons expanded with the arrival of the Harlem Railroad, which became part of Commodore Vanderbilt's vast New York Central system, as well as the Putnam Line Railroad, a division of the New York and New Haven Line.

In years gone by Brewster served as winter quarters for a number of small circuses, many of which were later consolidated by P. T. Barnum, who hailed from nearby Bridgeport, Connecticut. The colorful array of early American circus memorabilia and other collections is housed in the *1896 Old Town Hall of Southeast* (67 Main St., Brewster; 845–279–7500; southeastmuseum.org). Hours are 10 a.m. to 4 p.m., Tues through Sat, Apr through Dec. Donations are requested.

Visitors to the *Chuang Yen Monastery* in Carmel, home of the Buddhist Association of the United States, are greeted by ten thousand statues of the Buddha arrayed on the lotus terrace. Enter the cavernous Tang Dynasty–style Great Buddha Hall to view the largest Buddha statue in the Western Hemisphere, a thirty-seven-foot-high statue designed by Professor C. G. Chen. Chen also painted the 8-foot-high, 104-foot-long murals depicting scenes from the "Pure Land," or Amitabha Buddha, that cover the walls.

The Chuang Yen Monastery (2020 Rte. 301, Carmel; 845–225–1819; baus .org) welcomes visitors who wish to tour the buildings and grounds or to stay, study, and meditate. Hours are 9 a.m. to 5 p.m. daily; the grounds close promptly at 5.

In 1974, Philippa de Menil and Heinger Friedrich founded the nonprofit Dia Art Foundation, to hold their collections of works by important artists of the 1960s and 1970s. Located on thirty-one acres on the banks of the Hudson River, the museum occupies a historic printing facility that was built in 1929 by the National Biscuit Company (Nabisco). It houses works by such major artists as Andy Warhol, Max Neuhaus, Cy Twombly, Bridget Riley, Nancy Holt, Walter de Maria, and Richard Serra.

Dia: Beacon, Riggio Galleries (3 Beekman St., Beacon; 845–440–0100; diaart.org) is open 11 a.m. to 6 p.m. Fri through Mon, with last admission at 4:45 p.m. Guided tours are given every Sat at 1 p.m. The museum is closed on Thanksgiving, Christmas Eve, Christmas, New Year's Eve, and New Year's Day. The cafe and bookshop open at 11 a.m. year-round. Admission is $15 for adults, $12 for seniors, students, and visitors with disabilities and their care partners. Children under 12 are free.

Not all of the Hudson Valley landowners enjoyed fabulous riches. Most, in fact, lived fairly ordinary lives and farmed their own land. The *Van Wyck Homestead Museum* (also known as the Van Wyck–Wharton House), a National Historic Site in Fishkill, showcases the typical Dutch country farmhouse started in 1732 by Cornelius Van Wyck, which finally reached completion with the construction of the West Wing in the 1750s.

Like so many other farmhouses, the Van Wyck Homestead might have been forgotten by history had it not played a part in the American Revolution. Located along the strategic route between New York City and the Champlain Valley, the house became attractive to the Continental Army, which requisitioned it to serve as headquarters for General Israel Putnam. Fishkill served as an important supply depot for General Washington's northern forces from 1776 to 1783. Military trials were held at the house; one such event was reputedly the source used by James Fenimore Cooper for an incident in his novel *The Spy*. Today, the Fishkill Historical Society operates it as a museum of colonial life in the Hudson Valley. The house features a working colonial kitchen fireplace with a beehive oven, and an exhibit of Revolutionary War artifacts unearthed in the vicinity during archaeological digs.

The Van Wyck Homestead Museum (504 Rte. 9, Fishkill; 845–896–9560; fishkillhistoricalsociety.org) is open Memorial Day through Oct on Sat and Sun from 1 to 4 p.m. and by appointment. There is an admission charge of $2. Special events include craft fairs in September and at the holidays, a June midsummer festival, and a St. Nicholas Day holiday tour.

No trip through the Hudson Valley can be complete without some stops at local wineries, so make plans to enjoy three of the valley's best—all within fifteen minutes of one another. *Clinton Vineyards* (450 Schultzville Rd., Clinton Corners; 845–266–5372; clintonvineyards.com) offers gold medal–winning Riesling and Pinot Noir as well as its celebrated cassis, a full-bodied black currant dessert wine, and a number of others. It's open on weekend afternoons for tastings for $18 to $20, and visitors can add a local cheese and charcuterie plate for $20 with their tasting (reserve in advance). At the new *Milea Estate Vineyard* in Staatsburg (450 Hollow Rd.; 845–266–0384; mileaestatevineyard .com), visitors can sample the Chardonnay and Riesling that Japan Airlines selected to be served to first-class passengers jetting between Tokyo and New York. Reserve your place using the Open Table link on the website's Visit page. The third stop, *Millbrook Vineyards and Winery* (26 Wing Rd., Millbrook; 845–677–8383; millbrookwine.com), brings you to the first winery in the region to focus exclusively on vinifera grapes. Producing wine since the early 1980s, this winery features its Hunt Country family of red, white, and rosé wines as well as special reserve Pinot Noir and Cabernet Franc varieties. Open daily year-round, it offers tastings from noon to 5 p.m.

In 1847 Samuel F. B. Morse, inventor of the telegraph and Morse code, purchased one hundred acres of land and a seventeen-year-old Georgian house. With the help of his friend, architect Alexander Jackson Davis, he transformed the original structure into a Tuscan-style villa. Today, *Locust Grove, Samuel Morse Historic Site*, a unique combination of 150 acres of nature preserve, historic gardens, landscaped lawns, vistas, and architecture, is one of the most handsome of the Hudson River estates. In 1963 it became the first in the valley to be designated a National Historic Landmark.

Original family furnishings are exhibited in period room settings and include rare Duncan Phyfe and Chippendale pieces. Paintings include works by Morse himself as well as by artists such as George Inness. There's also a rare bound collection of *Birds of America* by J. J. Audubon. A replica of "the invention of the century" is on exhibit in the Morse Room.

Locust Grove, Samuel Morse Historic Site (2683 South Rd., Poughkeepsie; 845-454-4500; lgny.org), is open daily May through Oct, and on weekends in Apr, Nov, and Dec, from 10 a.m. to 5 p.m. Closed on Thanksgiving, Christmas Eve, Christmas Day, New Year's Day, and Easter. Admission is $12 for adults, $11 for seniors, and $6 for those between the ages of 3 and 18. There is no fee to walk the grounds, which are open from 8 a.m. to dusk.

Speaking of walking, don't miss the opportunity to enjoy some of the best views of the Hudson River from the middle of a brilliantly restored bridge, in what is now a state historical park. **Walkway over the Hudson** (60 Parker Ave., Poughkeepsie; 845-834-2867; walkway.org) in the heart of Poughkeepsie repurposes a nineteenth-century railroad bridge that was the first to cross the Hudson River between New York City and Albany. After fire damaged the bridge beyond repair in 1974, it stood dormant until a group of citizens came up with the inspired idea to renovate it and turn it into a park. The $38.8 million project actually turned out to be less expensive than demolishing the bridge would have been, and today it stands as the world's longest pedestrian bridge at 1.28 miles, 212 feet above the river's surface. Since its opening in October 2009, it has become a new meeting place for neighbors and friends throughout the river valley, and a terrific tourist destination as well. It's open daily sunrise to sunset and is free to visit.

You're now in the **Culinary Institute of America** (CIA) country. Founded in 1946 as a trade school to train returning World War II veterans in the culinary arts, the institute now stands as one of the most renowned culinary schools in the world. Among its distinguished graduates are *Gourmet* magazine executive chef and *Good Morning America* personality Sara Moulton; television personality and author Anthony Bourdain; and *Iron Chef*'s Cat Cora.

Since America launched its love affair with the Food Network, the CIA has become a veritable hub of culinary activity, attracting not only serious students and food professionals, but also enthusiastic foodies who sign up for the school's one-day courses and cooking boot camps. With forty-one state-of-the-art kitchens and bakeshops, the CIA is a food-lover's Eden.

The CIA plays a major role in making the Hudson Valley a culinary destination, serving as the setting for popular food and wine events and turning out students who have gone on to work in the region's restaurants. In addition, the five student-staffed restaurants on the CIA's 150-acre campus attract tens of thousands of food lovers each year, all eager to sample the "homework" turned out by the culinary stars of the future.

The **Ristorante Caterina de' Medici** (845–451–1011; ristorantecaterina demedici.com), open Mon through Fri for lunch and dinner, showcases the indigenous foods of Italy's various regions, as well as a prix-fixe Saturday pasta dinner with five pastas and Caesar salad, served family-style. The casual Al Forno Room, located within the Ristorante Caterina de' Medici, serves wood-fired pizza, salad, and antipasti.

The **Bocuse Restaurant** (845–451–1012; bocuserestaurant.com), open Tues through Sat, features classic French cuisine prepared with the most modern cooking techniques. The **American Bounty Restaurant** (845–451–1011; americanbountyrestaurant.com), open Tues through Sat for lunch and dinner, serves regional American dishes, while the Tavern at American Bounty provides more casual fare. The **Post Road Brew House** (ciarestaurantgroup.com/post-road-brew-house/), the newest CIA venue, provides "elevated" pub-style meals accompanied by craft beers brewed on-site. The **Apple Pie Bakery Café** (applepiebakerycafe.com), where CIA students learn their fine pastry skills, offers a selection of sandwiches, pastries, and breads, also available for takeout; it is open Mon through Fri, 8 a.m. to 6:30 p.m. Reservations are necessary for the formal restaurants but not for the Al Forno Room, Tavern, Brew House, or bakery.

President Franklin D. Roosevelt's accomplishments are the stuff of legend—the nation's only four-term president established Social Security, moved the country past the Great Depression, and presided over the US involvement in World War II, all from a wheelchair where polio confined him before he took office—but far fewer people know of his commitment to sustainable forestry. Take an hour or two while passing through Hyde Park to stroll through **Roosevelt Farm and Forest**, part of former Roosevelt property protected by the National Park Service. The last remaining acres of his own forest, saved from

Celebrate the Valley's Bounty

Don't miss the **Hudson Valley Wine & Food Fest**, held on the second weekend in September at the Dutchess County Fairgrounds. More than 150 wineries from throughout New York State, food trucks, farms, specialty food vendors, craft breweries, distilleries, and more gather for a celebration of food and beverages that draws visitors from all over the region. Celebrity chefs share their secrets in seminars and cooking demonstrations, and no one goes home hungry. Go to hudsonvalleywinefest .com for details and to purchase tickets.

development in 2004 by the Scenic Hudson Land Trust, demonstrate the results of scientific forestry: managing a timber crop with a balance between harvesting and environmental protection. He directed his staff to plant more than half a million trees here, creating a particularly pleasant woodland of native species: beech, poplar, tulip tree, maple, oak, hemlock, and others. Well-marked trails crisscross the forest, giving visitors a respite from Route 9 traffic and hours in the car. Find the trailhead at 4088 Albany Post Rd., Hyde Park; 845–337–8474; nps.gov/hofr. Open daily dawn to dusk.

Whenever First Lady Eleanor Roosevelt took time out from the many causes she championed before, during, and after her husband's presidency, she retreated to Val-Kill, a small fieldstone cottage that FDR had built for her in 1925 by a stream on the grounds of the Roosevelt family estate. The cottage became the permanent home for two dear friends, New York Democratic Committee coworkers Nancy Cook and Marion Dickerman, and whenever Eleanor returned home, she would opt to stay here rather than in the nearby family mansion presided over by Franklin's autocratic mother, Sara Delano Roosevelt.

In 1926 the women, along with Caroline O'Day, built a second, larger building to house Val-Kill Industries, intended to teach farm workers how to manufacture goods, thus keeping them from migrating to large cities in search of work. Until the business closed in 1936—a victim of the Great Depression—the workers manufactured replicas of Early American furniture, weavings, and pewter pieces. At this point, Mrs. Roosevelt converted the building into apartments for herself and her secretary, Malvina "Tommy" Thompson, and added several guest rooms. She renamed the building ***Val-Kill Cottage*** and wrote to her daughter, "My house seems nicer than ever and I could be happy in it alone! That's the last test of one's surroundings." Among the visitors to Val-Kill were John F. Kennedy, Adlai Stevenson, Nikita Khrushchev, and Jawaharlal Nehru.

After Mrs. Roosevelt died in 1962, several developers tried to take over her home, but they were thwarted when a group of concerned citizens organized to preserve the site. In 1977 President Jimmy Carter signed a bill creating the ***Eleanor Roosevelt National Historic Site*** (519 Albany Post Rd., Hyde Park; 845–229–9115; nps.gov/elro). Today visitors can tour the cottages and grounds daily, May through Oct, from 9 a.m. to 5 p.m.; and from Nov through Apr, Sat and Sun, 9 a.m. to 5 p.m. Admission is $8 for adults, free for children under 17.

Tucked at the top of a challenging trail through Val-Kill's adjacent woodland sits ***Top Cottage*** (nps.gov/hofr/planyourvisit/top-cottage.htm), FDR's secret hideaway where he went to "escape the mob," as he put it, of people clamoring for the attentions of the longtime president of the United States. Here he also shared a relationship with his companion Margaret "Daisy" Suckley, the nature of which has never been conclusively determined. Roosevelt entertained many a head of state up here, including British prime minister Winston Churchill, and he took time to read, write, and even birdwatch in this secluded setting. You can hike up to Top Cottage or get here by bus from **Home of Franklin D. Roosevelt National Historic Site** and enjoy a ranger-led tour of the surprisingly modest getaway. Open May through the third week in Oct, Mon through Fri, with tours departing from the Wallace Visitor Center at the FDR home at 11:10 a.m., 1:10 p.m., and 3:10 p.m.

Heading through Hyde Park, we're back in mansion territory—in addition to FDR's home, you can visit the **Franklin D. Roosevelt Presidential Library**, or **Vanderbilt Mansion National Historic Site**—but as we head north, we can see a difference in the architecture. Palaces such as **Staatsburgh**, formerly Mills Mansion State Historic Site, represent the glory days of industrial and financial captains—the so-called Gilded Age of the late nineteenth century. The idea behind this sort of house building was to live not like a country squire, but more like a Renaissance lord of an Italian city-state.

Ogden Mills finished his neoclassical mansion in 1896, but its story begins more than one hundred years earlier. In 1792, Morgan Lewis, great-grandfather of Mills's wife, Ruth Livingston Mills, purchased the property on which the Mills estate stands. Lewis, an officer in the revolution and the third post-independence governor of New York State, built two houses here. The first burned in 1832, at which time it was replaced by an up-to-date Greek Revival structure. This was the home that stood on the property when it was inherited by Ruth Livingston Mills in 1890.

But Ogden Mills had something far grander in mind for his wife's legacy. He hired a firm with a solid reputation in mansion building to enlarge the home and embellish its interiors—McKim, Mead, and White, a popular firm among wealthy clients.

The architects added two spacious wings and decked out both the new and the old portions of the exterior with balustrades and pilasters more reminiscent of Blenheim Palace than anything previously seen in the Hudson Valley. The interior was (and is) French, in Louis XV and XVI period styles—lots of carving and gilding on furniture and wall and ceiling surfaces, along with oak paneling and monumental tapestries.

Staatsburgh State Historic Site, 75 Mills Mansion Drive, Road #1, Staatsburg (845–889–8851; parks.ny.gov/historic-sites/staatsburgh/), is open from mid-Apr through Oct, Wed through Sat, 10 a.m. to 5 p.m., and Sun 11 a.m. to 5 p.m. It reopens after Thanksgiving through Dec. Admission is $5 for adults, $4 for seniors and students, free for children under 12.

Troutbeck, on the banks of the trout-filled Webatuck River in Amenia, is an English-style country estate that functions as a country inn. The 250-acre retreat, with its slate-roofed mansion with leaded windows, has undergone a recent renovation that brings modern amenities like forty-two-inch flatscreen televisions and broadband WiFi to your romantic weekend. The former home of poet-naturalist Myron B. Benton, Troutbeck served as a gathering place for celebrities during the early decades of the twentieth century. Ernest Hemingway, Sinclair Lewis, and Teddy Roosevelt are said to have been houseguests of the Springarn family, who owned the house from 1902 to 1978.

The restaurant, open to the public for daily lunch and dinner and Sunday brunch, benefits from the leadership of Michelin-starred chef Gabe McMackin and features a seasonal menu based on locally sourced Hudson Valley ingredients. Troutbeck, 515 Leedsville Rd., Amenia (845–789–1555; troutbeck.com), is open year-round.

The Wetmore family, which owns *Cascade Mountain Winery & Restaurant*, says of its product: "Regional wine is a way of tasting our seasons past. Last summer's sunshine, the snows of winter, rain, and frost; it's all there in a glass." You can sample the winery's Heavenly Daze red, Private Reserve white, or Harvest rosé at the vineyard, which offers tours and tastings on weekends from May to Nov, 11 a.m. to 5 p.m. The excellent restaurant serves lunch Thurs through Sun, and dinner on Sat. Cascade Mountain Winery and Restaurant is at 835 Cascade Mountain Road in Amenia (845–373–9021; cascademt.com).

Although its location is off the beaten path, the *Old Drovers Inn* is very much on the main track for those who love gourmet dining and superb accommodations. Winner of some of the industry's most prestigious awards, including AAA's Four Diamond Award and an award of excellence for its wine list and cellar from *Wine Spectator*, the inn, now a bed-and-breakfast, was also named one of the five Gourmet Retreats of the Year in Andrew Harper's Hideaway Report. Beautifully restored and in continuous use since it was built in 1750, the inn was originally a stop for cattle drovers, who purchased livestock from New England farmers and drove the animals down the post roads to markets in New York City.

Dinner entrees at the *Tap Room* restaurant reflect the kitchen's blending of American and European styles, with starters including the inn's signature cheddar cheese soup and Hudson Valley foie gras, and seasonal entrees ranging from country-fried quail and waffles to seared Faroe Island salmon, as well as a range of creative cocktails.

Like the food, the six guest suites promise romance and deliver it with stylish grace. Prices range from $199 to $249 for the cozy Rose Room overlooking the gardens, to $275 to $325 per night for the Gables 2, the wood-paneled third-floor room with a large private bath. American breakfast and high tea at 4 p.m. are included. Pets are permitted for a fee of $25 per day with advance approval.

Old Drovers Inn (196 E. Duncan Hill Rd., Dover Plains; 845–832–9311; old droversinn.com) serves lunch Fri, Sat, and Sun, and dinner nightly except Wed.

When twenty-one-year-old artist Peter Wing returned from fighting in Vietnam, he wanted to build a place where he could retreat from the world. He and his wife, Toni, who is also an artist, worked for the next twenty-five years to create **Wing's Castle**, a fabulously eccentric stone castle overlooking the Hudson Valley, on land Peter's family had run as a dairy farm. Eighty percent of the structure is made of salvaged materials from antique buildings.

Peter wasn't successful in retreating, however. Visitors from around the world stop in for tours and are surprised to learn that the castle is also the Wings' home. It's furnished with Victorian pieces, more than two thousand antiques, and mannequins dressed in period clothing. A seven-foot-deep moat that runs under the castle serves as a swimming pool, and twelve- and thirteen-foot hand-hewn rocks that Peter removed from an old building create Stonehenge East, a circle of pillars saluting the sun.

Wing's Castle (717 Bangall Rd., Millbrook; 845–677–9085; wingscastle.com) is open for tours only to paying guests of the bed-and-breakfast. Guests can choose one of the five eclectic rooms, including the Dungeon, a deliciously shadowy chamber with a medieval-style arched tunnel corridor to the Annex Suite next door. All accommodations include WiFi in the room and a generous continental breakfast. (No children or pets are permitted.) Rooms begin at $200 per night, with full occupancy of the Cottage, a two-bedroom suite for up to four people, at $400 per night.

Inspired by eighth-century Chinese garden maker Wang Wei, 1920s property owners Walter and Marion Burt Beck turned their 185 acres in Millbrook into **Innisfree Garden**. Walter Beck called the concept a "cup garden," drawing attention to something rare or beautiful and segregating it so that it can be enjoyed without distraction. The result is this endlessly varied landscape of contained spaces, each forming its own three-dimensional picture. Innisfree Garden (Tyrrel Road, Millbrook; 845–677–8000; innisfreegarden.org) is open early May to Nov 1, Wed through Sun, 10 a.m. to 5 p.m. Admission is $10 for adults, $5 for seniors 65+ and children 15 and under.

The **Old Rhinebeck Aerodrome**, three miles upriver from the town of Rhinebeck, is more than just a museum—many of the pre-1930s planes exhibited here actually take to the air each weekend. The three main buildings at the aerodrome house a collection of aircraft, automobiles, and other vehicles from the period 1900–1937 and are open throughout the week. On Saturday and Sunday, though, you can combine a tour of the exhibits on the ground with attendance at an air show featuring both original aircraft and accurate reproductions. Saturdays are reserved for flights of planes from the Pioneer (pre–World War I) and Lindbergh eras. On Sundays the show is a period-piece melodrama in which intrepid Allied fliers do battle with the "Black Baron." Where else can you watch a live dogfight?

All that's left at this point is to go up there yourself, and you can do just that. The aerodrome has on hand a 1929 New Standard D-25—which carries four passengers wearing helmets and goggles—for open-cockpit flights of fifteen minutes' duration. The cost is $100 per person for a fifteen-minute ride (with a two-person minimum), or $200 per person for a thirty-minute lighthouse and mansion tour (again, at least two people must ride), and rides are available on weekends, before and after the show, or on weekdays with advance reservations.

Old Rhinebeck Aerodrome (44 Stone Church Rd., Rhinebeck; 845–752–3200; oldrhinebeck.org) is open daily May through Oct from 10 a.m. to 5 p.m. On Sat and Sun from mid-June through mid-Oct, the air show begins at 2 p.m. Weekday admission is $12 for adults; $8 for seniors, children 6 to 17, and active-duty or retired military with ID; and free for children 5 and under. Admission for weekend air shows is $25 for adults; $20 for seniors and active duty or retired military with ID; and $12 for children ages 6 to 17. The plane rides cost extra, as mentioned above.

America's oldest continuously operating hotel, the **Beekman Arms**, opened for business as the Traphagen Inn in 1766. A meeting place for American Revolutionary War generals, the Beekman was also the site of Franklin Delano Roosevelt's election eve rallies from the beginning of his career right through his presidency. Visitors can choose from one of fourteen rooms in the inn, the motel, or the fifty-room **Delamater Inn** (845–786–7080), a block away, built in 1844 and one of the few early examples of American Gothic residences still in existence. The inn's accommodations include seven guest houses, several with fireplaces, clustered around a courtyard.

The Beekman Arms & Delamater Inn (6387 Mill St., Rhinebeck; 845–876–7077; beekmandelamaterinn.com) are open year-round. Rates range from $120 to $170 in the Arms, $100 to $125 in the contemporary motel, and $95 to $180 in the Delamater House. All rooms have a private bath, TV, phone, and a complimentary decanter of sherry. A two-night minimum stay is required weekends from May through October and holiday weekends. Lunch, dinner, and Sunday brunch are served in the Tavern at Beekman Arms, which also features a cozy, colonial-style taproom.

There was a time when every schoolchild worthy of a gold star knew that the *Clermont* was the first successful steamboat, built by Robert Fulton and tested on the Hudson River. Less commonly known, however, is that the boat formally registered by its owners as *The North River Steamboat of Clermont* took its name from the estate of Robert R. Livingston, chancellor of New York and a backer of Fulton's experiments. Clermont, one of the great family seats of the valley, overlooks the Hudson River near Germantown.

The story of Clermont begins with the royal charter granted to Robert Livingston in 1686, which made the Scottish-born trader Lord of the Manor of Livingston, a 162,000-acre tract that would evolve into the entire southern third of modern-day Columbia County. When Livingston died in 1728, he broke with the English custom of strict adherence to primogeniture by giving 13,000 acres of his land to his third son. This was Clermont, the Lower Manor, on which Robert of Clermont, as he was known, established his home in 1728.

Two more Robert Livingstons figure in the tale after this point: Robert of Clermont's son, a New York judge, and the judge's son, a member of the Second Continental Congress who filled the now-obsolete office of state chancellor. It was the chancellor's mother, Margaret Beekman Livingston, who rebuilt the house after it was burned in 1777 by the British (parts of the original walls are incorporated into the present structure).

The Livingston family lived at Clermont until 1962, making various enlargements and modifications to their home over time. In that year the house, its furnishings, and the five hundred remaining acres of the Clermont estate became the property of the State of New York.

The mansion at **Clermont State Historic Site** (also a National Historic Landmark) has been restored to its circa-1930 appearance; however, the collections are primarily half eighteenth- and half nineteenth-century French and early American. Tours of Clermont include the first and second floors. There are formal gardens, woodsy hiking trails, and spacious landscapes (perfect for picnics) on bluffs overlooking the Hudson.

Clermont (1 Clermont Ave., Germantown; 518–537–4240; friendsofclermont .org) is open Tues through Sun and on Mon holidays from 11 a.m. to 5 p.m. (last tour at 4:30). From Nov through Mar, hours are 11 a.m. to 4 p.m. (last tour at 3:30), weekends only. The grounds are open and free daily, year-round from 8:30 a.m. to sunset. The Visitor Center is open from Apr through Oct, Tues through Sun, and holidays that land on Mondays, 10:30 a.m. to 5 p.m.; Nov through Mar, weekends 11 a.m. to 4 p.m. The Heritage Music Festival is held in mid-July. Admission to the mansion is $5 for adults, $4 for seniors, and children under 12 are free.

Want to paddle a sea kayak around the Statue of Liberty? How about past Sing Sing Prison or up through the northern Hudson Highlands past Bannerman's Castle on Pollepel Island? *Atlantic Kayak Tours*, the largest sea-kayaking business in the tri-state area, offers these tours and many more throughout the waters of Connecticut, New Jersey, and the Empire State, and you don't need any experience to join up. They're at 320 West Saugerties Road in Saugerties (845–246–2187). The company also offers kayak tours and lessons on the Lower Hudson River at Norrie Point Paddlesport Center on the grounds of Norrie State Park. That facility is open on weekends from mid-May through mid-Sept; check atlantickayaktours.com for exact dates and hours.

Known for his mammoth landscapes and his theatrical presentations, Hudson River School master Frederic Edwin Church built a Persian Gothic castle, Olana, commanding a magnificent view of the river south of the town of Hudson.

Olana draws heavily upon Islamic and Byzantine motifs. Persian arches abound, as do Oriental carpets, brass work, and inlaid furniture. The overall aesthetic is typically Victorian, with no space left empty that could possibly be filled with things. What makes Olana atypical, of course, is the quality of the things.

Although Church employed as a consultant Calvert Vaux, who had collaborated with Frederick Law Olmsted on the design of New York's Central Park, the artist designed his own house. When scholars describe Olana as a major work of art by Church, they are not speaking figuratively; the paints for the interior were mixed on his own palette.

Olana State Historic Site (Route 9G, Hudson; 518–828–0135; olana.org) offers guided tours on Fri from 11 a.m. to 2 p.m., and Sat and Sun from 10 a.m. to 4 p.m. The grounds are open daily from 8 a.m. to sunset, with expansive gardens and five miles of carriage roads to explore, and one of the best views of the Hudson River Valley in the state. A number of outdoor tours are available; visit the website for the latest information.

More than seventy antiques shops fill five historic walking blocks on *Warren Street* in Hudson. Furniture, clocks, porcelains, rugs, ephemera . . . the antiques district is a collector's dream. Most shops are open Thursday through Tuesday. For information call the Hudson Antiques & Art Dealers Association at 518–822–9397 or check their website at hudsonantiques.net. For a complete list of shops, contact the Columbia County Tourism Department at (800) 724–1846.

On July 13, 1865, Barnum's American Museum, located at the corner of Ann Street and Broadway in Manhattan, and filled with the "wonders of the world," caught fire. Volunteer fire companies, some in newly introduced steam engines, rushed to the rescue and managed to save, among other things, "Old Glory," the flag that was flying from a mast on the roof.

Today Old Glory is one of just 2,500 fire-related articles on display at the **FASNY Museum of Firefighting**, which documents nearly three hundred years of firefighting history and houses one of the country's largest collections of firefighting apparatus and memorabilia. Of the sixty-eight firefighting engines on display, the majority are nineteenth-century hand pumpers, ladder trucks, and hose carts, including a 1725 Newsham, the first successful working engine used in New York.

The museum is next door to the Volunteer Firemen's Home, a health-care facility for volunteer firefighters who continue to volunteer, this time as museum guides.

The FASNY Museum of Firefighting (117 Harry Howard Ave., Hudson; 518–822–1875; fasnyfiremuseum.com) is open Wed through Sun, 10 a.m. to 4:30 p.m., except major holidays. Admission is $10 for adults, $5 for children 3 to 17, and free for children under age 3.

The home of Pulitzer Prize–winning lyrical poet and playwright Edna St. Vincent Millay still stands in Austerlitz, where she lived with her husband, Jan Boissevain, for twenty-five years. **Steepletop** (440 East Hill Rd., Austerlitz; 518–392–3362; millay.org) began as a 635-acre blueberry farm, to which the couple added a writing cabin, a Sears Roebuck–kit barn, and even a tennis court. Today you can visit the home of the woman who wrote such works as "Renascence," one of her most famous poems, as well as "The Ballad of the Harp Weaver," for which she won the Pulitzer. Its library has more than three thousand books, and 230 acres of open landscape complete the experience. Call or check the website for current hours.

It's easy to whisk right past the small town of Hillsdale, but let the curves in the road direct you into town to discover **Hillsdale General Store**, where you can stroll through antiques, china, household items, specialty items selected by local designers, and all the maple syrup and other local food products you can carry. In a building that has housed a retail store for well over one hundred years, this shop happens to be next door to one of our favorite ice-cream parlors in all of New York State: the **Village Scoop**, where you can get an ample portion of Jane's Homemade Ice Cream, one of the best brands in the Hudson River Valley. The Scoop also sells luscious baked goods, alcohol-free cocktails, and cheese boards if you need to stock your picnic basket as you pass through town.

The road less traveled can sometimes lead us to the nicest places. Route 23 out of Hillsdale to Craryville is such a road. It goes—via a right turn off Route 23 onto Craryville Road, and then a left onto West End Road and then right onto Rodman Road (or just follow the signs)—to ***Rodgers Book Barn***, a secondhand shop considered by many bibliophiles to be one of the best in the country. The barn—a two-story affair—is packed from floor to ceiling with some twenty thousand books. The collection is wonderfully eclectic: There are inexpensive '50s potboilers, tomes on European and American history, gardening books, rare out-of-print editions in dozens of categories, and undoubtedly a few of my own titles, as well as a cat or two. The shop's owner, Maureen Rodgers, encourages browsing to the point of inviting patrons to bring along a lunch to enjoy in the grape arbor next to the herb garden.

Rodgers Book Barn (467 Rodman Rd., Hillsdale; 518–325–3610; rodgers bookbarn.com) is open year-round, Fri through Sun, 11 a.m. to 4 p.m., and Mon and Thurs mornings by appointment.

The ***Crandell Theater*** first opened its doors on Christmas Day 1926. Today, Columbia County's oldest and largest movie theater, a Spanish-style building of brick and stucco, remains proudly independent in a world of chain-owned, cookie-cutter megaplexes. Get there early, grab a bag of freshly popped popcorn, and head for the balcony. You'll get a true blast from the past along with a first-run movie for only $7.50 a ticket for adults ($6.50 for members and children, as well as for matinees). The theater is at 48 Main Street in Chatham (518–392–3331; crandelltheatre.org).

East of Albany

The ***Shaker Museum and Library*** in Old Chatham lives in a collection of buildings located just twelve miles from Mount Lebanon, New York, where the Shakers established one of their first US communities. Formally known as the United Society of Believers in Christ's Second Appearing, the Shakers originated in Britain and relocated to America just prior to the revolution. A quietist, monastic order dedicated to equality between the sexes, sharing of community property, temperance in its broad sense, and the practice of celibacy, the sect peaked in the middle nineteenth century with about six thousand members. Today there are fewer than a dozen Shakers living in a community at Sabbath-day Lake, Maine.

Ironically, it is the secular aspects of Shaker life that are most often recalled today. The members of the communities were almost obsessive regarding simplicity and purity of form in the articles they designed and crafted for daily life; "Shaker furniture" has become a generic term for the elegantly uncluttered designs they employed. In their pursuit of the perfect form dictated by function, they even invented now ubiquitous objects, such as the flat broom.

Ring around the Collar

According to local lore, Mrs. Hannah Lord Montague of Troy spawned a new industry when, in 1825, she cut the soiled collars off her husband's otherwise clean shirts so she would only have to wash the dirty parts. This inspired *Cluett, Peabody & Company*, a manufacturer that provided button-on shirt collars to *Arrow Shirt Company*, a wardrobe staple for every working man in the 1910s and 1920s. In its heyday, the factory turned out four million collars every week, making it the most successful company in the United States in its time. Its Bleachery complex still stands in *Peebles Island State Park*, at the confluence of the Mohawk and Hudson Rivers here in Troy.

The Shaker Museum has amassed a collection of more than eighteen thousand objects, half of which are on display. The main building contains an orientation gallery that surveys Shaker history and provides highlights of the rest of the collection, and the library contains one of the two most extensive collections of Shaker material in the world. The cafe serves snacks and beverages.

The Shaker Museum and Library (88 Shaker Museum Rd. off County Route 13, Old Chatham; 518–794–9100; shakermuseumandlibrary.org) is open by appointment Mon through Fri, 9 a.m. to 5 p.m.

In 1624 a ship with thirty Dutch Walloons onboard sailed up the Hudson River and established a fur-trading station called Fort Orange, replacing the Fort Nassau trading post constructed here in 1617. Disputes back in the Netherlands pushed the community that sprang up around the fort to become the first permanent, independent Dutch settlement in New Netherland. Fort Orange managed to survive annual flooding, a massive smallpox outbreak, and dicey politics involving the Dutch West India Company, and became the city of Albany under English rule before the end of the century.

Across the river is the town of Rensselaer, named for the family who held the "patroonship," or feudal proprietorship, of the vast area on the east bank.

Born in the USA

During the War of 1812, Troy brickmaker Samuel Wilson opened a slaughterhouse and sold meat to a government contractor named Elbert Anderson. All of his beef and pork was stamped "US-E.A.," and soldiers made up a story that the "US," which stood for United States, actually stood for "Uncle Sam" Wilson. The Troy newspaper picked up the amusing anecdote on September 7, 1813, and thus was *Uncle Sam* born. A monument to his memory stands at the head of 101st Street in Troy.

Crailo, built in the early eighteenth century by the first patroon's grandson, recalls a time when the Dutch were still the predominant cultural presence in the area.

Crailo changed with time and tastes. A Georgian-style east wing, added in 1762, reflected the increasing influence of the English in the area; Federal touches were added later in the century. Since 1933 the house has served as a museum of the Dutch in the upper Hudson Valley. Exhibits include seventeenth- and eighteenth-century prints and archaeological artifacts, many from the Fort Orange excavation of 1970–71.

Crailo State Historic Site (9 1/2 Riverside Ave., Rensselaer; 518–463–8738; parks.ny.gov/historic-sites/crailo) is open mid-Apr through late Oct, with tours by reservation only from Wed through Sun at 11 a.m., 1 p.m., and 3 p.m. From Nov through Mar, visits are by appointment, Tues through Fri, 10 a.m. to 4 p.m. Tours are given on the hour and half hour; the last tour is at 4 p.m. It is also open Memorial Day, Independence Day, and Labor Day. Admission is $5 for adults, free for children 12 and under, and $4 for seniors and students 13 and up.

The *Children's Museum of Science and Technology* (CMOST) is the only science center in the capital area where parents and children can explore and make discoveries together. Recent programs featured birds of prey; an animated adventure exploring the nature of atoms and molecules; experiments on the nature of water; the technology of robots; and an exploration of the nature of color.

The Children's Museum of Science and Technology (250 Jordan Rd., Rensselaer Tech Park, Troy; 518–235–2120; cmost.org) is open Sept through June, Tues through Sun from 9 a.m. to 4 p.m.; July and Aug, Mon through Sat from 9 a.m. to 4 p.m. Admission is $8 per person for ages 2 and up; free for active-duty military.

Hoosic Valley

You may know that the Battle of Bunker Hill was not actually fought on Bunker Hill (it took place on Breed's Hill, in Charlestown, Massachusetts), but how many can identify another military misnomer of the revolution?

We're talking about the 1777 Battle of Bennington, an American victory that laid the groundwork for the defeat and surrender of General Burgoyne at Saratoga that October. The battle, in which American militiamen defended their ammunition and supplies from an attacking party made up of British troops, Tory sympathizers, mercenaries, and Indians, took place not in Bennington, Vermont, but in Walloomsac, New York. True, the stores that the British were after were stashed in the Vermont town, but the actual fighting took place on New York soil.

The State of New York today maintains **Bennington Battlefield State Historic Site** on a lovely hilltop in eastern Rensselaer County's Grafton State Park, studded with bronze and granite markers that explain the movements of the troops on the American militia's triumphal day. The spot is located at 5157 Route 67 and is open May 1 through Veterans Day, daily 8 a.m. to sunset. Visitors can check road conditions by calling Bennington Battlefield State Historic Site at (518) 860–9094 or by visiting parks.ny.gov/historic-sites/12/. On a clear day you can enjoy fine views of the Green Mountain foothills, among which Bennington's obelisk monument is prominent. Drive over to visit the monument and give the Vermonters their due—but really, doesn't "Battle of Walloomsac" have a nice ring to it?

Folk artist Will Moses, a great-grandson of the renowned primitive painter Grandma Moses, carries on the family tradition through his own art: minutely detailed paintings that reflect the charm and beauty of the tiny rural community where he lives. At **Mount Nebo Gallery** (60 Grandma Moses Rd., Eagle Bridge; 800–328–6326; willmoses.com), in the house where his famous ancestor developed her own artistic style, visitors can view and purchase painstakingly printed serigraphs of Will Moses's paintings, along with prints, etchings, note cards, puzzles, Christmas cards, illustrated books, posters, calendars, and more. The gallery is open Mon through Fri, 9 a.m. to 4 p.m.; Sat, 10 a.m. to 5 p.m.; Sun, noon to 5 p.m.

Our next stop on this ramble up the east shore of the Hudson offers proof that in this part of the world, the monastic spirit did not pass into history with the Shakers. Cambridge is the home of the **New Skete Monasteries**, a group of monks, nuns, and laypeople organized around a life of prayer, contemplation, and physical work. Founded in 1966 within the Byzantine Rite of the Roman Catholic Church, the New Skete Communities have been a part of the Orthodox Church in America since 1979.

Visitors to New Skete are welcome at the community's two houses of worship. The small Transfiguration Temple, open at all times, contains a number of icons painted by the monks and nuns, while the larger Holy Wisdom Church—open to visitors only during services—has, embedded in its marble floor, original pieces of mosaic that were brought from the 576 AD Church of Saint Sophia (Holy Wisdom) in Constantinople. Worship services are usually twice daily.

As in many monastic communities, the monks and the nuns of New Skete help support themselves through a wide variety of pursuits. An important part of their life is the breeding of German shepherds and the boarding and training of all breeds of dogs. The monks have even written four successful books, *How to Be Your Dog's Best Friend, The Art of Raising a Puppy, Let Dogs Be Dogs*, and *I & Dog: The New Skete Way.* At their gift shops they sell their own cheeses, smoked meats, fruitcakes, the famous New Skete cheesecakes, dog beds, religious cards made by the nuns, original painted icons, Christmas ornaments, and other items.

The convent is accessible from the village of Cambridge via East Main Street on Ash Grove Road, and the monastery is farther out of town on 273 New Skete Road. For information call the monks at (518) 677–3928 or the nuns at (518) 677–3810. The nuns' bakery is open Tues through Fri, 9 a.m. to 4 p.m.; Sat, 10 a.m. to 4 p.m. Their website is newskete.com.

No drive along Route 7 in eastern New York can be complete without a stop at the family-owned and -operated ***Potter Hill Barn*** (3864 NY 7, Hoosick Falls; 800–301–7776 or 518–686–7777; potterhillbarn.com), where shoppers find all kinds of country craft items, including ceramics, tableware, textiles, furniture, embroidered items, candles, lamps, dolls, wooden signs, baskets, and much more. Significantly different from other gift shops along this route, Potter Hill's merchandise is always high quality and includes many items crafted by local artisans, and the spacious store provides a relaxed shopping experience. It's open daily year-round except for Christmas Day, 10 a.m. to 5:30 p.m.

Places to Stay East of the Hudson

HOPEWELL JUNCTION

Le Chambord at Curry Estate
2737 Rte. 52
(845) 221–1941
curryestate.com

HUDSON

Hudson Bed and Breakfast
136 Union St.
(518) 929–6199
hudsonbandb.com

HYDE PARK

Journey Inn Bed & Breakfast
One Sherwood Pl.
(845) 229–8972
journeyinn.com

PEEKSKILL

Inn on the Hudson
634 Main St.
(914) 739–1500
innonthehudson.com

POUGHKEEPSIE

Best Western Plus the Inn & Suites at the Falls
50 Red Oaks Mill Rd.
(845) 462–5770
bestwestern.com/
en_US/book/hotels-
in-poughkeepsie/
best-western-plus-the-
inn-suites-at-the-falls/
propertyCode.33149.html

RHINEBECK

Bittersweet Bed & Breakfast
470 Wurtemburg Rd.
(845) 876–7777
bittersweetbedandbreakfast
.com

The Gables of Rhinebeck
6358 Mill St.
(631) 766–6871
thegablesrhinebeck.com

Whistlewood Farm Bed and Breakfast
52 Pells Rd.
(845) 876–6838
whistlewood.com

TARRYTOWN

Tarrytown House Estate and Conference Center
49 East Sunnyside Ln.
(914) 591–8200
tarrytownhouseestate.com

TIVOLI

Hotel Tivoli
53 Broadway
(845) 757–2100
hoteltivoli.org

TROY

Olde Judge Mansion
3300 Sixth Ave.
(518) 274–5698
oldejudgemansion.com

WHITE PLAINS

Renaissance Westchester Hotel
80 West Red Oak Ln.
(914) 694–5400
marriott.com/hotels/
travel/hpnsh-renaissance-
westchester-hotel/

Places to Eat East of the Hudson

BEACON

Sukhothai Restaurant
516 Main St.
(845) 790–5375
sukhothainy.com

GARRISON

Valley Restaurant at the Garrison
2015 US 9
(845) 424–3604
thegarrison.com

GERMANTOWN

Gaskins
2 Church Ave.
(518) 537–2107
gaskinsny.com

REGIONAL TOURIST INFORMATION EAST OF THE HUDSON

Columbia County Tourism
401 State St.
Hudson
(518) 828–3375
columbiacountytourism.org

Dutchess County Tourism
3 Neptune Rd.
Suite A11A
Poughkeepsie
(845) 463–4000 and
(800) 445–3131
dutchesstourism.com

Hudson Valley Tourism
(845) 291–2136 and
(800) 232–4782
travelhudsonvalley.org

Putnam County Tourism
40 Glendale Ave., third floor
Carmel
(845) 808–1015
visitputnam.org

Rensselaer County Tourism
1600 7th Ave.
Troy
(518) 270–2673
renscotourism.com

OTHER ATTRACTIONS WORTH SEEING EAST OF THE HUDSON

**Bardavon 1869
Opera House**
35 Market St.
Poughkeepsie
(845) 473–2072
bardavon.org

Boscobel
1601 Rte. 9D
Garrison
(845) 265–3638
boscobel.org

Frances Lehman Loeb Art Center
Vassar College
124 Raymond Ave.
Poughkeepsie
(845) 437–5632
fllac.vassar.edu

Kykuit (Rockefeller Estate)
381 N. Broadway
Sleepy Hollow
(914) 631–8200
hudsonvalley.org/historic-sites/
kykuit-the-rockefeller-estate/

Madame Brett Homestead
50 Van Nydeck Ave.
Beacon
(845) 831–6533
hudsonrivervalley.com/sites/
Madam-Brett-Homestead

Mary Flagler Cary Arboretum
2801 Sharon Tpke.
Millbrook
(845) 677–5343
tools.bgci.org/garden
.php?id=1308?id=1308

Montgomery Place Campus
Bard College
Campus Road
Annandale-on-Hudson
(845) 752–5000
bard.edu/montgomeryplace/

Philipsburg Manor
381 N. Broadway
Sleepy Hollow
(914) 366–6900
hudsonvalley.org/historic-sites/
philipsburg-manor/

Taconic State Park
253 Rte. 344
Copake Falls
(518) 329–3993
parks.ny.gov/parks/taconiccopake

Van Cortlandt Manor
525 S. Riverside Ave.
Croton-on-Hudson
(914) 631–8200
hudsonvalley.org/historic-sites/
van-cortlandt-manor/

Wilderstein Historic Site
330 Morton Rd.
Rhinebeck
(845) 876–4818
wilderstein.org

HOPEWELL JUNCTION

Le Chambord
at Curry Estate
2737 Rte. 52
(845) 221–1941
curryestate.com

KATONAH

Blue Dolphin Ristorante
175 Katonah Ave.
(914) 232–4791
bluedolphinny.com

POCANTICO HILLS

Blue Hill at Stone Barns
630 Bedford Rd.
(914) 366–9600
bluehillfarm.com

POUGHKEEPSIE

Cosimo's
120 Delafield St.
(845) 485–7172
cosimospoughkeepsie.com

RHINEBECK

The Tasting Room
Restaurant
3767 NY 9G
(845) 876–4480
gendroncatering.com

TARRYTOWN

Bistro 12
12 Main St.
(914) 909–2770
bistro12.net

The Adirondacks

For those who have no idea that New York State contains some of the most scenically splendid roads in the United States, take a drive north to the Adirondacks at just about any time of year. Brilliantly monochromatic as baby leaves burst forth throughout the region's heavily forested mountains, covered in wildflowers in summer, unsurpassed in beauty as the leaves turn amber, scarlet, and rusty red in fall, and grandly snowcapped in winter, these peaks provide the break from cityscapes every urban dweller needs—just as they did centuries ago, when the richest Hudson River Valley tycoons made their way up here to "rusticate" along the many lakes.

The Adirondacks count forty-two peaks that soar over 4,000 feet above sea level, including Mt. Marcy, near Lake Placid, the state's highest elevation at 5,344 feet.

The brainchild of a few enlightened souls in 1892, Adirondack Park protects more than six million acres of mountains, waterways, and open land, allowing the landowners of three million of those acres to continue to live, work, and develop within its borders. This permitted the rest of the wild lands to recover from the clear-cutting the logging industry had completed in the mid-nineteenth century, which had left denuded

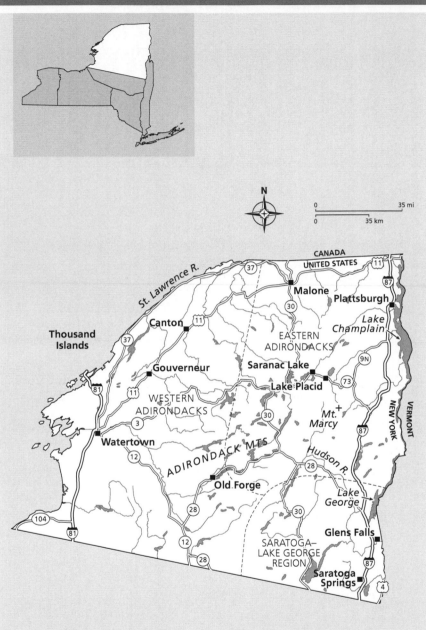

mountainsides to erode without their forest cover. Today these wide stretches of undeveloped land fairly burst with natural wonders, from chains of crystal lakes to burbling rivers, and from herds of white-tailed deer to gently whistling common loons.

Most visitors come here to experience the great outdoors, but on rainy or snowy days that make hiking, skiing, and boating unpleasant, there's still plenty to see between the high peaks. Museums and historic sites document the rich history of the land and its people, from the Native American nations to the settlers who carved towns out of the woods, building cabins and boats, and yes, even the comfortable outdoor chairs that take their name from this region.

(Note: The overall place-to-place direction followed in this chapter is counterclockwise—south to north to west.)

Saratoga–Lake George Region

To horse-racing fans, **Saratoga Springs** is simply "The Spa," an annual exodus from New York City, when the August races at **Saratoga Race Course** bring them out into the fresh air. Many fans book their hotel rooms a year in advance, everywhere from the stately old Adelphi Hotel to the national chains, to the many B&Bs housed in lovely old Victorian houses. But there's so much more to Saratoga than racing: rich history to discover, mineral springs to enjoy, and concerts and shows at the **Saratoga Performing Arts Center** (spac.org), summer home to the Philadelphia Orchestra and the New York City Opera and Ballet.

When puzzling over an exacta gets too taxing, relax and "take the cure" at the **Lincoln Baths** (65 South Broadway) or the **Roosevelt Baths & Spa** (39 Roosevelt Dr.), both built in the 1930s and modeled after the grand spas of Europe. Both were recently renovated and have added a full menu of facials, massages, and other treatments to complement the traditional effervescent mineral water bath, a uniquely relaxing experience.

The baths are a short stroll from the **Gideon Putnam Resort and Spa** (24 Gideon Putnam Rd.), the grand Georgian Revival–style edifice at the center of the 2,300-acre Saratoga Spa State Park. A gracious setting for every sort of leisure activity—tennis, golf, swimming, horseback riding, jogging, and, in winter, ice-skating and cross-country skiing—the hotel offers a luxurious, recently renovated setting, returning it to a time when the flamboyant interior designer Dorothy Draper envisioned bold colors and patterns for its grand lobby and gracious restaurants. Rates at the Gideon Putnam vary according to season, with rooms running from as low as $116, with many value-added romantic,

AUTHOR'S FAVORITES IN THE ADIRONDACKS

Adirondack Experience	John Brown Farm State Historic Site
Crown Point State Historic Site	Old Forge Hardware
Ferd's Bog	Paul Smith's VIC
Garnet Mine Tours	Saratoga National Historical Park
High Peaks Scenic Byway	Wild Center

golf, and spa packages offered. Call (800) 890–1171 or go to gideonputnam .com for more on the hotel and the baths.

Tradition says the Native Americans of the Saratoga region visited High Rock Spring as early as 1300 to gain strength from the "Medicine Spring of the Great Spirit." Centuries later, in 1771, Mohawk tribesmen from Johnstown carried Sir William Johnson, suffering from a wound received in the Battle of Lake George, on a litter to High Rock Spring. After a short stay, Johnson's health improved noticeably, and the reputation of the spring quickly grew.

The first person to recognize the commercial value of the mineral waters at Saratoga Springs may well have been John Arnold, who in 1774 purchased a crude log cabin built on a bluff overlooking High Rock Spring, improved it, and opened an inn. Thirteen years later, Revolutionary War hero Alexander Bryan purchased the inn, the only Saratoga hotel until 1801. Now the **Olde Bryan Inn**, the hotel has been a lodge, tavern, restaurant, and private dwelling, and is now a restaurant serving traditional American cuisine. Today you can enjoy chicken wings, burgers, a homestyle turkey dinner, fish and chips, a range of other dishes, and a piece of chocolate chip pie.

The Olde Bryan Inn (123 Maple Ave., Saratoga Springs; 518–587–2990) is open Sun through Thurs, 11 a.m. until 10 p.m.; Fri and Sat, 11 a.m. to 11 p.m. The tavern is open daily until midnight.

Between 1823 and 1889, industrious Saratogans bottled mineral waters from approximately thirty springs in Saratoga County and distributed them around the world, touting their medicinal and curative properties. The **National Bottle Museum**, housed in a 1901 former hardware store in Ballston Spa's historic district, documents the rise and decline of that industry. Through exhibits of antique bottles and glassmaking tools, videos, and artifacts, it tells the story of a time past, when young men were indentured to the owners of glass factories and apprenticed for fifteen years in order to become glassblowers in the

A Gas Explosion

The discovery of a process to extract carbonic gas (used to make carbonated beverages) from Saratoga Springs waters in 1890 was almost the resort's death knell. Over the next few decades, the burgeoning industry pumped many of its wells nearly dry. In 1910, to protect its natural resources, the state purchased 163 springs and 1,000 acres of land surrounding them, and constructed baths, a research institute, a Hall of Springs, and the Gideon Putnam hotel.

glasshouses that made bottles and jars by hand. It re-creates an industry and a way of life that have vanished from the American scene.

The National Bottle Museum (76 Milton Ave., Ballston Spa; 518–885–7589; nationalbottlemuseum.org) is open year-round, Tues through Sat, 10 a.m. to 4 p.m. and closed Sun and Mon. Admission is free.

For those born too late to see Secretariat or Seabiscuit in the flesh, the history and traditions of the sport are thoroughly chronicled at the *National Museum of Racing and Hall of Fame*, directly across from the Saratoga Race Course. Patrons enter the museum through an actual starting gate, complete with life-size representations of a horse, jockey, and starter. Some of the highlights: paintings of outstanding horses, the saddle and boots used by jockey Johnny Loftus on Man o' War, a Hall of Fame, and the actual skeleton of a thoroughbred. The film *What It Takes: Journey to the Hall of Fame* is shown in the theater. Video booths lining the walls provide films of some of racing's greats.

The National Museum of Racing and Hall of Fame (191 Union Ave., Saratoga Springs; 518–584–0400; racingmuseum.org) is open every day, year-round, 9 a.m. to 5 p.m.; closed on Thanksgiving Day and Christmas Day. Admission is $7 for adults and $5 for senior citizens, students, and children 6 to 18.

Folks in Saratoga Springs have been flocking to *Hattie's* for Southern fried chicken and biscuits since 1938. Chef Jasper Alexander prepares everything—slow-cooked barbecued spare ribs, Hoppin' John (black-eyed peas with chopped onion, salt and pepper, butter, and pork), blackened catfish, Creole jambalaya, gumbo—using authentic Louisiana recipes and methods, carrying on a tradition much prized by the eatery's loyal following. Hattie's (3057 Rte. 50, Saratoga Springs; 518–584–4790; hattiesrestaurant.com) is open Wed through Sat, 5 to 9 p.m.; Sat and Sun brunch, 10 a.m. to 2 p.m. Enjoy courtyard dining in the summer in one of the restaurant's four outdoor spaces.

Many people visiting the Saratoga Springs area skip the racetrack and the spas entirely and choose the destination because of its pivotal role in America winning the Revolutionary War. *Saratoga National Historical Park* tells the story of how American artillery on Bemis Heights blocked the advance of the British army under General John Burgoyne, thanks to some brilliant engineering of the fortifications by Polish colonel Thaddeus Kosciuszko that made them virtually impossible to break. In two battles separated by three weeks, Burgoyne lost more than twelve hundred men, more than twice the number sacrificed by the scrappy American army. As the standoff progressed, American troops arrived from throughout the northern colonies, eventually surrounding Burgoyne's forces with seventeen thousand men and forcing the British general's surrender. The battles turned the tide of the war in America's favor, and while it took another four years to bring it to a close, the British knew they fought at a disadvantage from this point forward. Visitors can pick up a CD at

ANNUAL EVENTS IN THE ADIRONDACKS

JANUARY

Lake George Polar Plunge
Lake George
(800) 705–0059
lakegeorge.com/polar-plunge/

Winter Birding Weekend
Long Lake
(518) 624–3077
adirondack.net/event/winter-birding-weekend-in-long-lake-139402/

FEBRUARY

Empire State Winter Games
Lake Placid
(518) 523–1655
orda.org

Winter Carnival
Saranac Lake
(518) 891–1990
saranaclake.com/events/
saranac-lake-winter-carnival

MARCH

Ticonderoga End of Winter Carnival
Ticonderoga
lakechamplainregion.com/events/
ticonderoga-end-of-winter-carnival

Maple Weekend at the International Maple Museum Centre
Croghan
(315) 346–1107
maplemuseumcentre.org

MAY

Adirondack Boreal Birding Festival
Blue Mountain Lake
(518) 548–3076
adirondackexperience.com/events/
adirondack-boreal-birding-festival-0

The Adirondack Paddlefest & Outdoor Expo
Inlet
(315) 369–6672
mountainmanoutdoors.com/adirondack-paddlefest.html

JUNE

Americade Motorcycle Rally
Lake George
(518) 798–7888
americade.com

Lake Placid Film Festival
Lake Placid
(518) 523–3456
lakeplacidfilmfestival.org

the visitor center to listen to while driving the battlefield's tour road, or call the number posted at the start of the tour for narration by mobile phone. Saratoga National Historical Park (648 NY-32, Stillwater; 518–664–9821; nps.gov/sara) is open daily, 9 a.m. to 5 p.m.; closed Thanksgiving Day, Christmas Day, and New Year's Day. Admission to this national park is free.

In June 1885, suffering from throat cancer and longing for fresh air and a healthier climate, President Ulysses S. Grant left his home in New York City for Saratoga County. He and his family moved into a summer cottage on top of Mt. McGregor, eight miles from Saratoga Springs. At the cottage he continued work on his memoirs and, two weeks after completing them, died on July 23, 1885.

LARAC Arts Festival
Glens Falls
(518) 523–3456
larac.org/festivals/

JULY

Can-Am Arts Festival
Sackets Harbor
canamfestival.com

Long Boat Regatta
Long Lake
(518) 624–3077
mylonglake.com/category/
long-boat-regatta/

AUGUST

Travers Festival Week
Saratoga Springs
(518) 584–3255
saratoga.com/race-track/travers-festival/

SEPTEMBER

Adirondack Balloon Festival
Queensbury
(518) 222–4593
adirondackballoonfest.org

Adirondack Wool and Arts Festival
Glens Falls
glensfalls.com/event/
adirondack-wool-arts-festival-79683/

Great Adirondack Moose Festival
Indian Lake
(518) 648–5112
adirondack.net/event/
adirondack-moose-festival-64386/

Inlet's Fall Festival
Inlet
adirondack.net/event/
inlets-fall-festival-153725/

OCTOBER

World's Largest Garage Sale
Warrensburg
(518) 623–2161
warrensburggaragesale.com

DECEMBER

First Night (New Year's Eve)
Saranac Lake
(518) 891–2484
adirondack.net/event/
first-night-saranac-lake-25223/

A Chip by Any Other Name . . .

In 1853, in an effort to please a finicky customer, cook George Crum at Moon's Lake House cut his potatoes paper-thin and deep-fried the slices. The crispy Saratoga Chips became potato chips, launching an entire snack industry.

The house at ***Ulysses S. Grant Cottage State Historic Site*** is preserved as Grant left it, from the bed where he died to the floral pieces sent from around the country. It is operated by the Friends of the Ulysses S. Grant Cottage, in cooperation with the New York State Office of Parks, Recreation, and Historic Preservation.

Grant Cottage State Historic Site (1000 Mt. McGregor Rd., Wilton; 518–584–4353; grantcottage.org) is open Labor Day through Nov 1, Fri through Sun, 9:30 a.m. to closing; call for current hours. Admission is $9 for adults, $7 for senior citizens, and $5 for children 6 to 17; children 5 and under are free.

The Hydes of Glens Falls—Charlotte Pruyn, heiress to the paper company fortune, and Louis Fisk Hyde of Boston—preferred painting to ponies, and spent a fortune amassing what became known as the ***Hyde Collection*** of American and European art. The couple began building the Florentine villa that would become their home-as-museum in 1912, in the mold of Boston tastemaker Isabella Stewart Gardner. With the help of connoisseurs such as Bernard Berenson, the Hydes acquired a collection spanning five centuries that included works by Rubens, Botticelli, Rembrandt, Seurat, Degas, Homer, Whistler, Picasso, Cézanne, and Matisse. No mere check-writers, the Hydes bought with expert eyes, building a visual anthology rich with important and expressive works.

The Hyde Collection opened to the public in 1963 after Mrs. Hyde's death at the age of ninety-six and underwent extensive restoration and renovations in 2004. The Hyde Collection (161 Warren St., Glens Falls; 518–792–1761; hydecollection.org) is open year-round Fri through Sun, 10 a.m. to 5 p.m.; closed Mon through Thurs and national holidays. Adults $12; seniors 60+ $10; students and children under 13 are free, as are veterans and active-duty military and their families.

Fans of James Fenimore Cooper's *The Last of the Mohicans* may take an interest in Glens Falls—not just the town, but the waterfall itself, and the shadowy cave hidden behind it. ***Cooper's Cave*** (Cooper's Cave Drive, Glens Falls; 518–761–3864; cityofglensfalls.com), referred to in the novel as the "dark and silent cave" beneath the thundering, pre-dam waters, became shelter for the book's two heroines and their guide as Hawkeye and his Mohican traveling companions continued on their journey. Today the dam harnesses the falls for water power to generate electricity for Finch Paper LLC and Boralex, Inc., but the cave itself—once a roadside attraction back in the mid-twentieth century— still provides a fun stop for literature and history buffs. Follow US 9 north into the village of South Glen Falls, and make an immediate left at the bridge, driving into a parking area and small park with interpretive signs about the falls and dam. You can view the cave from here. Open May 1 through Oct 31, dawn to dusk, free admission.

At the age of nineteen, Marcella (Kochanska) Sembrich made her operatic debut in Athens, Greece, singing in a number of the great opera houses in Europe before joining New York's Metropolitan Opera Company for its first season in 1883. She returned to Europe until 1898 and rejoined the Metropolitan Opera until 1909, when her farewell was the occasion for the most sumptuous gala in the Met's history at the time. Sembrich founded the vocal departments of the Juilliard School in New York and the Curtis Institute in Philadelphia, and served as a preeminent teacher of singing for twenty-five years. She often brought students to a studio near her summer home in Bolton Landing on Lake George. *The Marcella Sembrich Opera Museum*, in Mme. Sembrich's converted studio, displays operatic memorabilia she collected from her debut to her death in 1935.

Summer events include studio talks, a lakeside lecture series, a master class in voice, and occasional recitals or chamber concerts.

The Marcella Sembrich Opera Museum (4800 Lake Shore Dr., Bolton Landing; 518–644–9839; operamuseum.com) is open daily, June 1 through Sept 22, 10 a.m. to 12:30 p.m. and 2 to 5:30 p.m. Admission is free, with a suggested donation of $5 for adults 16 and over.

Better known as a summer party town than a posh resort area, *Lake George* has long attracted an eclectic crowd to its budget-friendly accommodations, restaurants, and activities from Memorial Day through the fall foliage season. Even so, you can get a taste of gracious living in Gilded-Age style at *The Sagamore* (not to be confused with the Great Camp Sagamore up in the mountains), a grand old hotel built on a seventy-acre private island off Bolton Landing at 110 Sagamore Road. Two long wings spread out toward the lake, giving many rooms a sparkling view of the water. Time-honored pleasures include formal dining in the Trillium restaurant; sipping afternoon tea (or perhaps a single malt scotch) on the veranda; sailing, swimming, tennis, racquetball, or even golf (the latter on the mainland); and de-stressing in the spa.

Rates at the Sagamore vary seasonally, starting in the mid-$200s per night for a room with no view to $798 a night for suites with a view in the summer season. Some suites and accommodations in the eleven-room Hermitage have higher rates. Call (866) 384–1944 or go to thesagamore.com for current rates and specials; reach the hotel on the local line at (518) 644–9400.

Eastern Adirondacks

Fort Ticonderoga, which stands on a promontory jutting into the southern end of Lake Champlain, provided the French with a southern defense in their struggle against Great Britain for control of Canada in 1755. Called Fort Carillon at the time, it was built of earth and timbers and later upgraded to stone, with four pointed bastions presenting an interlocking field of fire against attackers.

In 1758 the Marquis de Montcalm repelled a massive attack on the fort by the British, but a year later Lord Jeffrey Amherst captured the fort and renamed it Ticonderoga. Seventeen years later—three weeks after the Battles of Lexington and Concord—Ethan Allen and Benedict Arnold captured "Fort Ti" from the British "in the name of the Great Jehovah and the Continental Congress," giving the Americans their first victory of the revolution.

Last garrisoned in 1777, Fort Ti might be little more than a roadside marker had it not been for the efforts of the Pell family to protect the site since 1820. Stephen and Sarah Pell began a restoration of it in 1908, bringing it up to the standard we see today. Guides in eighteenth-century clothing provide historical interpretation for visitors, and a host of events, including live artillery demonstrations and fife and drum musters, help bring the fort to life.

Visitors can stride along the ramparts, view the earthworks built during both the French and Indian Wars and the American Revolution, examine the barracks, and visit the museum, which houses North America's largest collection of eighteenth-century artillery as well as paintings, furniture, and military memorabilia. Just outside the fort is the battlefield where, in 1758, Montcalm devastated the 42nd Highland ("Black Watch") Regiment.

Fort Ticonderoga (102 Fort Ti Rd., Ticonderoga; 518–585–2210; fort ticonderoga.org) is open daily from early May through late Oct, 9:30 a.m. to 5 p.m. Admission is $19.95 for adults, $17.95 for seniors, $12 for children ages 5 to 15, and free for children under 5. The America's Fort Café is open for breakfast, lunch, and snacks, and the Museum Store provides grab-and-go meals and snacks.

As a sidelight to a Fort Ticonderoga visit, drive to the summit of nearby ***Mt. Defiance*** for a panoramic view of the Champlain Valley. Extend your experience of this region with a seventy-five-minute narrated cruise tour of Lake Champlain aboard the *Carillon* ($40 adults and seniors, $25 children 5 to 12, free for children 4 and under), which operates from a dock at the Fort Ticonderoga property.

Located west of Ticonderoga, deeper in the Adirondacks, **Garnet Hill Lodge**, a remote resort on six hundred acres of land, provides easy access to the Barton family garnet mine. Members of the Barton family built the lodge in 1933 when they came to the area, creating a rustic Adirondack-style accommodation. But some of the rooms, complete with whirlpool baths and hot tubs, can no longer be described as "rustic," as they now feature all kinds of modern amenities and comforts. The resort offers a host of activities, including tubing, mountain biking, and a special course on fly-fishing. The lodge, at 39 Garnet Hill Road off of 13th Lake Road in North River (518–251–2444; garnet-hill.com), is open year-round. Rates range from $150 per night for a standard room to $219 per night for a balcony room; call for seasonal and multi-night rates.

Visitors can tour the **Barton Mines** and look for gemstones in the open pits at **Garnet Mine Tours** on Barton Mines Road. The mines represent one of the world's largest garnet deposits, with some of the largest garnet crystals in the world, and its flat character makes it easy to walk while searching for gemstones. The mines are open daily from late June through early Oct—9:30 a.m. to 5 p.m. Mon through Sat, 11 a.m. to 5 p.m. Sun—and on weekends through Columbus Day. Visitors must be escorted in the mines; the tour is $14.95 for adults, $10.95 for children ages 7 to 14, and $13.95 for seniors 60+. Call (518) 251–2706 or go to garnetminetours.com for information. Garnet Mine Tours begin at 1126 Barton Mines Rd. in North River.

Brandied French toast with sautéed apples is the breakfast specialty at **Goose Pond Inn** (518–251–3434; goosepondinn.com), a charming, antiques-filled, turn-of-the-century bed-and-breakfast just a mile from Gore Mountain Ski Center. The inn, open year-round, is on Main Street in North Creek. Rates begin at $155/night for a mid-week double, and the inn offers many special packages.

Superb food, an award-winning wine list, and elegant accommodations are hallmarks of Chestertown's **Friends Lake Inn**, consistently rated the number-one hotel in the Adirondacks on TripAdvisor. Built in the 1860s as

No Barking

"Adirondack" is an Anglicism of the Iroquois word for the Algonquin Indians, whom they called "Ha-De-Ron-Dah" or "bark-eaters" for their habit of eating certain types of tree bark.

a boardinghouse to accommodate tanners who worked in the city's major industry, the inn has seventeen guest rooms with turn-of-the-twentieth-century furnishings, private baths, and queen-size four-poster beds. Many rooms have panoramic views of the lake.

The dining room serves a New American cuisine featuring homemade pâtés, breads, and international desserts and has the largest wine cellar in northern New York. A full country breakfast, with treats like locally smoked bacon and mango crepes with raspberry coulis, is included in the rate.

The inn has a private beach for summer fun, a sauna, and an outdoor pool, and in winter its Nordic Ski Center grooms thirty-two kilometers of cross-country ski trails.

The Friends Lake Inn is on Friends Lake Road, Chestertown (518–494–4751; friendslake.com). Rates range from $329 to $429 per couple per night; ski packages and other multi-night rates are available.

For some distance north of Ticonderoga, Lake Champlain narrows enough for a single military installation to command both shores and govern the passage of ship traffic. This was the purpose of the two fortifications at **Crown Point State Historic Site** (parks.ny.gov/historic-sites/34). Serving as the staging area for French raids on English settlements in New England and the Hudson Valley in the late 1600s, Crown Point became the location of the French Fort St. Frederic, begun in 1734 and finished in 1737. The stone citadel defended the lake crossing with fifty cannons and swivel-mounted guns, and a garrison of 80 to 120 soldiers. It also provided a doctor, hospital, flour mill, and chapel for its troops and the residents of the town that sprang up around the fort, which in turn provided the fort's inhabitants with food and livestock.

The French defended the fort from British interlopers from 1755 to 1759, but when they heard that General Jeffrey Amherst and a swelled complement of troops were on their way, they demolished the fort and abandoned the remains. Amherst seized the remains and ordered it enlarged. Fort Crown Point became one of the largest star forts on the North American continent, with living quarters for up to five hundred people. When a 1773 fire reduced the fort to a "useless mass of Earth only," according to military engineer John Montresor, the British vacated it and left just a few soldiers as guard. This made it easy for American militiamen to capture the fort in 1775. The militia used it as headquarters for the navy until 1776.

Today a museum on the site displays artifacts uncovered at the site during extensive archaeological digs. Visitors can also have the pleasure of walking (or driving) across the Lake Champlain Bridge and enjoying the spectacular views of the lake from this nearly new span, and setting foot in Vermont on the other side.

The visitor center at Crown Point State Historic Site, at the Lake Champlain Bridge (21 Grandview Dr., Crown Point; 518–597–4666), is open May through Oct, Wed through Mon, 9:30 a.m. to 5 p.m. Grounds are open all year from sunrise to sunset. Admission to the museum is $4 for adults, $3 for seniors, and free for children 12 and under. There is an admission fee for each car on weekends and holidays. Group visits by advance reservation.

Tiny Essex, in the foothills of the Adirondacks on the shore of Lake Champlain, is one of the state's loveliest villages. Founded in the eighteenth century and one of the earliest European settlements on the lake, it is listed on the National Register of Historic Places and offers visitors a fascinating architectural overview: The streets are lined with homes and public buildings in a multitude of styles, including Federal, Greek Revival, Italianate, and French Second Empire. One of the homes, an 1853 Greek Revival twenty-room mansion called **Greystone** with eighteen-inch-thick cut stone walls (Elm Street across from the ferry dock; 518–963–8058 or 518–963–4650), took four years to complete and has been restored by its present owners, who have opened it for tours at 2 and 3:30 p.m. on Sat and Sun, from Memorial Day to Labor Day. Admission is free.

There are several lodging options in town, including the **Essex Inn** (2297 Main St.; 518–963–4400; essexinnessex.com), which has been operating almost continuously since it was built in 1810, making it one of the longest-lived structures in town. Extensively renovated in 1986, the inn has fourteen guest rooms, and rates, beginning at $195 to $395 per night, depending on the room, include a full breakfast. There are several restaurants in town, including one at the inn, which serves meals alfresco when the weather permits.

If you want to take a short boat ride, the **Essex–Charlotte Ferry** (802–864–9804; ferries.com/vt-ny-ferry-routes/charlotte-vt-essex-ny/) in town crosses the lake to Charlotte, Vermont, in just twenty minutes. If you're on foot, there's not much to see on the other side, but you can hop off and catch a return ferry in half an hour. The ferry does not operate when there is ice on the lake. The crossing is $4.50 per adult on foot, $2.25 for children 6 to 12, and free for children under 6. You can also cross with your vehicle for $10.75, which includes the car and driver; additional passengers pay the fees above.

For general information about Essex, visit the Adirondack Coast website at goadirondack.com, or call (518) 563–1000.

From here, it's time to drive into the heart of the Adirondacks—and the **High Peaks Scenic Byway** makes this the most spectacular driving experience you can have in New York State. Winding along NY Route 73 from southeast of St. Huberts to Saranac Lake (with a highly recommended side trip to Wilmington and Whiteface Mountain on NY Route 86), the scenic byway never disappoints in any season. Look forward to wildflowers and heavily forested, emerald mountainsides in spring and summer, magnificent displays of color in fall, and powdered icing over the trees between glistening snow fields in winter. The 24.2-mile road may be crowded with traffic during leaf-peeping season, but there's plenty of reason to proceed slowly to admire the views—and this congestion is nothing compared to what New York City dwellers tolerate during their daily commute. We had the pleasure of documenting this road in our book *Scenic Driving New York*, so if you would like a lively travelogue, it's readily available.

The *Adirondack Experience: The Museum at Blue Mountain Lake*, in the heart of the mountain region, chronicles the history of the Adirondacks and the way of life enjoyed by its residents. Located on a ridge overlooking Blue Mountain Lake, the museum rambles through twenty-two separate exhibit buildings on a thirty-acre compound. With a fully immersive, interactive permanent exhibition at its heart, the ADKX explores the bond between the natural setting and the people who live here, from the native Mohawk and Abenaki tribes to miners, lumber operations, great camp founders, and luminaries including Teddy Roosevelt. A restored turn-of-the-century cottage houses a large collection of rustic "Adirondack furniture," currently enjoying a revival among interior designers, and local fine artists receive recognition as well, from the Hudson River School to later periods.

The Adirondack Experience: The Museum at Blue Mountain Lake (9097 SR 30, Blue Mountain Lake; 518–352–7311; theadkx.org) is open daily from Memorial Day weekend through Columbus Day, 10 a.m. to 5 p.m. Admission is $15 for adults; $13 for 62 and over; $8 for ages 6 to 12, students, and military personnel; under 6 free. Allow three to five hours for your visit.

Of the roughly thirty-five Gilded Age Adirondack "Great Camps" that survive, one of the most spectacular—and least known—is *Camp Santanoni* in Newcomb, part of a 12,900-acre estate within the Adirondack Forest Preserve. Robert and Anna Pruyn of Albany commissioned architect Robert H. Robertson to design their camp, a partly Japanese-inspired, six-building log complex on the shores of Newcomb Lake. The main lodge buildings, completed in 1893, required 1,500 spruce trees for their construction. The buildings' common roof, covering sixteen thousand square feet and composed of fifty-eight distinct planes, was conceived to resemble a bird in flight.

Saved from demolition and placed on the National Register of Historic Places following their 1972 acquisition by the state, the more than forty-five buildings standing on the estate are under the care of the New York State Department of Environmental Conservation, the town of Newcomb, and Adirondack Architectural Heritage, which has undertaken a massive program of stabilization and restoration.

Unusual even among remote Great Camps, Santanoni's three complexes of buildings remain accessible only on foot. From the rambling gate lodge—itself a mammoth six-bedroom structure, incorporating a stone gateway arch—visitors can hike, bicycle, or cross-country ski five miles on a gravel carriage road to reach the lake and main lodge. In summer you can rest for the night at one of eight primitive campsites before beginning the trip back, or go on to Moose Pond, which is even deeper within the preserve.

Interns posted at the gate lodge and main lodge during the summer months can provide interpretive information on the property, and a program of three guided tours is offered. For tour schedules and general information on Santanoni, contact Adirondack Architectural Heritage, 1790 Main St., Keeseville, 12944 (518–834–9328; aarch.org/santanoni/).

We can learn by studying a subject in a museum, but even the best museum in the world can't convey how it feels to walk among mountains that are almost one million years old. *Siamese Ponds Wilderness Region* in western Warren County provides hundreds of miles of state-maintained trails and tote roads that wind over hills and mountains and past streams, ponds, and lakes. Choose a short hike along 13th Lake or a loop trail past John Pond, or plan a longer trek and camp in one of the primitive campsites at the Siamese Ponds, in the heart of the wilderness. Rockhounds will love exploring the passageways and valleys through a wide variety of rock formations, carved by Ice Age glaciers and eons of tumbling rocks carried along mountain streams. Hikers may find veins of minerals and semiprecious stones on these exposed rock walls.

Siamese Ponds Wilderness Region has entrance points from Stony Creek, Thurman, Wevertown, Johnsburg, North Creek, and North River. Learn more at dec.ny.gov/lands/53172.html.

With its thirty-one-acre campus, resident naturalists, and live exhibits, the *Wild Center* serves as a base camp for the Adirondacks. Here you can explore hands-on nature exhibits and encounter hundreds of live animals that live in the woods and waters: rare native trout, river otters, porcupines, and even turtles the size of walnuts.

Three trails wind through the Wild Center. The Wild Walk takes visitors into the treetops along sturdy bridges to get a completely different perspective on the natural world around them. Visitors can climb up a stairwell in the "snag," a tree some four stories tall, watch for eagles in their nests near the walkway, and even climb into an eagle's "nest" built for humans. Additional trails at ground level lead to a boardwalk around Greenleaf Pond and raised overlooks at the oxbow marsh on Raquette River. If you like, you can take a guided canoe paddle on the Raquette River on any afternoon the weather permits.

The Wild Center is located at 45 Museum Dr., Tupper Lake (518–359–7800; wildcenter.org). From Columbus Day to Memorial Day, hours are Fri through Mon from 10 a.m. to 5 p.m. From Memorial Day to Columbus Day, the museum is open daily from 10 a.m. to 5 p.m. An adult ticket is $20; a youth ticket (ages 5 to 17) is $12; a senior 65+ or military ticket is $18. Children 4 and younger are free.

The most iconic of the Adirondack camps, **Great Camp Sagamore**'s twenty-seven buildings on Raquette Lake were built in 1897 by William West Durant, who sold the camp in 1901 to Alfred Vanderbilt as a wilderness retreat. After Vanderbilt died on the *Lusitania* in 1915, his widow continued to entertain family and friends as "the hostess of the gaming crowd" for the next thirty-nine years.

Visitors to Sagamore can take a two-hour guided tour (self-led tours are not permitted) and, with reservations, stay overnight in one of the double-occupancy rooms (twin beds, bathroom down the hall) in conjunction with one of the camp's scheduled programs. Buffet meals are served in the dining hall overlooking the lake. Twenty miles of hiking trails, canoeing, and a semi-outdoor bowling alley all make a visit here a true Adirondack experience.

Sagamore (1105 Sagamore Rd., Raquette Lake 13436; 315–354–5311; sagamore.org) has guided daily tours at 10 a.m. and 1:30 p.m. from mid-June to Labor Day, Sat and Sun at 1:30 p.m. from Memorial Day weekend to mid-June. Tours from Labor Day to mid-Oct (check the website for beginning and end dates) are at 1:30 p.m. daily. Admission is $18 for adults, $16 for seniors and military with ID, and $10 for students.

More than 435 species of plants and trees, 18 varieties of orchids, and 28 varieties of ferns thrive in the Adirondacks' largest block of remote public land—the 79,487-acre **Moose River Plains Complex**, which is also home to boreal bird species including Canada jay, olive-sided flycatcher, boreal chicka-dee, mourning warbler, and others. There are more than forty miles of roads and many miles of trails to explore, and camping is provided at 140 primitive sites. Trail maps and other information can be found at the New York Department of Environmental Conservation website: dec.ny.gov/lands/53596.html.

Nearby, just off Uncas Road in Inlet, **Ferd's Bog** features a five-hundred-foot boardwalk that provides access to a rare open bog mat. Among the numerous unusual plants growing here are several species of rare orchids, including the white-fringed, rose Patagonia, and grass pink. Also watch for bug-eating pitcher plants. Birders come here to look for Canada jay, olive-sided flycatcher, yellow-bellied flycatcher, black-backed woodpecker, the increasingly rare American three-toed woodpecker, boreal chickadee, Lincoln's sparrow, and white-crowned sparrow, as well as many more common species that nest and breed in this unusual habitat.

Ferd's Bog is administered by New York State's Department of Environmental Conservation (DEC). For information call 518–897–1310 or visit dec.ny .gov/outdoor/84702.html.

The View Center for Arts and Culture (3278 SR 28, Old Forge; 315–369–6411; viewarts.org) opened in its current form in 2011 after sixty years of moves from the founder's front lawn to the Thendara train station. Now well established in its own facility, the center offers year-round exhibitions and programs, including fine art, music and theater performances, classes in pottery, basketry, and other creative arts, as well as a space for special events. Memorial Day through Oct 7: Mon through Sat, 10 a.m. to 4 p.m.; Sun, noon to 4 p.m. Fall and winter: Mon through Sat, 10 a.m. to 4 p.m.; closed Sun. General admission is $10, free for children under 18.

"The Adirondacks' Most General Store," serving the area since 1900, has become a tourist attraction in its own right, and most visitors can't pass through the town of Old Forge without stopping at ***Old Forge Hardware*** (104 Fulton St., Old Forge; 315–369–6100; oldforgehardware.com). Recently expanded to include one of the Adirondacks' most comprehensive book departments as well as every houseware your cabin, camp, or cottage requires, Old Forge Hardware provides a wonderful diversion on a rainy day. Be sure to pick up a bumper sticker featuring the stylized face of Henry, the Old Forge Hardware dog (while this pup is long gone, there are always a couple of pooches wandering around the store). It's open daily year-round except Easter, Thanksgiving, Christmas, and New Year's Day. Hours vary with the season, so call ahead.

Stillwater Reservoir, which abuts Pigeon Lake Wilderness, Five Ponds Wilderness, Pepperbox Wilderness, and Independence River Wild Forest, more than qualifies as an off-the-beaten-path destination. Both routes to the reservoir, from either Lowville or the Old Forge–Eagle Bay area, include ten-mile drives along narrow dirt roads through the wilderness. The site's very remoteness has contributed to its increasing popularity over the years, and the New York Department of Environmental Conservation, which oversees the area, has restricted camping along the shoreline to designated sites, or to at least 150 feet inland from the reservoir's high-water mark.

Camping beyond this perimeter, however, remains relatively unrestricted and affords some of the region's best opportunities for wilderness tenting, as well as fine flat-water canoeing, motorboating (proceed with caution; there are numerous navigational hazards), fishing (splake, bass, perch, and bullheads), snowmobiling, and cross-country skiing.

Campsites at the 6,700-acre reservoir are free of charge and available on a first-come, first-served basis. For more information, visit the New York DEC page on Stillwater at dec.ny.gov/outdoor/34382.html, or call (315) 376–3521.

Explore one of the world's largest ice arena complexes at the *Olympic Sports Complex* in downtown Lake Placid. The venue for the 1932 and 1980 Winter Olympic Games, it's perhaps best remembered as the site of the 1980 "Miracle on Ice," the unlikely victory of the young US hockey squad over the USSR's powerhouse Red Army team. The complex has four indoor rinks, a museum, a cafeteria, and a gift shop and is open for public skating from late June through early Sept on weekdays for just $5 (skate rental is $3). There are ice shows here most Saturday nights throughout the summer months.

If you're looking for a bit more stimulation, how about rocketing down the only dedicated bobsled, luge, and skeleton run in America on a wheeled sled at a speed of more than sixty miles per hour? The sleds at the Olympic Sports Complex are piloted by professional drivers and brakemen and operate from late June through mid-Oct, Wed through Sun from 10 a.m. to 12:30 p.m. and 1:30 to 4 p.m. The fee is $65 for the bobsled and $45 for the luge; the ride is subject to weather and bobsled run conditions.

Other activities at the complex include biathlon target shooting (late June through Labor Day), Wed through Sun, 10 a.m. to 4 p.m., with a charge of $5 for five rounds; and mountain biking on Mt. Van Hoevenberg (rentals available). From early July through late August, freestyle aerial skiing demonstrations (the skiers end up in the pool) are held on Wednesday at the Olympic Jumping complex, and, on Saturday, Nordic ski jumping is held at the ninety-meter jump.

For information on all of these activities as well as special events, call the Olympic Center Main Office, Lake Placid, at (518) 523–1655.

A sauna and a massage are never more welcome than after a day on the wind-chilled ski slopes, and fortunately, Lake Placid is home to the *Mirror Lake Inn Resort and Spa* (77 Mirror Lake Dr.), one of the country's top small hotels. It's best known for its award-winning kitchen, with both the casual dining and the formal restaurant enjoying flawless service and spectacular views of the lake. Rates for standard rooms start at $199 during the week and $399 on weekends. Call (518) 523–2544 or go to mirrorlakeinn.com to find out about their special food and wine events.

John Brown's body lies a-moulderin' in the grave, according to the old spiritual, and that grave is in North Elba, near Lake Placid, part of the *John Brown Farm State Historic Site*. Brown, a militant abolitionist, led the 1859 raid on the US arsenal at Harpers Ferry, Virginia, in hopes of arming black slaves to revolt against their masters. The plan failed, and Brown was executed and buried here, along with two of his sons and several of his followers who were killed at Harpers Ferry.

Brown moved to this area in 1849, trying to establish an agricultural community called Timbucto for free Blacks. This well-intentioned scheme failed, and Brown joined his sons in Kansas during the volatile 1850s, when the struggle to decide whether the territory would be admitted to the Union as a slave state or a free state earned it the nickname "Bleeding Kansas." Brown, of course, made a name for himself in Kansas, taking part in the clash at Osawatomie.

The farmhouse at the John Brown Farm State Historic Site (115 John Brown Rd., Lake Placid; 518–523–3900; parks.ny.gov/historic-sites/johnbrownfarm) is open daily (except Tues) from May 1 to Oct 31, 10 a.m. to 5 p.m. The grounds are open all year during daylight hours. Admission is free.

At the **Adirondack Guideboats Woodward Boat Shop**, Chris Woodward builds Adirondack guideboats using the same techniques that Willard Hanmer, one of the boat's original builders, used back in the 1930s—and he's making them in the same building. The boats—the style is indigenous to the region between Saranac Lake and Old Forge—are used for hunting and guiding. Chris also makes and sells paddles, seats, and oars as well as boat accessories. The shop, at 3 Hanmer Ave., Saranac Lake (518–891–3961), is open by appointment. Call ahead to make sure he'll be there.

In 1887 Robert Louis Stevenson set sail from Bournemouth, England, for a small farmhouse in Saranac Lake, the village he dubbed "the Little Switzerland in the Adirondacks." He lived here with his family, writing *The Master of Ballantrae* and *The Wrong Box*, skating at nearby Moody Pond, and enjoying life in the mountains. His wife, Margaret, wrote to a friend, "We are high up in the Adirondack Mountains living in a guide's cottage in the most primitive fashion. The maid does the cooking (we have little beyond venison and bread to cook) and the boy comes every morning to carry water from a distant spring for drinking purposes. It is already very cold but we have caulked the doors and windows as one caulks a boat, and have laid in a store of extraordinary garments made by the Canadian Indians."

Today the cottage, preserved in its original state, holds the country's largest collection of Stevenson's personal mementos, including his Scottish smoking jacket with a sprig of heather in the breast pocket, original letters, and his yachting cap. There's a plaque here donated by Mount Rushmore sculptor Gutzon Borglum, who regarded Stevenson as "the great sculptor of words."

The **Robert Louis Stevenson Memorial Cottage** (11 Stevenson Ln., Saranac Lake; 518–891–1462; robertlouisstevensonmemorialcottage.com) is open July through Columbus Day weekend, Tues to Sun, 9:30 a.m. to noon and 1 to

Elves Wanted

Many places call themselves *Santa's Workshop*, but how many are actually located in the North Pole? North Pole, New York, that is. This forerunner of modern theme parks opened in 1949, the brainchild of Lake Placid businessman Julian Reiss and designer/artist Arto Monaco. The result of this collaboration was a fantasy village populated by storybook characters, where children can ride the Candy Cane Express or the Christmas Carousel; visit with Santa and Mrs. Claus; mail out cards post-marked "North Pole, NY" and "Santa's Workshop"—and generally make merry.

Santa's Workshop is in the High Peaks area of Adirondacks Park at 324 Whiteface Memorial Highway (Route 431), 1½ miles northwest of the intersection with Route 86 in the town of Wilmington (518–946–2211; northpoleny.com). Check the website for the current general admission prices and for the many options for packages that include lodging and special activities. The park is open from mid-July through late Dec, generally on Sat and Sun. Hours vary; in early Dec, the park is open Sunday evenings; as the holidays approach, it's open Mon through Fri evenings as well.

From mid-Nov through mid-Dec, two-night family packages are offered; they include lodging (at various nearby properties), breakfasts and dinners, entertainment, and admission to Santa's Workshop.

4:30 p.m. The rest of the year it is open by appointment. Admission is $10 for adults; free for children under 12. Group rates are available.

Approximately 130,000 year-round residents live in Adirondack Park's 105 towns and villages, but 43 percent of the total acreage is state-owned, constitutionally protected "forever wild" land. To best get a sense of the park, stop at one of two visitor interpretive centers run by local colleges: ***Paul Smith's Visitor Interpretive Center*** (the VIC; 8023 NY 30; 518–327–3000; paulsmiths.edu/vic/); or ***the Center for Nature Interpretation in the Adirondacks*** on the State University of New York's Environmental Science and Forestry's Newcomb campus (5922 NY 28N, Newcomb; 518–582–2000; esf.edu/aic/). Both are open daily year-round, from 9 a.m. to 5 p.m., except Thanksgiving and Christmas. Admission is free. Both facilities feature miles of nature trails for birding, butterfly watching, hiking, cross-country skiing, and other outdoor pursuits.

How It's Done

Park administrators from throughout the world have come to New York State to study the management of Adirondack State Park.

The Adirondacks and, in fact, much of New York State, were once the territory of the Iroquois Confederacy. Perhaps the most politically sophisticated of all the tribal groupings of North American Indians, the Iroquois actually included five distinct tribes—the Mohawks, Senecas, Onondagas, Oneidas, and Cayugas—who were later joined by the Tuscaroras to form the "six nations" of the confederation. The history and contemporary circumstances of the Iroquois are documented in the *Six Nations Indian Museum*, a "living museum" that presents its material from a Native American point of view.

The museum, opened in 1954, was built by the Faddens, members of the Mohawk Nation, and is still operated and staffed by members of that family. The museum's design reflects the architecture of the traditional Haudenosaunee (Six Iroquois National Confederacy) bark house. The longhouse is a metaphor for the confederacy, symbolically stretching from east to west across ancestral territory.

A visit to the museum—jam-packed with artifacts—is a reminder that for centuries before Europeans arrived, the Iroquois built a society. Throughout the season Native Americans visit to talk about their histories, cultures, and their people's contributions to contemporary society.

The Six Nations Indian Museum (1462 County Route 60, Onchiota; 518–891–2299; sixnationsindianmuseum.com) is open daily except Mon from July 1 through Labor Day, 10 a.m. to 5 p.m., and by appointment in June and Sept. Call ahead to find out the current admission price.

If you're looking for an opportunity to experience five-hundred-million-year-old rock faces the way William Gilliland did when he navigated the Ausable River in 1765, look no further than *Ausable Chasm* (2144 Route 9; 518–834–7454; ausablechasm.com), one of the most popular destinations in the Adirondacks. The river and its two cascades, Horseshoe and Rainbow Falls, provided water power for settlers' mills and Atlantic salmon to feed their families, leading this area north of Willsboro to blossom throughout the late eighteenth and nineteenth centuries. Today the mills and lumber operations are gone, but visitors can explore the gorge on guided hikes that lead to hidden caves, behind the mist of the falls, and past the ruins of a horseshoe mail factory. Open year-round, 9 a.m. to 4 p.m.; open until 5 p.m. from the end of June through Labor Day. Closed Thanksgiving, Christmas Eve, Christmas Day, and New Year's Day. Admission is $17.85 for adults, $9.95 for children ages 5 to 12, and free for children under 5; there are additional fees for raft or tube float tours and the Riverwalk; many package prices available.

Once a part of the corridor used by trading and war parties in the days of the French and Indian Wars, the area around Plattsburgh, on Lake Champlain, had settled into a peaceful mercantile existence by the end of the eighteenth century. Here William Bailey built the **Kent-Delord House** in 1797, and it passed through multiple hands until Henry Delord purchased it in 1810. A refugee from the French Revolution who had served as a justice of the peace in Peru, New York, before moving to Plattsburgh, Delord remodeled the house in the fashionable Federal style of the era. He moved in at the completion of renovations in 1811, thus beginning more than a century of his family's residence here.

Just three years later, the War of 1812 came to Plattsburgh as British forces thrust southward along Lake Champlain. But the Delords' friend, Commodore Thomas Macdonough, thwarted the British in the Battle of Plattsburgh, and the house escaped undamaged despite heavy fighting in the area.

The continued story of the Kent-Delord House might be that of any home of a provincial bourgeois family during the nineteenth century. The difference, of course, is that this house has survived remarkably intact. It offers a fine opportunity to see how an upper-middle-class family lived from the days just after the revolution through the Victorian age, and, not incidentally, it houses a distinguished collection of American portrait art, including the work of John Singleton Copley, George Freeman, and Henry Inman.

The Kent-Delord House Museum (17 Cumberland Ave., Plattsburgh; 518–561–1035; kentdelordhouse.org) is open Mar and Apr by appointment; May through Dec, Tues through Sat, from noon to 4 p.m.; the last tour begins at 3:15 p.m. Admission is $5 for adults, $3 for students.

Yarborough Square (672 Bear Swamp Rd., Peru; 518–643–7057) carries the works of about two hundred artists and craftspeople from the United States and Canada, including a large collection of stoneware, porcelain, and raku pottery, metal sculptures, candles, and handcrafted jewelry—everything from recycled glass to wrought-iron pieces. The gallery, which also represents several painters and numerous craftspeople, is truly a North Country find. It's open daily from 10 a.m. to 6 p.m.

Alice T. Miner herself created the Chazy museum that bears her name. A pioneer in the colonial revival movement and wife of railroad industrialist and

But What about Butter?

In earlier times, the mothers of Iroquois maidens arranged the marriages of their daughters. A girl would acknowledge her mother's choice by putting a basket of bread at the prospective bridegroom's door. If he and his mother accepted, they would send a basket of food back to the girl and her family. If the offer was turned down, the girl's offering would remain untouched.

philanthropist William H. Miner, she opened the museum in 1824 and worked for the next twenty-six years, until her death, to assemble the fifteen-room collection. Included in the exhibit are period furniture; miniature furniture once toted about by traveling salesmen; a large collection of china, porcelain, and glass; early samplers; War of 1812 muskets; and other objects of early Americana.

The *Alice T. Miner Museum* (9618 Main St., Chazy; 518–846–7336; miner museum.org) is open May through Dec, Tues through Sat, with guided tours at 10 a.m., noon, and 2 p.m. Admission is $3 for adults, $2 for seniors 65+, and $1 for students. Children under 5 are free.

Western Adirondacks, Saint Lawrence Valley, and Thousand Islands

The *Akwesasne Cultural Center* is dedicated to preserving the past, present, and future of the Akwesasne Mohawk people, whose history in the area dates back thousands of years. The museum houses more than three thousand artifacts and an extensive collection of black-ash splint basketry; it also offers classes in such traditional art forms as basketry, quillwork, and water drums. The library holds one of the largest Native American collections in northern New York and includes information on indigenous people throughout North America.

Akwesasne Cultural Center (321 State Route 37, Hogansburg; 518–358–2461; akwesasneculturalcenter.org) is open daily year-round except Sun and major holidays. In July and Aug it is open Mon through Fri, 8:30 a.m. to 4:30 p.m. From Sept to June it is open Mon from 12:30 to 5:30 p.m.; Tues through Thurs, 8:30 a.m. to 8:30 p.m.; Fri, 8:30 a.m. to 4:30 p.m.; and Sat, 11 a.m. to 3 p.m. Suggested museum contribution is $2 for adults and $1 for children ages 5 to 16.

Horace Greeley famously said, "Go west, young man," and that's just what young Frederic Remington did. Born in 1861 in Ogdensburg, on the St. Lawrence Seaway, Remington quit Yale at the age of nineteen and headed for wide-open spaces. He spent five years traveling, taking in the vistas and the cowboys and horses that would inspire his paintings and sculpture. By 1885 he was already making his name as an illustrator and artist. Remington died in 1909 at the peak of his popularity, so his widow bequeathed the artist's collection of paintings and sculpture to the Ogdensburg Public Library; the collection now forms the Frederic Remington Art Museum, housed in the 1810 house where Mrs. Remington lived until her death.

The collection includes bronzes, oil paintings, and hundreds of pen-and-ink sketches by Remington, as well as pictures he collected by his contemporaries, including Charles Dana Gibson and Childe Hassam.

The *Frederic Remington Art Museum* (303 Washington St., Ogdensburg; 315–393–2425; fredericremington.org) is open from May 15 through Oct 15, Mon through Sat from 10 a.m. to 5 p.m., and Sun from 1 to 5 p.m.; from Oct 16 to May 14, hours are Wed through Sat from 11 a.m. to 5 p.m. and Sun from 1 to 5 p.m. Closed New Year's Day, Easter, Thanksgiving, and Christmas Day. Admission is $10 for adults, $7 for students ages 16 through college, $9 for senior citizens 65+, and free for children 15 and under.

While Frederic Remington looked west for artistic inspiration, hotel magnate George C. Boldt turned instead to his native Germany. Boldt's creativity wasn't a matter of putting paint to canvas or molding bronze, however. He intended to build the 120-room *Boldt Castle*, Rhineland-style, on one of the Thousand Islands in the St. Lawrence River.

Boldt, who owned the Waldorf-Astoria in New York and the Bellevue-Stratford Hotel in Philadelphia, bought his island at the turn of the century from a man named Hart, but that isn't why it is named Heart Island. The name derives from the fact that the hotelier had the island physically reshaped into the configuration of a heart, as a token of devotion to his wife, Louise, for whom the entire project was a monumental expression of his love.

Construction of the six-story castle and its numerous outbuildings began in 1900. Boldt hired masons, woodcarvers, landscapers, and other craftspeople from all over the world to execute details ranging from terra-cotta wall inlays and roof tiles to a huge, opalescent glass dome. He planned and built a smaller castle as a temporary residence and eventual playhouse, and he built an underground tunnel for bringing supplies from the docks to the main house. There were bowling alleys, a sauna, an indoor swimming pool—in short, it was to be the sort of place that would take years to finish and decades to enjoy.

Throw Away the Key

Many years ago, the village of Mannsville, 21 miles south of Watertown, became the site of an unusual orphan asylum. The Klan Haven Home occupied a big frame house set on three hundred acres, where boys could train in agriculture and girls learned what was then called "domestic science." The curriculum probably also included a brand of social studies, because the home was run by the Ku Klux Klan for some thirty orphaned children of Klan members. It has long since ceased to operate.

What's in the Water?

The St. Lawrence River is renowned for game fishing. Among the most common: large- and smallmouth bass, Northern pike, yellow perch, and walleye.

But there weren't enough years left. Louise Boldt died suddenly in 1904, and George Boldt, heartbroken, wired his construction supervisors to stop all work. The walls and roof of the castle were by this time essentially finished, but crated fixtures such as mantels and statuary were left where they stood, and the bustling island fell silent. Boldt never again set foot in his empty castle, on which he had spent $2.5 million.

Boldt died in 1916, and two years later Edward J. Noble, the inventor of Life Savers candy, bought the island and its structures. Noble and his heirs ran the deteriorating castle as a tourist attraction until 1977, when they gave it to the Thousand Islands Bridge Authority, which has invested millions of dollars in rehabilitation efforts to preserve the historic structure.

Boldt Castle, Heart Island, Alexandria Bay (315–482–9724; boldtcastle .com), is accessible via tour boat from the upper and lower docks on James Street in Alexandria Bay, as well as to tour boat patrons departing from Gananoque or Rockport, Ontario. The castle is open from Mother's Day to the first week in Oct, Fri through Sun, 10:30 a.m. to 6:30 p.m.; and Mon through Thurs, 11 a.m. to 5 p.m. Admission is $10 for adults (13 and up) and $7 for children ages 5 to 12; children 4 and under are free.

If you find the most appealing aspect of George Boldt's heyday to be the sleek mahogany runabouts and graceful skiffs that plied the waters of the Thousand Islands and other Gilded Age resorts, make sure you find your way to the ***Antique Boat Museum*** in Clayton. The museum is a freshwater boat-lover's dream, housing slender, mirror-finished launches; antique canoes; distinctive St. Lawrence River skiffs; handmade guideboats—about two hundred historic small craft in all.

The Antique Boat Museum takes no sides in the eternal conflict between sailing purists and "stinkpotters," being broad enough in its philosophy to house a fine collection of antique outboard and inboard engines, including the oldest outboard known to exist. The one distinction to which it rigidly adheres pertains to construction material: All of the boats exhibited here are made of wood.

The Antique Boat Museum (750 Mary St., Clayton; 315–686–4104; abm.org) is open from early May through mid-Oct, daily except Wed, from 9 a.m. to 5

Dressing Up for Dinner

The former Thousand Islands Inn had a claim to fame: It invented Thousand Island salad dressing, serving it to the dining public in the early 1900s. The dressing, with its many flecks of colorful minced vegetables evoking "thousands" of islands, was created by Sophia LaLonde for her husband, a guide, to serve to fishing parties as part of their shore dinners. One of his clients, a New York City stage actress named May Irwin, loved the dressing and gave it the name Thousand Island. She also gave the recipe to George C. Boldt, owner of Boldt Castle and New York's Waldorf-Astoria Hotel. He ordered his maître d', Oscar Tschirky, to put it on the hotel menu.

The original recipe is a family secret, but here's James Beard's recipe that comes close: Blend ½ cup chili sauce, 1 finely chopped pimiento, 1 tablespoon grated onion, and 2 tablespoons finely chopped green pepper with 1 cup mayonnaise.

p.m. Admission is $14 for adults, $12 for seniors 65+; $8 for students ages 7 to 17; free for children 6 and under. Blue Star military can bring five additional family members for a total price of $40. Tour and boat ride packages are also available on the museum's website.

While in Clayton, there's one thing no visitor should miss: a sample of **River Rat Cheese**, the cheddars that make New York State cheeses a favorite with shoppers from all over the country. River Rat's cheeses range from mild cheddar to the sharpest of the sharp, aged fourteen years before they appear in the store at 242 James Street. There's a variety for every taste, from flavored cheeses to "squeaky" curds, and many are packaged with Adirondack sausage and other local products like maple syrup, Rita's famous mustards and horseradish, trail mixes, chocolates, and all kinds of snacks. Call (800) 752–1341, or check out the selection at riverratcheese.net to get your mouth watering before you visit.

Are you yearning to sail to a foreign land? **Horne's Ferry**, the only international auto/passenger ferry on the St. Lawrence River, crosses over to Wolfe Island, Ontario, Canada, in just ten minutes. The ferry makes hourly crossings from 8 a.m. to 7:30 p.m. daily from late Apr through late Oct. Rates are $15 each way for a car and driver, and $2 for additional passengers or pedestrians. Call (315) 783–0638 or visit hferry.com.

The only place in the northeastern United States to see prairie smoke, a flower whose feathery plumes expand as it goes to seed, is in **Chaumont Barrens Preserve**, a Nature Conservancy property on Van Alstyne Road in Jefferson, with a unique "alvar" landscape characterized by a mosaic of austere, windswept vegetation. Alvar sites lie scattered along an arc from here, through

Ontario to northern Michigan. Scientists hypothesize that the landscapes, distinguished by a linear pattern of vegetation, were formed during the retreat of the last glacier approximately ten thousand years ago, when a huge ice dam burst and a torrent swept away all surface debris and dissolved limestone bedrock along cracks and fissures.

The rare combination of extreme conditions at Chaumont have created a two-mile landscape of exposed outcrops, fissures, moss gardens, patches of woods, shrub savannas, and open grasslands.

Chaumont Barrens is open daily from a half hour before sunrise until a half hour before sunset. For information call (585) 546–8030 or (315) 387–3600, or visit nature.org/en-us/get-involved/how-to-help/places-we-protect/central-chaumont-barrens/.

The international cooperation exemplified by the *St. Lawrence Seaway*, and the peaceful coexistence that allows pleasure craft to sail unimpeded along the boundary waters of the St. Lawrence River and Lake Ontario, are things we take for granted today, but this state of affairs has hardly existed since time immemorial. Barely more than a century ago, the US Navy kept an active installation at *Sackets Harbor Battlefield*, on Lake Ontario's Black River Bay, against the possibility of war with Canada. During the War of 1812, this small lakeport actually did see combat between American and British forces.

When the war began, Sackets Harbor was not yet a flourishing American naval port. It was from here, in April 1813, that the Americans launched their attack upon Toronto; a month later, the British turned the tables on the depleted American garrison and attacked the shipyard. The defenders repulsed the attack but lost most of their supplies to fire in the course of the struggle—not because of British determination, but because a young American lieutenant ordered half a million dollars' worth of naval supplies burned rather than allowing them to fall into British hands. Sackets Harbor remained in American control for the rest of the war.

Ski NY

When powder falls, so many skiers think about heading for the Green Mountains of Vermont; but there are more than thirty fantastic ski resorts here in New York, including the 4,867-foot Whiteface Mountain, site of two Olympic downhill runs. This peak in the heart of the Adirondack State Park boasts the greatest vertical drop in the East, as well as a thirteen-acre terrain park and a 450-foot super half-pipe. Get weather updates and other information on New York ski stations at skiandrideny.com.

Today's visitor to Sackets Harbor can still see many of the facilities of the old naval base, including officers' homes and sites associated with the 1813 battle.

Sackets Harbor Battlefield State Historic Site (504 West Main St., Sackets Harbor; 315–646–3634; sacketsharborbattlefield.org) is open Memorial Day to Labor Day, Mon through Sat from 10 a.m. to 4:30 p.m., and Sun from 1 p.m. to 4:30 p.m. During the last week of Aug and the first week of Sept, the site is closed Mon and Tues (but open on Labor Day). Call to check the admission fee.

The *International Maple Museum Centre*, dedicated to preserving the history and evolution of the North American maple syrup industry, houses three floors of antique sugaring equipment, logging tools, and artifacts. There are replicas of a sugarhouse and a lumber camp kitchen, and the American Maple Hall of Fame. The museum hosts three all-you-can-eat pancake breakfasts a year—in February, May, and September—to raise funds. There is also an ice-cream social around July 1, with entertainment and maple treats; a Maple Weekend in mid-Mar; and, in Dec, "Christmas in Croghan," with hot chocolate and maple cream on crackers. Call for dates.

The International Maple Museum Centre (9756 State Route 812, Croghan; 315–346–1107; maplemuseumcentre.org) is open Fri, Sat, and Mon, 11 a.m. to 4 p.m. from Memorial Day to June 30; daily except Sun, 11 a.m. to 4 p.m. from July 1 to early Sept. Admission is $5 for adults; $2 for children 5 to 12; $10 per family (two adults with up to four children).

The *North American Fiddler's Hall of Fame & Museum*, dedicated to "each and every fiddler who ever made hearts light and happy with his lilting music," preserves, perpetuates, and promotes the art of fiddling and the dances pertaining to the art. Run by the New York State Old Tyme Fiddlers' Association, which is headquartered in the same building, it displays artifacts and collects tapes of fiddlers and inducts a new member (or members) into its Hall of Fame each year. The museum, at 1121 Comins Road in Redfield, is open during all scheduled events and by appointment. Every Sun afternoon from Memorial Day to the first Sun in Oct there's also a free concert (donations are welcome). For information call (315) 599–7009 or visit nysotfa.com/hall-of-fame.

In the latter part of the nineteenth century, Joseph and John Moser emigrated from Alsace-Lorraine to Kirschnerville. They cleared a plot of land, built a dwelling, purchased farm animals, and then brought the rest of their family from overseas. The Mosers were Mennonites, and three generations lived and worshiped here until the 1980s, when a group purchased the farm to preserve as a living history of the life and faith of the area's settlers.

Today the *Adirondack Mennonite Heritage Farm*, under the auspices of the Adirondack Mennonite Heritage Association, tells of the life of the early

Amish-Mennonite settlers. In addition to exhibits in the farmhouse, visitors can see a Worship Room with the original benches (meetings were held in homes on a rotational basis until 1912, when the Croghan Mennonite Church was built). There are also a number of outbuildings, including a granary with a display of early tools and equipment.

On the first Saturday of July, the farm holds a special, day-long Zwanzigstein Fest, which features traditional Mennonite foods and crafts, a petting zoo, bread and butter and ice-cream making demonstrations, and horse-pulled wagon rides. The highlight of the day is the mini-auction of quilts, "comforts," and antiques.

The Mennonite Heritage Farm (8778 Erie Canal Rd., Croghan; 315–346–1122; mennoniteheritagefarm.com) is open varying hours during July and Aug, or by appointment. Admission is charged only for the Zwanzigstein Fest, but donations are gratefully accepted at any time.

The 2,100-acre **Whetstone Gulf State Park**, built in and around a three-mile-long gorge cut in the eastern edge of the Tug Hill plateau, provides one of the most spectacular scenic vistas east of the Rocky Mountains. Mostly undeveloped, the park has fifty-six campsites, six of which are stream-front, a picnic area along Whetstone Creek, a man-made swimming area, and several hiking and cross-country ski trails (one circles the gorge). A five-hundred-acre reservoir above the gorge, stocked with tiger muskie and largemouth bass, provides canoeing and fishing.

Whetstone Gulf State Park (6065 W Rd., Lowville; 315–376–6630; parks.ny .gov/parks/92/) is open Memorial Day through Sept, and Dec 15 through Mar 15, with admission charged during the summer months. Limited facilities are available in winter, but the heated Beach Building has restrooms and is open from the second week in Dec until the first week of Mar. To reserve a campsite call the New York State Campsite and Cabin Reservation Program at (800) 456–CAMP. Admission is $7 per vehicle on peak days and $6 on non-peak days, with the toll booth open 9 a.m. to 9 p.m. from two weeks before Memorial Day until two weeks after Labor Day.

The man who built **Constable Hall**, William Constable Jr., received a rather generous birthright: four million acres of Adirondack wilderness. His father purchased the property with two other New York City real-estate speculators and ultimately became the principal owner and chief developer. The senior William Constable sold large tracts to European and American land companies and families from New England, launching the settlement of the North Country. In 1819 the younger Constable built a Georgian mansion here, patterned on a family-owned estate in Ireland, and five generations of the Constable family lived in this splendid home until 1947, when the house became a museum. The original deed is just one of the family mementos displayed at the home, which still has many of its original furnishings.

Constable Hall (5909 John St., Constableville; 315–397–2323; constablehall .org) is open Wed through Sat from 10 a.m. to 4 p.m., and Sun from 1 to 4 p.m. Admission is $6 for adults and $4 for children under 12.

Barely a dozen lighthouses in North America allow visitors to stay overnight. *Salmon River (Selkirk) Lighthouse*, built in 1838 on Lake Ontario at the mouth of the Salmon River, provides an overnight stay that must be much more comfortable than the original lighthouse keeper experienced. Listed on the National Register of Historic Places, the centrally heated lighthouse sleeps up to ten people in four bedrooms (two single and four double beds), and it has a kitchen, living room, bathroom, high-definition television, and high-speed WiFi. Salmon River Lighthouse can be rented from Apr through early Dec for $225 to $325 per night Sun through Thurs; $275 to $375 Fri and Sat; or $1,500 per couple for a week. The lighthouse is part of a five-acre compound that includes a charter fishing fleet, cabins, boat rentals, and a launch ramp. For information contact Lighthouse Marina, 5 Lake Road Extension, Pulaski (315–509-4208; salmonriverlighthousemarina.com).

Just north of Utica, in the foothills of the Adirondacks, you'll find *Steuben Memorial State Historic Site*. Baron Frederick von Steuben was a Prussian officer who in 1777, at the age of forty-seven, emigrated to the United States to help drill the soldiers of the Continental Army. He arrived at the American winter encampment at Valley Forge, where morale was flagging and discipline had deteriorated in the face of hunger and bitter cold. Von Steuben rose to the occasion: Washington's troops might not have had boots, but they learned how to march in file, perform classic military drills, and become proficient with the bayonet. He even found time to write a masterful treatise on military training, *Regulations for the Order and Discipline of the Troops of the United States*.

The United States rewarded von Steuben handsomely, acknowledging his contribution to the new nation's victory as second only to Washington himself. Among his other rewards, he received sixteen thousand acres of land in upstate New York. He built a simple two-room log house and lived out the rest of his summers here until his death in 1794. The house that stands here today is a replica, and the drillmaster himself is buried beneath an imposing monument not far from here.

The Steuben Memorial State Historic Site (9941 Starr Hill Rd., Remsen; 315–768–7224, 315–655–3200; parks.ny.gov/historic-sites/2/) is open from Memorial Day to Labor Day, Wed through Sat, 10 a.m. to 5 p.m.; Sun and Mon holidays, 1 to 5 p.m. The grounds are open daily, dawn to dusk. Guided tours are available; call ahead. Admission is free.

Places to Stay in the Adirondacks

ALEXANDRIA BAY

The Edgewood Resort
22467 Edgewood Rd.
(315) 482–9923
theedgewoodresort.com

GLENS FALLS

Glens Falls Inn
25 Sherman Ave.
(518) 409–4204
glensfallsinn.com

KEENE

Bark Eater Inn
124 Alstead Hill Rd.
(518) 576–7100
barkeater.com

LAKE LUZERNE

The Lamplight Inn
231 Lake Ave.
(800) 262–4668
lamplightinn.com

LAKE PLACID

Golden Arrow Lakeside Resort
2559 Main St.
(844) 209–8080
golden-arrow.com

Whiteface Lodge Lake Placid
7 Whiteface Inn Ln.
(518) 523–0505
thewhitefacelodge.com

NORTH CREEK

Phoenix Inn Resort
307 Main St.
(518) 251–2200
phoenixinnresorts.com

ROCK CITY FALLS

The Mansion Inn
801 Rte. 29
(888) 996–9977
(518) 885–1607
themansionsaratoga.com

SARANAC LAKE

Hotel Saranac
100 Main St.
(518) 891–6900
hotelsaranac.com

SARATOGA SPRINGS

Adelphi Hotel
365 Broadway
(518) 678–6000
theadelphihotel.com

Batcheller Mansion Inn
20 W. Circular St.
(518) 584–7012
batchellermansioninn.com

TUPPER LAKE

The Timber Lodge
1472 NY 30
(518) 359–2320

WARRENSBURG

Merrill Magee House
3 Hudson St.
(518) 260–7729
merrillmagee.com

Seasons Bed and Breakfast
3822 Main St.
(518) 623–3832
seasons-bandb.com

Places to Eat in the Adirondacks

ALEXANDRIA BAY

Riley's by the River
46 James St.
(315) 482–7777
rileysbytheriver.com

LAKE LUZERNE

Waterhouse Restaurant
85 Lake Ave.
(518) 696–3115
waterhouse-restaurant.com

LAKE PLACID

Great Adirondack Brewing Company
2442 Main St.
(518) 523–1629
adirondackbrewing.com

Top of the Park
2407 Main St., 2nd Fl.
(518) 523–3632
topofthepark.bar

MAYFIELD

Lanzi's on the Lake
1751 NY 30
(518) 661–7711
lanzisonthelake.net

RAY BROOK

Tail O' the Pup BBQ
1186 NY 86
(518) 891–0777
tailofthepupbbq.com

REGIONAL TOURIST INFORMATION FOR THE ADIRONDACKS

Adirondacks Regional Tourism Council
PO Box 911
Lake Placid
adk.com

Lake George Regional Chamber of Commerce
2176 US 9
(518) 668–5755
lakegeorgechamber.com

Lake Placid Convention and Visitors Bureau
2608 Main St.
Lake Placid
(518) 523–2445
lakeplacid.com

North Country–Plattsburgh Chamber of Commerce
7061 Rte. 9
Plattsburgh
(518) 563–1000
northcountrychamber.com

The 1000 Islands International Tourism Council
43373 Collins Landing
Alexandria Bay
(800) 847–5163 or
(315) 482–2520
visit1000islands.com

Saranac Lake Chamber of Commerce
39 Main St.
(518) 891–1990
saranaclake.com

Saratoga Convention and Tourism Bureau
60 Railroad Pl., Ste. 301
Saratoga Springs
(518) 584–1531
(844) 947–4922
discoversaratoga.com

Saratoga County Chamber of Commerce
297 Broadway
Saratoga Springs
(518) 584–3255
saratoga.org/tourism/

Town of Webb Visitor Information Center
3140 NY 28
Old Forge
(877) 653–3674
(315) 369–6983
oldforgeny.com

Warren County Tourism Department
1340 NY 9
Lake George
(800) 958–4748
visitlakegeorge.com

Whiteface Mountain Regional Visitors Bureau
5753 NY 86
Wilmington
(518) 946–2255
(888) 944–8332
whitefaceregion.com

SARATOGA SPRINGS

Olde Bryan Inn
123 Maple Ave.
(518) 587–2990
oldebryaninn.com

TUPPER LAKE

Raquette River Brewing
11 Balsam St. #2
(518) 359–5160
raquetteriverbrewing.com

OTHER ATTRACTIONS WORTH SEEING IN THE ADIRONDACKS

Gore Mountain
793 Peaceful Valley Rd.
North Creek
(518) 251–2411
goremountain.com

High Falls Gorge
4761 NY 86
Wilmington
(518) 946–2278
highfallsgorge.com

Natural Stone Bridge and Caves
535 Stone Bridge Rd.
Pottersville
(518) 494–2283
stonebridgeandcaves.com

Plattsburgh State Art Museum
SUNY, 101 Broad St.
Plattsburgh
(518) 563–7709
plattsburgh.edu/plattslife/arts/art-museum/index.html

Wilder Homestead: Almanzo Wilder Farm
177 Stacy Rd.
Malone
(518) 483–1207
almanzowilderfarm.com

The Mohawk Valley

Drums along the Mohawk, Leatherstocking Trail, "I got a mule and her name is Sal/Fifteen miles on the Erie Canal . . . "—the lore of the Mohawk Valley penetrated the national consciousness centuries ago and continues to spark the imagination. It's no wonder: The valley provided the first passage between the East Coast and the Great Lakes via "Clinton's Ditch," the nickname skeptics gave to Governor Dewitt Clinton's outlandish idea to dig a canal nearly four hundred miles long; and countless Americans have passed through here via Native American trails, Commodore Vanderbilt's "Water Level Route" of the New York Central Railroad, and today's New York State Thruway. Here Jesuit missionaries met their end at the hands of the Iroquois, James Fenimore Cooper's Deerslayer stalked, and homesteaders struck out for the Midwest along a water-filled ditch, in barges pulled by draft animals. Surely this is one of the most storied corridors of the original thirteen colonies.

Along the way, people settled into towns and made things—guns in Ilion, pots and pans in Rome, gloves in Gloversville. A great deal of the state's agricultural bounty still comes from this region: dairy products from more than six hundred thousand cows (more than twelve billion pounds of

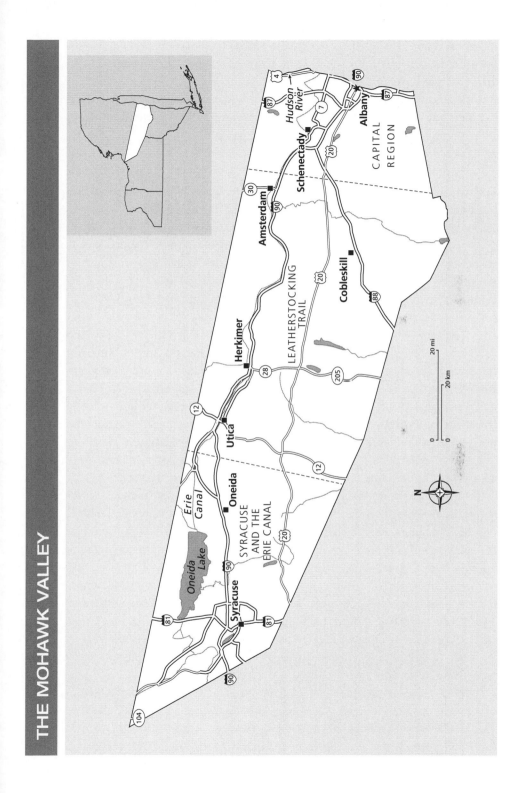

THE MOHAWK VALLEY

milk get produced here every year), apples from the nation's third-largest producer of the bright red fruit, and grapes that make New York's wines some of the best in the country.

This chapter begins in Albany and heads west to Syracuse, loosely following the route of the Mohawk River as well as the New York State Thruway.

Capital Region

The capital of the Empire State, Albany today has all the trappings of a government seat: posh homes and restaurants, traffic, and massive "official" architecture—namely the beautiful and ornate *State Capitol building*, partly designed by H. H. Richardson, and the four monolithic, marble-clad state office towers so closely associated with the grandiose visions of the late governor Nelson Rockefeller. But visit the *Albany Institute of History & Art* to discover the culture of Albany and the upper Hudson River Valley from the seventeenth century to the present.

Works by Hudson River School painters, including Cole, Durand, and Cropsey, receive their due here, but the institute possesses fine examples of an even older regional genre: portraits of the seventeenth- and eighteenth-century Dutch settlers of the Hudson Valley. These pictures echo the Dutch genre paintings that left us a detailed record of the comforts of burgher life in the Netherlands. It's easy to imagine the people in the portraits surrounded by the institute's wonderful collection of early Hudson Valley furniture and silver.

The Albany Institute of History & Art (125 Washington Ave., Albany; 518–463–4478; albanyinstitute.org) is open Wed through Sat from 10 a.m. to 5 p.m., and Sun from noon to 5 p.m. Admission is $10 for adults, $8 for seniors 62+ and students with ID, and $6 for children ages 6 to 12; free to children under 6.

The Schuylers were among the earliest of the Dutch settlers of the upper Hudson Valley and were involved throughout the colonial period in trading, agriculture, land development, and local politics. Until recently, the most renowned member of the family was Philip Schuyler (1733–1804), whose manorial home is today preserved as the *Schuyler Mansion State Historic Site*. Thanks to the Broadway hit *Hamilton*, we now know a great deal more about Schuyler's two elder daughters: Elizabeth, the wife of Alexander Hamilton (their wedding took place in this house in 1780); and her politically savvy older sister, Angelica.

Philip Schuyler designed the elegant mansion himself in the Georgian style, with rose-colored brick walls, graceful fenestration, and a double-hipped roof (the awkward hexagonal brick entry vestibule is an 1818 addition). He furnished it largely with purchases he made during a 1761–62 trip to England;

today it houses an excellent collection of colonial and Federal period furnishings. After Schuyler died in 1804, this architectural gem was sold and used as an orphanage before being acquired by the state in 1912.

The Schuyler Mansion State Historic Site (32 Catherine St., Albany; 518–434–0835; parks.ny.gov/historic-sites/33/) is open mid-Apr through Oct, Wed through Sun, 11 a.m. to 5 p.m.; Nov through mid-Apr by appointment. Also open on Memorial Day, Independence Day, and Labor Day. Admission is $5 for adults, $4 for senior citizens and students, and free for children 12 and under.

In 1774 Mother Ann Lee, founder of the Shakers, left England with a small band of followers and came to New York City. A few years later the group established the country's first Shaker settlement in a town named Watervliet (now part of the town of Colonie).

Today the **Shaker Heritage Society** maintains a memorial to this historic settlement. Among the points of interest are a garden with some one hundred varieties of herbs (herbs were one of the early Shakers' major trade crops), the Ann Lee Pond nature preserve, and the Shaker Cemetery, where Lee and many of her followers are buried. The museum and gift shop are in the 1848 Shaker Meeting House, on the grounds of the Ann Lee Home.

The Shaker Heritage Society (25 Meeting House Rd., Albany; 518–456–7890; shakerheritage.org) is open Mar to early Oct, Tues through Sat, 10 a.m. to 4 p.m.; Oct 7 through Dec 19, Wed through Sat (Tues through Sat after Nov 19), 11 a.m. to 5 p.m.; closed July 4 and Thanksgiving Day. A donation of $5 per person is suggested.

One of Philip Schuyler's interests during his later years was the development of a canal and lock system in New York State. In the three decades after his death, canal building really hit its stride in the United States, turning formerly sleepy villages into canal boomtowns involved in the lucrative transport of goods between New York City and the Great Lakes, and on into the new

AUTHOR'S FAVORITES IN THE MOHAWK VALLEY

Chittenango Falls State Park	Glimmerglass Festival
Dinosaur Bar-B-Que	Peebles Island State Park
Farmers' Museum	Saranac Brewery
Fenimore Art Museum	Stickley Museum
Fly Creek Cider Mill	

American territories acquired through the Louisiana Purchase. One such town is *Waterford*, located near Cohoes just upriver from Albany.

Founded by the Dutch as Halfmoon Point in the early 1620s at the confluence of the Mohawk and Hudson Rivers, Waterford was incorporated under its present name in 1794 and remains the oldest incorporated village in the United States. In 1799 it became the head of sloop navigation on the Hudson, but its glory days of commerce came later, in the 1820s, when the new Champlain and Erie Canals made the town an important way station on a statewide transportation system.

ANNUAL EVENTS IN THE MOHAWK VALLEY

JANUARY

Schenectady Soup Stroll
Downtown Schenectady
facebook.com/
events/2478822629044568/

FEBRUARY

Albany Wine & Chocolate Festival
Albany
wineandchocolatefestivals.com/events/
albany-ny-wine-and-chocolate-festival/

MARCH

Restaurant Week
Schenectady
discoverschenectady.com/events/
annual-events/

APRIL

Brewtica Craft Beer Event
Utica
brewtica.com

Utica Wine & Chocolate Festival
wineandchocolatefestivals.com/events/
utica/

MAY

Tulip Festival
Albany
(518) 434–2032
albanyevents.org/events/Albany-Tulip-
Festival_2_event_main.htm

JUNE

Annual Baseball Hall of Fame Classic
Cooperstown
(888) HALL–OF–FAME
baseballhall.org

Old Songs Festival of Traditional Music
Altamont
(518) 765–2815
oldsongs.org

Syracuse Polish Festival
polishscholarship.org

Taste of Syracuse
Downtown Syracuse
tasteofsyracuse.com

JULY

Glimmerglass Opera Festival
Cooperstown
(607) 547–2255
glimmerglass.org

It wasn't long before the railroads superseded the canal system, but Waterford prospered as a small manufacturing center during the nineteenth century. The legacy of this era is the village's lovely residential architecture, much of it in the regionally significant "Waterford" style characterized by Federal details and Dutch-inspired single-step gables. Such architectural distinctions have earned the village center inclusion on the National Register of Historic Places. The historic district is the subject of tours given during Canalfest, on the second Saturday of May each year. It features boat rides, hayrides, a boat show, a craft fair, food, and entertainment.

National Baseball Hall of Fame Induction Weekend
Cooperstown
(888) HALL–OF–FAME
baseballhall.org

New York State Blues Festival
Clinton Square
Syracuse
nysbluesfest.com

Syracuse Arts & Crafts Festival
Syracuse
(315) 422–8284
downtownsyracuse.com/events/signature/syracuse-arts-crafts-festival/ac

Syracuse Nationals Car Show
NY State Fairgrounds
syracusenationals.com

AUGUST
The Great New York State Fair
Syracuse
(800) 234–4797 or
(315) 487–7711
nysfair.ny.gov

SEPTEMBER
Capital Region Apple & Wine Festival
Altamont Fairgrounds
albany.com/fall/apple-festival/

LarkFest One-Day Street Festival
Albany
albany.com/things-to-do/larkfest/

OCTOBER
Halloween at Howe Caverns
Howes Cave
(518) 296–8900
howecaverns.com

LaFayette Apple Festival
LaFayette
(315) 677–3644
lafayetteapplefest.org

NOVEMBER
Schenectady Holiday Parade
Schenectady
(518) 372–5656
albany.com/holiday/annual-events/schenectady-holiday-parade/

DECEMBER
Festival of Trees
Syracuse
(315) 474–6064
everson.org/connect/events/FOT19

First Night
Albany
albany.com/holiday/new-years/

> ## Short and Steamy
>
> The country's first railroad, with an eleven-mile track, ran between Albany and Schenectady.

From April through October in the village center at Erie Canal Lock 2, a series of outdoor exhibits details the history of the 1823 canal and the present-day barge canal.

Waterford attractions outside the village center include the **Champlain Canal**, this section of which was dug in 1823 and is still filled with water; the **Waterford Flight**, a series of five locks on the still-operating New York State Barge Canal, whose 169-foot total rise is the highest in the world; a state park at Lock 6; and **Peebles Island State Park**, the former home of the Cluett, Peabody & Company shirt factory, once the most successful manufacturing enterprise in the United States. **Waterford Historical Museum and Cultural Center** (2 Museum Ln., Waterford; 518–238–0809; waterfordmuseum.com) is open May through Oct, Tues through Sat from 10 a.m. to 3 p.m., and Sun from 12:30 to 3 p.m. Admission is $6 adults, $5 children and seniors; free for children under 6.

Leatherstocking Trail

The Erie Canal and the feats of engineering involved in building it are the focus of **Schoharie Crossing State Historic Site** at Fort Hunter. The site preserves seven canal-related structures dating from three periods of the waterway's construction or expansion, with interpretive displays that explain their use. The visitor center has an exhibit on the Erie Canal and information on the site and surrounding area. The 1850s-built Putnam's Canal Store, at Yankee Hill Lock 28 on Queen Anne's Road (2.2 miles east of the visitor center), served canal travelers for many years and now houses an exhibit on Erie Canal stores.

The **Erie Canalway National Heritage Corridor towpath**, a 363-mile stretch of paved or otherwise improved walking and bicycling trail, passes the Schoharie site and continues all the way to Buffalo to the west and Waterford to the east. Plan to walk a segment of the flat, easy trail for a mile or so to get a sense of the tranquil setting offered by one of the busiest waterways of the nineteenth century. With mules and human drivers pulling barges along the canal from towpaths on either side, travel down the Erie could not be called fast—but it glided along more easily and carried more heavy goods than a wagon crossing on land could possibly have managed.

Schoharie Crossing State Historic Site (129 Schoharie St., Fort Hunter; 518–829–7516; parks.ny.gov/historic-sites/27/) is open May through Oct 31 and Memorial Day, Independence Day, and Labor Day, Wed through Sat from 10 a.m. to 4 p.m., and Sun from 1 to 4 p.m. The grounds are open all year during daylight hours. Admission is free.

Long before there were canals or barges in this part of New York State, the waters of the Mohawk and its tributaries carried the canoes of the Iroquois. The empire of the Five Nations—Cayuga, Mohawk, Oneida, Onondaga, and Seneca—dominated the open lands, and the Mohawk built a palisaded village of longhouses called Ossernenon at present-day Auriesville. In 1642, a Mohawk party returned from a raid with three French and twenty Huron captives in custody. Among the French were a Jesuit priest, Isaac Jogues, and his lay assistant, René Goupil.

Goupil made an error that turned out to be fatal: He tried to teach a child the sign of the cross. Mohawks interpreted this as spellcasting and tomahawked the young assistant to death. Jogues fared somewhat better, living among the Mohawk until a trading foray to Fort Orange, when Dutch traders rescued him so he could return to Europe. Eventually he sailed to Quebec and then volunteered to go back to Ossernenon in May 1646, as part of a group attempting to ratify a peace treaty with the Mohawks. Perhaps he could have predicted that he would be recaptured near the village, this time by a faction of the tribe favoring continued hostilities. Both he and a lay companion, Jean Lalande, were killed by tomahawk-wielding Mohawks in October of that year. Canonized by the Roman Catholic Church in 1930 along with five Jesuit missionaries martyred in Canada, Jogues, Goupil, and Lalande are honored at the **National Shrine of the North American Martyrs** in Auriesville.

The New York Province of the Society of Jesus, the same Jesuit order to which Isaac Jogues belonged, maintains the shrine on the hilltop site of the

At Least They Don't Run

The leather leggings worn by Yankees who settled in this area gave birth to the region's nickname, the Leatherstocking Trail. James Fenimore Cooper immortalized the name in his *Leatherstocking Tales*, which recounted the adventures of fictional wilderness scout Nathaniel "Natty" Bumppo. Cooper is buried in the family plot in Cooperstown's Christ Church cemetery.

original Mohawk village of Ossernenon. Six hundred verdant acres surround the building, making it a particularly spiritual and satisfying stop for Jesuit pilgrims and those of other faiths who simply come to learn the history it represents. The shrine accommodates forty thousand to fifty thousand visitors each year, celebrating mass in the vast Coliseum, the central altar of which suggests the palisades of a Mohawk village; a Martyrs' Museum tells the story of the men honored here, and rustic chapels and a retreat house provide more opportunities for worship.

For information on the schedule of observances at the National Shrine of the North American Martyrs (136 Shrine Rd., Fultonville), call (518) 853–3939 or visit ourladyofmartyrsshrine.org. Open daily from mid-Apr through Oct 19 (Martyrs' Feast Day), 9 a.m. to 6 p.m.; the gift shop is open 10 a.m. to 3 p.m. The museum is open Fri through Wed in the afternoon throughout the season and is closed on Thurs. Admission is free; donations are accepted.

The French Catholic missionaries working among the Indians in the seventeenth century were not without their successes. The most famous name among Mohawk converts of that era is Kateri Tekakwitha, the "Lily of the Mohawks," born at Ossernenon and baptized at what is now the village of Fonda, where the *Saint Kateri Tekakwitha National Shrine and Historic Site* is located. Maintained by the Conventual Franciscan Order, the shrine commemorates the life of the Native American girl who lived half of her life here before moving to the community of converts established by the French at Caughnawaga, near Montreal, where she died in 1680 at the age of twenty-four. (In 1980, on the tercentenary of her death, Pope John Paul II announced the beatification of Kateri Tekakwitha, the last step before canonization in the Catholic Church. She was canonized in 2012.)

Aside from its religious connections, the Fonda site has been identified by archaeologists as the location of a Mohawk village, also called Caughnawaga. The shrine's Native American exhibit contains artifacts dug from the village site and other sites across the country, and is located on the ground floor of a revolutionary-era Dutch barn that now serves as a chapel.

Fitting Famous Fingers

Daniel Storto is the last of a breed—he's the only custom glove maker left in Gloversville. Settling in the one-time glove capital of America in 2002, Storto set up shop to carry on his business of handcrafting gloves for clients such as Whoopi Goldberg, Diane Keaton, and Madonna. Learn more at danielstorto.com.

The *Saint Kateri Tekakwitha National Shrine and Historic Site* (3636 NY 5, Fonda; 518–853–3646; katerishrine.com) is open daily from May 1 to Oct 31, 9 a.m. to 6 p.m. Candle Chapel, the outdoor sanctuary, and hiking trails are open dawn to dusk year-round. Admission is free. Check the website for mass times.

Just north of Fonda and nearby Johnstown is Gloversville, home of the *Fulton County Museum*. The town adopted this name in 1828 instead of Kingsborough, its original name, in homage to the linchpin of the local economy in those days: tanning and glove making. Here at the museum is the state's only glove-manufacturing display, a complete small glove factory of the last century, donated to the museum and reassembled in its original working format. Exhibits include collections of military, sports, technology, and public service items, and even the findings of several paranormal investigations completed at the museum.

The Fulton County Museum (237 Kingsboro Ave., Gloversville; 518–725–2203) is open Memorial Day weekend through Labor Day weekend, Thurs through Sun from noon to 4 p.m.; Sept through Columbus Day weekend, Sat and Sun from noon to 4 p.m.; and mid-Oct through the end of May on Sat only, 9 a.m. to noon. Admission is free; donations are accepted.

Fate plays a capricious hand in deciding for which industries a town will be noted. Gloversville got gloves; Canajoharie, our next stop along the Mohawk, got chewing gum—specifically the Beech-Nut Packing Company, of which town native Bartlett Arkell was president in the 1920s. Because of Arkell and his success in business, Canajoharie also came into possession of the finest independent art gallery of any municipality its size in the United States: the *Arkell Museum at Canajoharie*.

Arkell's beneficence to his hometown began with his donation of a new library in 1924. Two years later he donated the funds to build an art gallery wing on the library, and over the next few years he gave the community the magnificent collection of paintings that forms the bulk of the gallery's present holdings.

With continued growth of the collection, this institution has become not merely an art gallery with a library attached, but an art gallery with a small town attached. The roster of American painters exhibited here includes Hudson River School artists Albert Bierstadt (*El Capitan*), John Kensett, and Thomas Doughty; world-famous artists Gilbert Stuart (George Washington portrait), John Singer Sargent, and Winslow Homer make this an unusually robust gallery for a community of this size. John Singleton Copley, Thomas Eakins, George Inness (*Rainbow*), and James McNeill Whistler (*On the Thames*) represent the eighteenth and nineteenth centuries, while twentieth-century painters include

Charles Burchfield, Reginald Marsh, N. C. Wyeth, Andrew Wyeth (*February 2nd, 1942*), Edward Hopper, Thomas Hart Benton, and Grandma Moses; also featured is a Frederic Remington bronze, *Bronco Buster*. Add a collection of eighty Korean and Japanese ceramics, the gift of the late Colonel John Fox, and you have all the more reason—as if more were needed—to regard Canajoharie's museum as a destination in itself.

The Arkell Museum at Canajoharie (2 Erie Blvd., Canajoharie; 518–673–2314; arkellmuseum.org) is open Tues through Fri, 10 a.m. to 5 p.m.; Sat and Sun, noon to 5 p.m.; closed Mon. Adults $9, seniors and students $6.50, free for active-duty military and children ages 11 and under.

Life was tough in the Mohawk Valley in 1750, when Johannes Klock built the farmhouse-fortress preserved today as the ***Fort Klock Historic Restoration***. Located above the river at St. Johnsville, Fort Klock is a reminder that defensible stout-walled outposts were not unique to the "Wild West" of the late 1800s; in 1750 the Mohawk Valley was the Wild West.

Like his neighbors scattered along the river, Johannes Klock engaged in fur trading and farming. Canoes and bateaux could be tied up in the cove just below the house, yet the building itself stood on high enough ground and at a sufficient distance from the river to make it easily defensible should the waters of the Mohawk bring foes rather than friendly traders. The stone walls of Fort Klock are almost two feet thick and are dotted with "loopholes" that allowed inhabitants to fire muskets from protected positions within.

Now restored and protected as a registered National Historic Landmark, Fort Klock and its outbuildings, including a restored Dutch barn, tell a good part of the story of the Mohawk Valley in the eighteenth century—a time when the hardships of homesteading were made even more difficult by the constant threat of the musket, the tomahawk, and the torch.

Fort Klock Historic Restoration (7203 NY 5, St. Johnsville; 518–568–7779; fortklockrestoration.org) is open from Memorial Day through mid-Oct, Tues through Sun, 9 a.m. to 5 p.m. Call the site to find out the admission fee.

The ***Iroquois Indian Museum*** details the history of the Iroquois Confederacy, but it also specializes in researching the pre-revolutionary Schoharie Mohawk who lived here. The museum traces the history of the Mohawk and other nations of the confederacy, using Iroquois art as the jumping-off point for exploration. The main building at the museum resembles an Iroquois longhouse, with an outdoor amphitheater for storytelling and performances. Two log homes at the edge of the museum's forty-five-acre nature park were moved from Canada's largest Iroquois community, the Six Nations Reserve. A Children's Iroquois Museum on the ground floor uses a hands-on approach to help interpret the adult museum for youngsters.

The Iroquois Indian Museum (324 Caverns Rd., Howes Cave; 518–296–8949; iroquoismuseum.org) is open daily from July 1 through Labor Day weekend, Mon through Sat from 10 a.m. to 6 p.m. and Sun from noon to 6 p.m.; Apr, May, June, and Labor Day through Dec, open Tues through Sat from 10 a.m. to 5 p.m. and Sun from noon to 5 p.m. It is closed Jan through Mar. Admission is $8 for adults, $6.50 for senior citizens and students ages 13 to 17, and $5 for children ages 5 to 12.

Renovating a building takes a lot of effort; restoring an entire section of a town is a Herculean undertaking, as visitors to **Sharon Springs** will immediately appreciate. The erstwhile resort community, whose waters were said to equal those of Germany's Baden-Baden in therapeutic value, thrived in the mid- to late 1800s when people came seeking cures for everything from "malarial difficulties" to "biliary derangements."

Don't miss the self-guided Historic Main Street tour. Twenty plaques lining both sides of the road describe the village's golden era with stories, architectural facts, diary excerpts from the 1860s, and hundreds of photos from the nineteenth century.

Several lodgings in the historic district are opening as they are restored. Among them: the **Edgefield B&B** (518–284–9771; edgefieldbb.com), an English country house–style inn at 153 Washington St. The **Country Manor Inn** (629 Rte. 20; 518–284–6036; facebook.com/countrymanorinn) turns an early 1800s manor into a guesthouse with three single rooms and three suites, with a panoramic, ninety-mile view of the Mohawk Valley all the way to the mountains from the manor's back lawn.

The handsomely restored **American Hotel**, an 1847 National Register of Historic Places building at 192 Main Street, has nine rooms with private baths (breakfast included), a pub, and a restaurant with a menu of classic American favorites. It serves dinner nightly in spring and summer, closing Mon through Wed in the off-season, as well as Sunday brunch (518–284–2105; americanhotelny.com).

For information on Sharon Springs and the progress of a number of restoration efforts, visit sharonsprings.com.

Just out of town, **Clausen Farm** (106 Clausen Ridge Dr., Sharon Springs; 518–231–2097; clausenfarm.com), a forty-seven-acre Victorian estate dating back to the late 1700s, offers safari-style "glamping"—camping in luxury—with great views of the Mohawk Valley. Call for current rates.

To sports fans, **Cooperstown** is practically synonymous with baseball. Devotees come from all over the country to visit the **National Baseball Hall of Fame and Museum**, but many miss the three-story **National Baseball Hall of Fame Library**, located in a separate building connected to the museum. It's a treasure trove of baseball: a collection of more than 2.5 million items, including clippings, photographs, books, videos, movies, recordings—practically everything ever said or written about baseball. Established in 1939, the library is used by researchers but is open to visitors, who are invited to browse at their leisure. During your visit be sure to include the fifty-six-seat Bullpen Theater, where visitors can view the best in baseball highlight films and footage of the game's greatest plays.

The National Baseball Hall of Fame Library (25 Main St., Cooperstown; 607–547–7200; baseballhall.org/about-the-hall/477) is open daily, 9 a.m. to 5 p.m., with half-hour tours throughout the day, during summer months. Museum visitors can enter the library at no additional charge over the entry fee of $25 for adults, $20 for seniors 65+, $18 for veterans, $15 for children 7 to 12, and free for active-duty military and children 6 and under.

But there's so much more to Cooperstown than baseball. It's the quintessence of small-town America, founded in 1786 on the southern shore of Otsego Lake by William Cooper, father of author James Fenimore Cooper. Stand on the veranda of the historic *Otesaga Resort Hotel* at sunset (perhaps with a beverage), looking out over the eighteenth green to the incredible expanse of clear blue water reflecting an impressionist's palette of colors. You'll see why Cooper called it "Glimmerglass" in his *Leatherstocking Tales*. Built in 1909 by the Clark family, discreet patriarchs of Cooperstown, the Otesaga is at once a part of and apart from Main Street's small-town charms, just a short walk from its front gates. This landmark Georgian Revival edifice, with its mammoth white-columned entry contrasting with the redbrick structure, offers guests a complete destination. In addition to lodgings, guests enjoy fine dining, a cozy pub, and excellent recreation in the form of the vintage 1909 Devereux Emmett-designed Leatherstocking Golf Course, rated among the top public courses in the East.

At the Otesaga Resort Hotel (60 Lake St., Cooperstown; 800–348–6222 or 607–547–9931; otesaga.com) rates vary seasonally, starting at $179 a night for a standard double room. Ask about the many golf and holiday packages.

Just down the street from the Otesaga, the *Fenimore Art Museum* is a splendid showcase for the New York State Historical Association, featuring changing exhibits of works largely from the eighteenth through the early twentieth centuries, with an emphasis on paintings, early photographs, textiles, and other items relating to the American experience. Among the works are Hudson River School paintings by such luminaries as Thomas Cole and Asher B. Durand, folk art, and period furniture and paintings associated with Mr. Cooper.

The museum's $10-million, 18,000-square-foot American Indian Wing exhibits the Eugene and Clare Thaw Collection of American Indian Art, more than 700 masterpieces spanning 2,400 years that highlight the artistry of North

America's indigenous peoples. The Great Hall features a selection of large-scale objects from regions throughout North America.

The museum, overlooking the lake, has a formal terrace garden and restaurant with outdoor seating that overlooks the lake.

Right across the street is the twenty-three-acre **Farmers' Museum**, a cluster of historic buildings where the trades, skills, and agricultural practices of nineteenth-century rural New York State come to life. The museum's 1845 Village Crossroads is made up of ten early nineteenth-century buildings all built within one hundred miles of Cooperstown and moved here as life-size working exhibits. Among the buildings are a tavern, blacksmith's shop, one-room schoolhouse, and print shop. All are furnished in period style, and the museum interpreters perform the tasks appropriate to each building. Buy penny candy at Todd's General Store, meet farm animals, and be sure to see the Cardiff Giant, the fake petrified corpse of a ten-foot-tall man that became the centerpiece of one of the most impressive scams perpetrated on the American public in the 1800s.

Be sure to include a visit to the fascinating Seneca Log House, at one time the home of a traditional Seneca family. The site re-creates the daily life of a Seneca family in the 1840s, while docents demonstrate crafts of the period, including basketmaking, beadwork, and the making of tourist-related objects. Special seasonal events take place here throughout the year: an old-time Fourth of July, the September Harvest Festival, and a Candlelight Evening at Christmastime that features sleigh rides and hot wassail.

The Farmers' Museum (5775 Lake Rd.; 607–547–1450; farmersmuseum.org) in Cooperstown is open Apr, May, Oct, and Nov, Tues through Sun, 10 a.m. to 4 p.m. June through Sept it's open daily, 10 a.m. to 5 p.m. Admission for adults is $5 Mon through Fri, $7.50 Sat and Sun; $3 for children 7 to 12; free for children 6 and under.

The Fenimore Art Museum (5798 NY 80, Cooperstown; 607–547–1400; fenimoreartmuseum.org) is open Apr, May, and Oct through Dec, Tues through Sun, 10 a.m. to 4 p.m.; open daily June through Columbus Day, 10 a.m. to 5 p.m. General admission is $10, free to children 12 and under.

Of course, many travelers first discover the myriad charms of Cooperstown through baseball—the Hall of Fame events or one of the popular fantasy camps in which wanted-to-be players rub elbows and play games with retired baseball stars at **Doubleday Field**, just off Main Street. Fans of the movie *A League of Their Own* may recognize the wonderfully old-timey diamond enclosed by bleachers.

"When the building starts shaking, they've started making," says *USA Today* of **Fly Creek Cider Mill & Orchard**, a turn-of-the-century water-powered mill where visitors can watch apple cider being made and chow down on a host of cider-related products, including hot spiced cider, cider floats, and cider mill donuts. There's also a duck pond, a Tractorland kids' area with a paved tricycle track, and a gift shop selling everything from bagged cheese curds to home accessories. It's at 288 Goose Street, Fly Creek (607–547–9692; flycreekcidermill .com), and is open daily from mid-May until mid-Dec, 9 a.m. to 6 p.m.

Built in the early nineteenth century by one of the state's last great land-owning families, **Hyde Hall**, a New York State Historic Site, may be the finest example of a neoclassical country mansion north of the Mason-Dixon line. The estate's builder, George Clarke, secretary and lieutenant governor of the British Province of New York from 1703 to 1743, wanted to build a home similar to the one he'd left behind in Cheshire, England. He retained Philip Hooker, one of America's foremost early nineteenth-century architects, and kept copious records of the house's construction, furnishing, and decoration, allowing twenty-first-century restorers to replicate many of the original features as they worked. Don't miss the **Hyde Hall Covered Bridge** on your way through Glimmerglass State Park to the estate: It's the oldest still-existing covered bridge in the entire United States.

Hyde Hall (267 Glimmerglass State Park Rd., Cooperstown; 607–547–5098; hydehall.org), overlooking Otsego Lake, is open for tours daily in May, June, Sept, and Oct, 10 a.m., noon, and 2 p.m.; weekends, 10 a.m. to 5 p.m. (last tour at 4 p.m.). In July and Aug it's closed Wed, but tour hours are the same, with an additional daily tour at 4 p.m. Closed when there are events on-site. Admission is $15 for adults, $12 for seniors, military, and children 6 to 17; free for children under 5.

Just across the road from the state park, the professional, non-profit Glimmerglass Festival produces a selection of three operas and one musical theater production every summer, each with a full orchestra. Check this year's schedule at glimmerglass.org for performance dates and shows, and see if there's a lecture, cabaret, concert, symposium, or other special event on the day you're planning to visit—recent speakers have included US Supreme Court Justice Ruth Bader Ginsberg and Tony-winning Broadway composer Stephen Sondheim. Some of today's hottest opera stars have performed at Glimmerglass, and there's always the opportunity to see the next generation of performers before the rest of the world discovers them; 7300 Highway 80, Cooperstown; 607-547-2255; glimmerglass.org.

Outstanding hospitality and gourmet breakfasts are the hallmarks of the **Landmark Inn** (64 Chestnut St., Cooperstown; 607–547–7225; landmarkinn cooperstown.com), an elegant 1856 mansion in the heart of Cooperstown. The inn features eleven rooms, all with private bath, cable TV, refrigerators, and air-conditioning at their smoke-free B&B. Weekends May through Oct require a two-night minimum stay, and kids are very welcome.

At one point in the nineteenth century, 80 percent of the hops produced in America came from within a forty-mile radius of Cooperstown. The **Brewery Ommegang**, on a 135-acre former hops farm alongside the Susquehanna River, carries on the region's proud tradition, using traditional Belgian brewing techniques, including specialty malts, Syrian and Saaz hops, rare spices such as curaçao orange peel and paradise grain, and open fermentation, bottle-conditioning, and warm cellaring. Judge the result for yourself: The brewery is open for half-hour tours year-round, daily from noon to 6 p.m. Adults only, $5 per person; beer tasting with six different brews following the tour: $10.

Brewery Ommegang is at 656 County Route 33, paralleling Route 28 and midway between Cooperstown and Milford (607–544–1800; ommegang.com).

Herkimer diamonds, found just north of Ilion at Middleville, aren't really diamonds; nor are they generally very valuable. But they're a load of fun to try to find, and the **Ace of Diamonds Mine & Campground**—once known as the Tabor Estate, where the diamonds were first dug—can provide you with all the tools to begin your hunt.

The "diamonds" are really clear quartz crystals found in a rock formation called dolomite, buried about four hundred million years ago. Surface water containing silicon seeped down through the earth, where it became trapped in pockets in the dolomite. Tremendous heat and pressure caused the crystals to form, and over the years erosion, weathering, and water have exposed the strata. The crystals at the Ace of Diamonds are found in pockets in the rock and in soil surrounding the weathered rock. They're primarily used for mineral specimens, but ones of gem quality can be appropriate for arts and jewelry.

Ace of Diamonds Mine & Campground (84 Herkimer St., Middleville; 315–891–3855; herkimerdiamonds.com) is open daily Apr 1 through Oct 31 from 9 a.m. to 5 p.m. There is a digging fee of $12 per person for ages 8 and older, and $6 for children 4 to 7. Children ages 3 and under are free. You are welcome to bring your own hand tools, or you can rent gardening tools, a hammer, a chisel, and a bucket for $1 each. (Sledgehammers are $4.)

From Ilion it's just a short hop down the thruway to Utica and a pair of worthwhile museums. The **Munson-Williams-Proctor Arts Institute** places a good deal of emphasis on community accessibility and service, with free group tours, a speakers' bureau, and children's art programs, as well as free admission and a modestly priced performing arts series (some performances take place at the nearby Stanley Performing Arts Center). Their collection of paintings is strong in nineteenth-century genre work and the Hudson River School, as well as such moderns as Calder, Picasso, Kandinsky, and Pollock;

they also have comprehensive art and music libraries; a sculpture garden; and even a children's room where patrons can leave their kids for supervised play while they enjoy the museum. Fountain Elms, a beautifully restored 1850 home in the Italianate Victorian style, stands near the institute, with four period rooms on the ground floor that exemplify Victorian tastes. At Christmas, Victorian ornamentation adorns the house in grand holiday style.

The Munson-Williams-Proctor Arts Institute (310 Genesee St., Utica; 315–797–0000; mwpai.org) is open Tues through Sat 10 a.m. to 5 p.m. and Sun 1 to 5 p.m.; closed major holidays.

Once you retrieve your little ones from the children's room at the institute, take them next to a museum of their own, *Utica Children's Museum*, founded by the city's Junior League—but check first to see if the museum has reopened in its new location in the Parkway District of Utica (the opening there is scheduled for spring 2022). Since 1980 it occupied its own five-story, thirty-thousand-square-foot building, which it kept chock-full of participatory and hands-on exhibits concentrating on natural history, the history of New York State, and technology. The museum closed in March 2020 to begin the moving process, but this has been slowed by the COVID-19 pandemic. Call 315–724–6129 or check uticacm.org for reopening information.

If you've lived in upstate New York for decades, you probably remember Utica Club, the beer touted by talking beer steins Schultz and Doolcy. Such a staple of the area's culture could not simply vanish when the brand became part of FX Matt Brewing Company, so you can still find the characters illustrated on T-shirts when you tour what is now the *Saranac Brewery*, and Utica Club remains on tap in the 1888 Tavern there. Saranac Brewing Company is the second-oldest family-owned brewery—and twelfth-largest—in the country. In addition to the Saranac family of beers and Utica Club, it also produces McKenzie's Hard Ciders, Jed's Mules, and Saranac soft drinks.

You can tour the brewery and then sample the wares for free in the 1888 Tavern (the brewery makes 1888 Tavern Root Beer for kids and teetalers). The tour includes a visit to the seven-story brew house, the fermenting and aging cellars, and the packaging plant.

Saranac Brewery (830 Varick St., Utica; 315–624–2490; saranac.com) is open for tours year-round. June 1 through Labor Day, tours are given Mon through Sat from 1 to 4 p.m., every hour on the hour. On Sun, tours are given at 1 and 3 p.m. The rest of the year, tours are given Fri and Sat at 1 and 3 p.m. (closed major holidays). Advance reservations are recommended. Admission is $5 for adults and free for children 12 and under. Free parking is available in the Tour Center Concourse at the corner of Court and Varick Streets.

Heading west, make a stop at **Chittenango Falls State Park** (2300 Rathburn Rd., Cazenovia; 315–492–1756; parks.ny.gov/parks/130/) to see one of the hidden gems of central New York. The 167-foot cascade of water tumbles over a series of limestone and dolomite ridges in Chittenango Creek, and you can view this magnificent sight at the end of a half-mile walk, from the comfort of a sturdy bridge across the gorge. Open daily dawn to dusk. The New York State parks may charge an entrance fee on weekends from Memorial Day to Labor Day.

Syracuse and the Erie Canal

Back in 1790, the Holland Land Company sent its young agent, John Lincklaen, to America to scout investment possibilities. Two years later he reached the area around Cazenovia Lake, between present-day Rome and Syracuse, and his enthusiasm led his firm to invest in 120,000 acres here. A village, farms, and small businesses soon sprang up, with Lincklaen remaining in a patriarchal and entrepreneurial role that in 1807 allowed him to build himself a magnificent Federal mansion, today preserved at the **Lorenzo State Historic Site**.

The little fiefdom of Lorenzo offers an instructive glimpse into why New York is called the Empire State. Lincklaen and the descendants of his adopted family, who lived here until 1968 (the same year that the house, with its contents, was deeded to the state), were involved with many of the enterprises that led to the state's phenomenal growth during the nineteenth century—road building, canals, railroads, and industrial development.

The mansion, surrounded by twenty acres of lawns and formal gardens, sits on the shores of a four-mile-long lake. It is rich in Federal-era furnishings and the accumulated possessions of a century and a half of Lincklaens, including a fine selection of Hudson River School artworks. In the latest renovations, Zuber & Cie of Rixheim, France, used their original nineteenth-century printing blocks to reproduce an 1870 wallpaper originally hung in Lorenzo in 1901.

Generating Green Power

The **Fenner Wind Farm** stands on a 120-acre site along a ridge in Madison County, not far from Cazenovia. Twenty 328-foot-high windmills with 100-foot blades each produce 1.5 megawatts of electricity—collectively, enough to power 7,800 homes when operating at full capacity.

These projects are part of an ongoing process to fully restore the site to its turn-of-the-century beauty.

Lorenzo State Historic Site (17 Rippleton Rd., Cazenovia; 315–655–3200; parks.ny.gov/historic-sites/15/) is open from early May through Oct 31, Wed, Thurs, and Sat, and holidays that fall on Monday from 10 a.m. to 5 p.m.; Sun, 1 to 5 p.m. The grounds are open all year, 8 a.m. to dusk. Admission is $5 for adults, $4 for seniors, and free for children 12 and under.

Adding to the already considerable charm of the Mohawk Valley is *Skana: The Spa at the Turning Stone Resort and Casino* (5218 Patrick Rd., Verona; 800–771–7711; turningstone.com/spa/skana), the 17,000-acre resort, gaming, entertainment, and golf complex run as an enterprise of the Oneida Indian Nation.

The 33,000-square-foot state-of-the-art spa, salon, and fitness facility—the name is the Oneida word for "peace"—has twelve treatment rooms, including one private VIP spa suite and a couple's suite. The 10,000-square-foot fitness center has an indoor pool for laps and aquatic classes, cardiovascular training machines, and an exercise studio with cushioned flooring for daily group and private classes.

Around the turn of the twentieth century, the Arts and Crafts Movement swept America. It was an aesthetic revolution that rejected the superfluous ornamentation of Victorian furniture, advocating a return to clean lines, honest craftsmanship, and sturdy construction. Gustav and Leopold Stickley, leaders of the movement, began making Craftsman—also known as Mission—furniture.

Today Mission furniture has regained its early popularity, and the Stickleys continue to lead the industry with craftsmanship that remains true to the spirit of the original movement. To see how they maintain the highest levels of quality, visit the museum that commemorates the craft and see originals of the same fine pieces that the company continues to make today.

The Stickley Museum (300 Orchard St., Fayetteville; 315–682–5500; stickley .com/museum) is open Tues, 8 a.m. to 5 p.m.; Wed through Fri, 8 a.m. to 4:30 p.m.; Sat, 10 a.m. to 5 p.m. Call to check the current admission fee.

Hunt for your own Stickley treasures at the *Madison-Bouckville Outdoor Antiques Show*, the state's largest antiques event, held the third weekend in August in Bouckville. More than one thousand dealers from the United States and Canada sell antiques and collectibles at stalls spread over ninety acres of farmland. A Dixieland band is on hand to provide entertainment, and a shuttle provides transportation to and from the parking lots. For information call (315) 824–2462 or check madison-bouckville.com.

At the beginning of the nineteenth century, a swamp south of Oneida Lake became Syracuse, a city that grew around the salt industry and the Erie Canal.

Today visitors can see the last of the "weighlock" buildings that once dotted the waterway. Built in 1850 in Greek Revival style, this weigh station for canal boats today houses the *Erie Canal Museum*.

Exhibits in the Weighlock Gallery include a sixty-five-foot replica of a canal boat. The Frank Buchanan Thomson, named after a late museum director, offers a look at a typical Erie Canal vessel's crew quarters, immigrant accommodations, and cargo storage. The museum experience also includes a hands-on display of canal equipment and explanations of the engineering involved in connecting Albany and Buffalo by means of a 363-mile artificial waterway, with eighty-three locks and eighteen aqueducts. The job wasn't easy, but the result was the longest and most successful canal in the world.

The Erie Canal Museum (318 Erie Blvd. East, Syracuse; 315–471–0593; erie canalmuseum.org) is open Mon through Sat from 10 a.m. to 3 p.m.; closed on New Year's Day, Easter Sunday, July 4, Thanksgiving Day, and Christmas Day. Admission is free; a $10 donation per person is suggested.

From swamp to canal boomtown, Syracuse was a major commercial and industrial center by the end of the nineteenth century and ready for culture with a capital C. The *Everson Museum of Art* was founded by George Fisk Comfort, who had been instrumental in establishing New York City's Metropolitan Museum and who served as founder and dean of the College of Fine Arts at Syracuse University. Comfort established the Syracuse Museum of Fine Arts, which had its first exhibition in 1900. This initial show featured the work of impressionists such as Monet, Sisley, and Pissarro, as well as older, more recognized masters.

Renamed the Everson Museum in 1959 following a large bequest from Syracuse philanthropist Helen Everson, the museum moved in 1968 into its present quarters, a massive, modernist concrete structure that was architect I. M. Pei's first museum building. Its three exhibition levels contain nine galleries and a fifty-foot-square, two-story sculpture court.

The Everson Museum has extensive holdings of American art, including colonial portraits (one very famous one of George Washington), the works of nineteenth-century genre and luminist painters, and paintings by twentieth-century artists such as Robert Henri, John Sloan, Grandma Moses, Maxfield Parrish, Reginald Marsh, and Grant Wood. Its extensive collection of American ceramics may be the nation's premier collection in this field, with holdings dating from 1000 AD to the present. Here are pre-Columbian Native American vessels, colonial and nineteenth-century pieces, and contemporary functional and art pottery; the collection totals more than six thousand pieces.

The Everson Museum of Art (401 Harrison St., Syracuse; 315–474–6064; everson.org) is open Wed and Fri from noon to 5 p.m., Thurs noon to 8 p.m.,

A Tale of Salt City

Charles Dickens visited Syracuse, once also known as "Salt City," in 1869 to give a reading in the Weiting Opera House. He stayed in the Syracuse Hotel and wrote:

"I am here in a most wonderful out-of-the-world place, which looks as if it had begun to be built yesterday, and were going to be imperfectly knocked together with a nail or two the day after tomorrow. I am in the worst inn that ever was seen, and outside is a thaw that places the whole country under water. . . .

"We had an old buffalo for supper and an old pig for breakfast and we are going to have I don't know what for dinner at 6. In the public room downstairs, a number of men (speechless) with their feet against window frames, staring out the window and spitting dolefully at intervals. . . . And yet we have taken in considerably over 300 pounds for tomorrow night."

Sat 10 a.m. to 5 p.m., and Sun noon to 5 p.m. Closed holidays. Admission is $8 for adults, $6 for seniors 65+ and students, and free for children 12 and under.

If you've always wondered where salt comes from, visit the **Salt Museum** near Syracuse, "The City That Salt Built." At one time the area supplied the entire nation with the "white gold." The museum, constructed of timbers from former salt warehouses, explains the method of turning brine into salt, a process that endured until the 1920s.

The Salt Museum, in Onondaga Lake Park (106 Lake Dr., Liverpool; 315–451–7275; onondagacountyparks.com/parks/onondaga-lake-park/salt-museum/), is open mid-May through mid-Oct, Sat and Sun, noon to 5 p.m. Admission is free.

No trip through Syracuse is complete unless it includes a stop at **Dinosaur Bar-B-Que** (246 W. Willow St., Syracuse; 315–476–4937, dinosaurbarbque .com), the original restaurant that has become the signature rib joint in New York State. Not only are the meaty, fall-off-the-bone pork ribs smoked to perfection, but the many side choices—from creamy, lightly spiced macaroni and cheese to simmered greens with smoked turkey—explain Dinosaur's enduring popularity. A good-sized meal for two or for a family won't break the bank, either, even if you choose a combination platter with brisket, chicken, or sausage in addition to your quarter-rack. Don't forget the cornbread with its sticky honey glaze. Open Sun through Thurs, 11 a.m. to 9 p.m.; Fri and Sat, 11 a.m. to 10 p.m.

Places to Stay in the Mohawk Valley

ALBANY

Angels Bed and Breakfast
96 Madison Ave.
(518) 426–4104
angelsbedandbreakfast
.com

Desmond Hotel
660 Albany-Shaker Rd.
(800) 448–3500
desmondhotelsalbany.com

FAYETTEVILLE

The Craftsman Inn & Suites
7300 Genesee St.
(315) 637–8000
craftsmaninn.com

LITTLE FALLS

Gansevoort House Inn & Galleries
42 West Gansevoort St.
(315) 823–3969
gansevoorthouse.com

SCHENECTADY

Belvedere Inn
1926 Curry Rd.
(518) 630–4020
belvedereinnny.com/home

Parker Inn & Suites
424 State St.
(518) 688–1001
parkerinnandsuites.com

SCOTIA

The Glen Sanders Mansion
1 Glen Ave.
(518) 374–7262
glensandersmansion.com

SYRACUSE

Jefferson Clinton Suites
416 S. Clinton St.
(315) 425–0500
jeffersonclintonsuites.com

REGIONAL TOURIST INFORMATION IN THE MOHAWK VALLEY

Albany County Convention & Visitors Bureau
25 Quackenbush Sq.
Albany
(518) 434–1217 or
(800) 258–3582
albany.org

Capital Region Chamber of Commerce
5 Computer Dr. South
Albany
(518) 431–1400
schenectadychamber.org

Cooperstown/Otsego County Tourism
20 Chestnut St.
Cooperstown
(607) 322–4046
visitcooperstown.com

Fulton County Gateway to the Adirondacks
2 North Main St.
Gloversville
(800) 676–3858
(518) 725–0641
44lakes.com

Syracuse Convention & Visitors Bureau
109 S. Warren St., Ste. 10
Syracuse
(315) 470–1910
visitsyracuse.com

Places to Eat in the Mohawk Valley

ALBANY

Jack's Oyster House
42 State St.
(518) 465–8854
jacksoysterhouse.com

Nicole's
556 Delaware Ave.
(518) 436–4952
nicolescatering.com

COOPERSTOWN

Bocca Osteria
5438 NY 28
(607) 282–4031
boccaosteria.com

Origins Café at Carefree Gardens
558 Beaver Meadow Rd.
(607) 437–2862
originscafe.org/locations

The Tunnicliff Inn & Restaurant
34 Pioneer St.
(607) 547–9611
tunnicliffinn.net

ROTTERDAM

Center Stage Deli
2678 Hamburg St.
(518) 355–7791
centerstagedeli.com

SCHENECTADY

Bourbon Street Bar & Grill
2209 Central Ave.
(518) 382–1110
bourbonstreetcolonie.com

OTHER ATTRACTIONS WORTH SEEING IN THE MOHAWK VALLEY

Fort Stanwix National Monument
200 N. James St.
Rome
(315) 338–7730
nps.gov/fost/

Historic Cherry Hill
523½ South Pearl St.
Albany
(518) 434–4791
historiccherryhill.org

Howe Caverns
Caverns Road
Howes Cave
(518) 296–8990
howecaverns.com

New York State Capitol
State Street and Washington Avenue
Albany
(518) 474–2418
empirestateplaza.ny.gov

New York State Museum
Empire State Plaza
Albany
(518) 474–5877
nysm.nysed.gov

Proctors Theater
432 State St.
Schenectady
(518) 346–2604
proctors.org

Schenectady Stockade Area
Front Street
Schenectady
(518) 372–5656
discoverupstateny.com/packages/4779/
stockade-historic-district/

Ten Broeck Mansion
9 Ten Broeck Pl.
Albany
(518) 436–9826
tenbroeckmansion.org

SCOTIA

The Glen Sanders Mansion
1 Glen Ave.
(518) 374–7262
glensandersmansion.com

SYLVAN BEACH

Harpoon Eddie's
611 Park Ave.
(315) 762–5238
sylvanbeach.com/harpoons

SYRACUSE

Apizza Regionale
260 W. Genesee St.
(315) 802–2607
apizzaregionale.com

Kitty Hoynes Irish Pub & Restaurant
301 W. Fayette St.
(315) 424–1974
kittyhoynes.com

The Finger Lakes

Between New York's north coast along Lake Ontario and the Pennsylvania border, you'll find the region that rivals the Adirondacks for the title of the most enchantingly beautiful part of the state. South of the Lake Ontario plain, glaciers carved long, slender furrows, scooping out the soil and rock and piling it on either side of each gorge; when the glacial ice melted, it filled these deep ruts to turn them into a set of glimmering lakes. The hills that rest among and around the lakes became foothills of the Appalachian Mountains to the south—and the soil the glaciers piled here so effortlessly just happens to be perfect for growing grapes, especially the vinifera varieties, the ones that grow well in France, Germany, and other parts of Europe.

The aptly named Finger Lakes extend roughly north and south across an eighty-mile swath of the state, offering vistas so reminiscent of parts of Switzerland that it's no wonder the city at the northern end of Seneca Lake was named Geneva. Dedicated to the cultivation of familiar grape varieties like Chardonnay, Riesling, Cabernet Franc, and Pinot Noir, as well as new grapes bred specifically to thrive in New York's legendary winters, the Finger Lakes region has been named the top

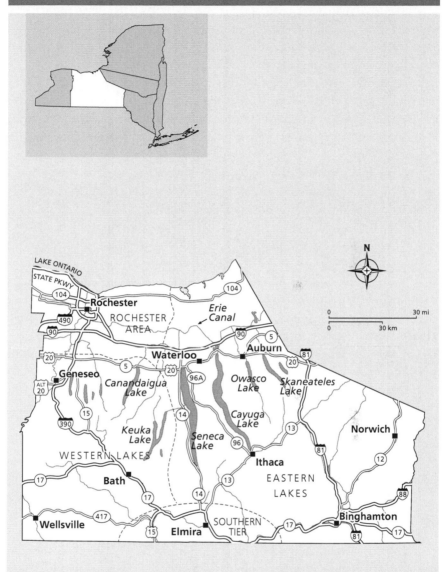

wine region in the country two years in a row by *USA Today*. More than 120 wineries make this region the top producer of wine in New York State—so there's plenty of variety along the shores of each lake to delight passionate oenophiles as well as more casual enthusiasts and tasting newbies.

Scenes of well-tended vines in rows along steep hillsides may put you in mind of Europe, but the Finger Lakes region is rich in Americana. Here are museums of coverlets and horse-drawn carriages, as well as tales of the Revolutionary War. You'll even find Mark Twain's study and a museum devoted to Memorial Day.

We'll approach this area from the south, beginning near the Pennsylvania border and continuing up toward Rochester, then heading east along the New York State Thruway and the northern Finger Lakes.

The Southern Tier

Mark Twain is revered for his tales of life on the Mississippi, but in fact, he wrote many of the stories here in New York, in a charming little summer house now located on the campus of Elmira College and preserved as the ***Mark Twain Study***.

In 1870 Twain married an Elmira woman named Olivia Langdon, and for years the author and his family took leave of their palatial Hartford home to spend many productive summers with Olivia's sister, Mrs. Theodore Crane. Mrs. Crane and her husband lived on a farm outside Elmira, where in 1874 they built Twain a freestanding octagonal study, with windows on all sides and a massive stone fireplace. Here Twain wrote *Tom Sawyer* and completed sections of *Huckleberry Finn, Life on the Mississippi, A Connecticut Yankee in King Arthur's Court*, and other works. It was, he said, "the loveliest study you ever saw."

The Langdon family donated the study to Elmira College in 1952 when it became difficult to maintain and protect from vandalism, whereupon it was removed to its present site on campus.

The Mark Twain Study (800 Park Pl., Elmira; 607–735–1941; marktwain studies.com/about/mark-twains-study) is open from mid-June to Labor Day, Mon through Sat from 9 a.m. to 5 p.m., and Sun from noon to 5 p.m. Call to arrange off-season visits.

Head up Jerusalem Hill Road in Elmira to the ***Hill Top Inn Restaurant's*** (171 Jerusalem Hill Rd., Elmira; 607–732–6728; hill-top-inn.com) outdoor terrace for a great view of the Chemung Valley along with satisfying traditional American cuisine. The Sullivan family has been greeting and feeding patrons here since 1933, with a menu of American staples including steak, broiled seafood, and lamb, as well as Italian dishes like veal marsala; homemade desserts

AUTHOR'S FAVORITES IN THE FINGER LAKES

Bully Hill Vineyards	Hill Cumorah
Corning Museum of Glass	Letchworth State Park
Dr. Konstantin Frank Vinifera Wine Cellars	Lively Run Goat Dairy Farm and Creamery
Dryden Theatre	National Susan B. Anthony Museum & House
Ganondagan State Historic Site	
Glenn H. Curtiss Museum	Ristorante Lucano
Harriet Tubman National Historical Park	Taughannock Falls State Park

are a specialty. The Hill Top Inn Restaurant is open for dinner Mon through Sat beginning at 5 p.m., and in June, July, and Aug from 4 to 8 p.m. Closed some holidays. Reservations are recommended.

The three-story Italianate mansion **Lindenwald Haus Inn**, with its twelve renovated Victorian suite apartments, has been a popular place to stay since it was built in 1876 to house widows of the Civil War. Every room features a living area, bedroom, and private bathroom, and each floor features a shared kitchen and common area. The five-acre grounds are dotted with fruit trees; guests are welcome to walk, bike, or swim.

Lindenwald Haus Inn (1526 Grand Central Ave., Elmira; 866–669–3327; linden waldhausinn.business.site) is open year-round. Visit the website and click "Get Quote" for a personalized price quote for your stay.

When Mark Twain's study was at its original site on his in-laws' Quarry Farm, it commanded a lovely view of the undulating hills along the Chemung River Valley. Little did Twain suspect that a few decades after his death, these same hills would attract recreationists content not merely to walk the trails and pastures but instead to soar quietly far above them. By the 1930s Harris Hill,

Sundae's Cool

While other cities may lay claim to the invention of the sundae, Ithaca has the earliest documentation, dating back to April 5, 1891: a newspaper advertisement announcing the "Cherry Sunday, a New 10 Cent Ice Cream Specialty Served Only at Platt & Colt's Famous Day and Night Soda Fountain."

outside Elmira, had become the "Soaring Capital of America." The **National Soaring Museum** keeps the science and sport of motorless flight vigorously alive, offering visitors earthbound exhibits and the opportunity to go aloft in sailplanes piloted by experienced professionals. The museum houses the world's largest exhibit of contemporary and historic sailplanes, along with displays explaining the development of soaring and its relation to the parallel fields of meteorology and aerodynamics. You can even climb into a cockpit simulator, similar to those used to teach soaring, and learn what the experience of controlling a motorless plane is like.

You can also arrange to get off the ground yourself at the museum or at the **Harris Hill Soaring Corp. Visitors' Center**, which has a staff of competent pilots licensed by the FAA. Just check in at the Harris Hill Gliderport—the rides are available all summer long and on weekends throughout the year, weather permitting. Even if you don't go up yourself, it's fun to watch the graceful, silent flights and landings of the sleek sailplanes.

ANNUAL EVENTS IN THE FINGER LAKES

MARCH

Central New York Maple Festival
Marathon
(607) 849–3278
maplefest.org

MAY

Rochester Lilac Festival
Rochester
(585) 473–4482
lilacfestival.com

JUNE

Ithaca Festival
Ithaca
(800) 273–3646
ithacafestival.org

Strawberry Festival
Owego
owego.org/strawberry-festival

Waterfront Festival
Watkins Glen
(607) 535–3003
thewaterfrontfestival.com

JULY

Corn Hill Arts Festival
Rochester
cornhillartsfestival.com

Finger Lakes Grassroots Festival
Trumansburg
(607) 387–5098
grassrootsfest.org

Finger Lakes Wine Festival
Watkins Glen
(607) 535–2486
flwinefest.com

AUGUST

Empire Farm Days
Seneca Falls
(800) 218–5586
empirefarmdays.com

The National Soaring Museum (51 Soaring Hill Dr., Elmira; 607–734–3128 for office or 734–0641 for glider field; soaringmuseum.org) is open daily May through Oct from 10 a.m. to 5 p.m. (closed some holidays), and Nov through Apr from 10 a.m. to 4 p.m. It's closed Mon and Tues in Jan and Feb. Admission is $9 for adults, $8 for seniors 60+, and $5 for children ages 7 to 18; it's free to children 6 and under. Call regarding schedules and cost of sailplane flights.

Upstream along the Chemung River is Corning, indelibly associated with the Corning, Inc., glass company and the ***Corning Museum of Glass (CMOG)***. Recently renovated and reimagined, the spectacular CMOG explores 3,500 years of glass and glassmaking, with exhibitions, demonstrations, science and technology galleries, and one of the most fascinating (and fragile) museum stores you will ever come across. Visitors can make their own glass projects using hot glassworking, flameworking, fusing, or sandblasting, supervised by experienced glassworkers. Visit cmog.org to book your experience online before you go. Corning Museum of Glass (1 Museum Way; 800–732–6845 or 607–937–5371; visit

Monroe County Fair
Henrietta
(585) 662–5543
mcfair.com

Park Avenue Festival
Rochester
(585) 473–4482
rochesterevents.com

SEPTEMBER

Golden Harvest Festival
Baldwinsville
(315) 451–7275
onondagacountyparks.com/
parks/beaver-lake-nature-center/
golden-harvest-festival/

Grand Prix Festival
Watkins Glen
(607) 535–3003
grandprixfestival.com

Naples Grape Festival
Naples
naplesgrapefest.org

OCTOBER

Letchworth Arts & Crafts Show
Mount Morris
(585) 237–3517
artswyco.org/lacs/

NOVEMBER

Lights on the Lake
Onondaga Lake Park
(through early Jan)
Liverpool
(315) 451–7275
lightsonthelake.com

DECEMBER

Dickens Christmas
Skaneateles
(315) 685–0552
skaneateles.com/calendar/
annual-events/dickens-christmas

As in Life, So in Death

Elmira's Woodlawn Cemetery, burial place of Mark Twain, also contains the graves of Union and Confederate Civil War soldiers. The Confederates are facing south, and the Union graves surround them—exactly as the Union soldiers surrounded their prisoners of war when all died in a nearby railroad accident during the war.

.cmog.org/) is open daily, 9 a.m. to 5 p.m., year-round. Adults $20; seniors 62+, military, and college students $17; free to children 17 and under.

Vitrix Hot Glass Studio, in Corning's historic Market Street district, provides a more intimate environment in which magnificent glass pieces are created by traditional glassblowing techniques. Vitrix turns out some of the country's finest handblown glass pieces, as it has since 1959. Vitrix Hot Glass Studio (77 West Market St., Corning; 607–936–8707; vitrixhotglass.com) is open Mon through Sat from 10 a.m. to 8 p.m., and Sun from 11 a.m. to 6 p.m. Glassblowers are at work Mon through Fri, 9 a.m. to 4 p.m.

The *Rockwell Museum of Western Art* owes its existence almost entirely to Robert F. Rockwell, an area native and former proprietor of a small department store chain whose interest in western art dates to his youth spent on a Colorado ranch. He began collecting seriously in the late 1950s, acquiring works by masters of "cowboy" art such as Charles M. Russell and Frederic Remington, as well as by landscapists of the caliber of Albert Bierstadt and Thomas Hill and animal artists A. F. Tait and Carl Rungius.

Rockwell's protean interests went beyond western art and sculpture to include an area dear to him as a Corning resident: the beautiful art glass created by Frederic Carder, cofounder of the Steuben Glass Works, which was later incorporated into Corning Glass Works, now Corning, Inc. Rockwell even collected antique toys.

By the 1980s, Rockwell's collections were too extensive to be casually shown in his department stores. He needed a museum, and he found a suitable venue in Corning's old city hall, a Romanesque Revival structure built in 1893. Corning, Inc., acquired the building from the city for $1, renovated it, and in 1982 the Rockwell Museum opened. At present it houses the largest collection of western art on the East Coast, more than two thousand pieces of Carder Steuben glass, Navajo weavings, antique firearms, Indian artifacts, and a toy collection as well.

The Rockwell Museum of Western Art (111 Cedar St., Corning; 607–937–5386) is open daily, 9 a.m. to 5 p.m. In summer it stays open until 7 p.m. The museum is closed Thanksgiving, Christmas Eve, Christmas Day, and New

Year's. Admission is $11.50 for adults, $10.50 for seniors 62+ and military, and $5.50 for students. Youths 17 and under are free.

Western Lakes

The westernmost Finger Lakes region nurtured one of twentieth-century America's great speed demons. At Hammondsport, on the southern tip of Keuka Lake, the **Glenn H. Curtiss Museum** chronicles the lifework of this native son, who was also a serious pioneer in motorcycling and aviation.

Glenn Hammond Curtiss started out, as did the Wright brothers, in the bicycle business. He quickly turned to motorcycles, building a V-8–powered bike on which he sped more than 136 miles per hour in 1907. He also built engines that powered lighter-than-air craft, and in that same year he became involved with Dr. Alexander Graham Bell and other enthusiasts in the "Aerial Experiment Association." Curtiss's engineering helped lift the association's Red Wing airplane off the ice of Keuka Lake on the first public flight (as opposed to the Wrights' secret 1903 experiment) of a heavier-than-air craft in the United States.

Glenn Curtiss's accomplishments over the next twenty years dominated the adolescence of aeronautics. In 1910 he landed a plane on water for the first time, and in 1911 he became the first American to receive a pilot's license. In 1919 a Curtiss "flying boat" made the first transatlantic crossing by air. Meanwhile he had built his Curtiss Aeroplane and Motor Company into an industrial giant, employing ten thousand men at the peak of production during World War I. Sensing the traveling trends of the motor age, he even manufactured the first successful house trailers. Following a merger, the company became Curtiss-Wright, producer of World War II aircraft such as the Navy Helldiver and the P-40 of "Flying Tigers" fame.

The museum, founded in 1960, houses seven historic aircraft and three reproductions; one of the latter is a flyable replica of the inventor's 1908 June Bug.

The Glenn H. Curtiss Museum (8419 State Route 54; 607–569–2160; glennhcurtissmuseum.org) is open daily from May 1 through Oct 31, 9 a.m. to 5 p.m.; from Nov 1 through Apr 30, it is open daily from 10 a.m. to 4 p.m. Admission is $13.50 for adults, $12 for seniors 65+, $10 for students, and free for children ages 6 and under.

There's hardly anyplace more off the beaten path than **Dr. Konstantin Frank Vinifera Wine Cellars**, on the western banks of Keuka Lake. Yet oenophiles still wend their way through the vineyards to reach the tasting room, eager to sip the Pinot Noirs, the Gewürztraminers, the sparkling wines, and especially the Rieslings. Dr. Frank's wines have won dozens of gold medals and have been ranked among the country's best wines by tastemakers like *Wine Spectator* magazine, making Dr. Frank one of the first to bring New York vintages into the national spotlight.

Back in the 1950s, when Dr. Frank arrived from Europe speaking not a word of English, vintners in the Finger Lakes were using indigenous American grapes to make rudimentary wines. A doctor of viticulture in his native Ukraine, Dr. Frank believed that the *Vitis vinifera*, the wine grapes of Europe, could be cultivated here, even with the cold winters. He proved it by grafting the varietal vines onto hardy rootstock, and today we can savor the fruits of his labor. Seek out Dr. Konstantin Frank Vinifera Wine Cellars at 9749 Middle Road, Hammondsport (800–320–0735; DrFrankWines.com), or purchase some of Dr. Frank's finest at your local wine merchant.

Dr. Frank's success inspired the neighboring vineyards to follow his lead, sparking a revolution in the New York wine industry. Explore this and a century and a half of winemaking history at the **Greyton H. Taylor Wine Museum**, on the grounds of **Bully Hill Vineyards**. The Taylor Wine Museum (8843 G. H. Taylor Memorial Dr., Hammondsport; 607–868–3610; fingerlakeswine country.com/listings/greyton-h-taylor-wine-museum/865/) is open from mid-May through Oct 31, Mon through Sat from 10 a.m. to 5 p.m., Sun from 11:30 a.m. to 5 p.m. The visitor center offers wine tastings every half hour and tours every hour. Donations are welcome. A restaurant next door specializes in moderately priced homemade pasta and dishes prepared with wine.

For a different perspective on the Taylor legacy, plan to stop at Bully Hill Vineyards before you leave this end of Keuka Lake. The creation of Walter Taylor, an executive vice president at Taylor Wines, Bully Hill got its name and its delightfully cocky attitude from a schism between the Taylors over the way Taylor Wines used grape juice from outside of New York in its wines under a veil of secrecy. Walter spoke out against the practice and found himself out of a job, so he started his own winery. Soon after, when Coca-Cola bought out

Uncork New York

Visitors can either let serendipity be their guide to the Finger Lakes' 120-plus wineries, taking a leisurely drive through the area and stopping when the spirit moves, or they can carefully plan a tasting route with the help of several websites: finger lakeswinecountry.com; senecalakewine.com (877–536–2717); keukawinetrail.com (800–440–4898); cayugawinetrail.com (800–684–5217); and newyorkwines.org (315–924–3700). You can find listings of wineries as well as places to eat, shop, and stay overnight; download the information you need or request maps and brochures.

Taylor Wines, they slapped Walter with a court order that prevented him from using the Taylor name on Bully Hill bottles. Imprinting "Wine Without Fear" and similar messages on the corks in his bottles, Walter Jr. built a reputation for wine with a chip on its shoulder, touting the slogan "They have our name and heritage, but they didn't get our goat." Bully Hill's semi-dry Love My Goat red and Goat white have become some of the most popular and most affordable wines in the Finger Lakes. Call (607) 868–3610 or visit bullyhillvineyards.com for tour and tasting times.

Although far less well known than southeastern Pennsylvania for its Amish and Mennonite populations, the Finger Lakes region long ago attracted members of these peaceful and industrious sects, because of its rich farmland and relative isolation from modern big-city hubbub. One of the most valued and enduring of Amish and Mennonite traditions is quiltmaking, and at **The Quilt Room** in Penn Yan, more than two hundred quilts and wall hangings reveal the meticulous artisanship of women from the surrounding area. In addition to the quilts on display—many of them one of a kind—the Quilt Room can engage quilters to create special-order goods based on any of several thousand traditional designs. Repair work is available as well.

The Quilt Room (1870 Hoyt Rd., Penn Yan; 315–536–5964; quiltroom.com) is open year-round; call for hours.

If you're looking for seclusion—and magnificent mountain views—check out the **Vagabond Inn**. The 7,000-square-foot inn stands in splendid isolation on top of a mountain in the Bristol range. Popular with honeymooners, the inn has a 60-foot-long great room with two massive fieldstone fireplaces, a Japanese garden, and an in-ground pool.

Don't be hasty in choosing a room: Each of the five suites has its special charms. For example, the Bristol has its own fireplace, a Jacuzzi for two (with views of the mountains), and rents for $275 in season. The Lodge, also for $275, has a huge river-stone fireplace and hot-tub chamber. Rates include breakfast. The Vagabond Inn (3300 Sliter Rd., Naples; 585–554–6271; thevagabondinn .com) is open all year.

If you're visiting the area in late September, you might be just in time to sample one of the region's most unusual delicacies—Naples grape pie. Local bakeries produce more than ten thousand grape pies six weeks of the year, beginning with the start of the annual Naples Grape Festival. If you're there any other time of the year, stop in for a slice at **Arbor Hill Grapery and Winery**. They serve them up all year, along with their wines and other wine food products, in a restored eighteenth-century building that once served as the local post office. They also serve casual lunches at Brews & Brats, featuring locally sourced sausages and other ingredients.

Arbor Hill (6461 BB State Route 64, Naples; 585–531–4113) is open daily from May through the first week in Jan, Mon through Sat from 10 a.m. to 5 p.m., and Sun from 11 a.m. to 5 p.m.; open weekends only from Jan to May.

If you'd like to pick up a whole grape pie on your way out of Naples along the shore of Canandaigua Lake, stop at **Monica's Pies** (7599 State Route 21; 585–374–2139). Monica Kay Schenk has been hailed as the best piemaker in the area, and her grape pies are a melt-in-your-mouth delicacy throughout the Finger Lakes. She and her staff also make twenty-four other kinds of pies, jams, jellies, conserves, and even quiches and chicken pot pie. Open Jan 1 through Apr 30, 9 a.m. to 5 p.m.; May 1 through Dec 31, 9 a.m. to 6 p.m.

At the southeast corner of the Alfred University campus is the **Stull Observatory**, considered to be one of the finest teaching observatories in the Northeast. It exists largely through the efforts of John Stull, who built or rebuilt all of the telescopes and many of the buildings. There are five major telescopes at the observatory: a nine-inch refractor dating from 1863, a sixteen-inch Cassegrain reflector, and fourteen-, twenty-, and thirty-two-inch Newtonian reflectors.

The Stull Observatory at Alfred University, Alfred (607–871–2208; alfred.edu/about/map/stull-observatory.cfm), offers public viewings (weather permitting) at the following times: Sept, Oct, Nov, Feb, Mar, and Apr, Fri from 9 to 11 p.m.; May, June, and July, Thurs from 10 p.m. until midnight. Admission is free.

Nearly eight thousand ceramic and glass objects—from pottery shards left behind by ancient civilizations, to works that reflect the cutting edge of ceramic technology—are housed at the **Alfred Ceramic Art Museum**, formerly the Schein-Joseph International Museum of Ceramic Art. The museum is a teaching and research arm of the New York State College of Ceramics at Alfred University. Among its permanent collections are tomb sculptures from the Neolithic period through the Yuan dynasty, Chinese funerary jars, and works by artists such as Charles Fergus Binns, Walter Ostrom, Mary Roettger, Rosanjin Kitaoji, and Bernard Leach.

The museum is located on the northeast corner of Main and Pine Streets on the Alfred campus (607–871–2421; ceramicsmuseum.alfred.edu). It is open Wed through Sat, 10 a.m. to 5 p.m. Admission is $7 for adults; $5 for seniors 55+; $3 for local residents within twenty-five miles, students outside of Alfred, and military; free for children 17 and under.

In July 1937 a freight train pulled into Alfred Station carrying thirty-five bells from Antwerp, Belgium. Eighteen of the bells, which weighed a total of 5,153 pounds (one, called the Bourdon, weighs about 3,850 pounds), were made in 1674 by Pieter Hemony, a famous Netherlands bellfounder. They were hung in a wooden tower overlooking the valley and, shortly thereafter, the **Davis Memorial Carillon** rang out over the hills for the first time.

A carillon is a musical instrument consisting of twenty-three or more cast bronze cup-shaped bells, which are precisely tuned so that many bells can be sounded together to produce a harmonious effect (the bells are stationary; only the clappers move). If you're lucky enough to be in the vicinity on one of the days that the carillonneur is performing, you can hear just how harmonious a sound the carillon (which now has forty-seven bells) can make. The carillon plays four times a week when classes are in session. In addition, the Wingate Memorial Summer Carillon Recital Series brings guest recitalists to perform Tuesday evenings in the month of July.

For information contact the Alfred University Division of Performing Arts in Alfred (607–871–2562; alfred.edu/about/map/carillon.cfm). There is no admission fee.

At the 14,427-acre **Letchworth State Park**, nicknamed the "Grand Canyon of the East," the Genesee River cascades down more than twenty waterfalls as it winds its way north through a series of beetling gorges, some almost six hundred feet high. Visitors can drive through the park on a seventeen-mile-long road that parallels the gorge or hike one of twenty hiking trails of varying difficulty and length.

Accommodations at the park include a campground, cabins, and the yellow-and-white Victorian **Glen Iris Inn** (585–493–2622; glenirisinn.com) overlooking Middle Falls, which offers comfortable rooms starting at $125 and suites from $220 from early Apr to early Nov. Houses are available from $310 to $480. The inn, the former home of William Pryor Letchworth, has welcomed guests since 1914. Glen Iris serves three meals a day from a menu of traditional American fare and offers a special picnic menu.

Just across from the inn, the **Letchworth Museum** is stuffed with exhibits relating to the park's history. On a hill in back of the museum is the grave of Mary Jemison, the "white woman of the Genesee." A prisoner of the Seneca from the age of fifteen, she eventually married a chief and later became a leader of her adopted people. Under the Big Tree Treaty of 1797, she was granted a large parcel of land along the river and lived there until she moved to Buffalo Creek Reservation. William Letchworth had her remains brought back and interred here in 1910.

Letchworth State Park, Genesee State Park and Recreation Region (1 Letchworth State Park, Castile; 585–493–3600; parks.ny.gov/parks/letchworth), is open year-round. There is an admission fee of $8 per day per car on weekends off-season; and daily from Memorial Day weekend through Oct. The museum is open daily from May through Oct between 10 a.m. and 5 p.m. A $1 donation is requested.

For those who would rather float over the falls than drive alongside them, **Balloons Over Letchworth** offers flights in a seven-story hot-air balloon. The voyages, which last approximately one hour (guests should plan on a total time of 2½ to 3 hours), end with a champagne celebration and cost $295 for one person or $179 each for three or more. There is a $10 surcharge per person during the month of October. The launch area is at the Middle/Upper Falls picnic area, a thousand feet south of the Glen Iris Inn (585–493–3340; balloon soverletchworth.com).

While at the park, tour the $25 million **Mt. Morris Dam**, which, since it began operating in 1952, has prevented flood damages estimated at $1 billion. For information call (585) 658–4220.

Just west of Canandaigua Lake, the little town of Bristol has become renowned for pottery, hand-thrown and hand-decorated by "the Wizard of Clay," master potter Jamie Kozlowski, son of the original Wizard, Jim Kozlowski, at **The Wizard of Clay Pottery**. The production facilities and retail stores are housed in seven geodesic domes Jim designed himself.

Jamie and his staff fire all pieces at a temperature of 2,265°F, which makes them extremely hard and durable, then treat them with a specially formulated glaze that gives them a richly colored finish. The Wizard's most original pottery is decorated with delicate imprints from real leaves gathered from the Bristol hills.

The Wizard of Clay Pottery (7851 Route 20A, Bristol; 585–229–2980; wizard ofclay.com) is open daily from 9 a.m. until 5 p.m.; closed major holidays.

The town of Horseheads got its name in 1789 when settlers coming into the valley came upon the bleached skulls of packhorses left behind by General John Sullivan after his battle against the Six Nations of the Iroquois. The **Horseheads Historical Society Museum**, in the former train depot at the corner of Broad and Curns Streets, exhibits cartoons and paintings by the nationally renowned humorist Eugene Zimmerman, better known as "Zim." He lived in a home he designed at the corner of Pine and West Mill Streets. It's now maintained by Historical Tours and open for tours by appointment. Zim also designed the bandstand in Teal Park.

The Horseheads Historical Society Museum is at the Depot (312 West Broad Street & Curns Street, Horseheads; 607–739–3938; horseheadshistorical .com). Open Tues, Thurs, and Sat from noon to 3 p.m., or by appointment.

Wings of Eagles Discovery Center houses an impressive collection of aircraft dating from World War II to the present, as well as exhibits tracing the development of flight. It also has a flight simulator in which visitors can experience virtual flight and gain an understanding of what it's like to fly in the cockpit of a warplane.

Wings of Eagles, Elmira-Corning Regional Airport (339 Daniel Zenker Dr., Horseheads; 607–358–4247; wingsofeagles.com), is open Fri through Sun, 10 a.m. to 3 p.m. Admission is $7 for adults, $5.50 for senior citizens, and there is a family rate of $18 for two adults and three children.

Greater Rochester Area

"Spend a day in the nineteenth century," reads the invitation of the *Genesee Country Village & Museum*, the state's largest living history museum. Located in Mumford on the southern outskirts of Rochester, the fifty-plus reconstructed buildings represent different periods in the development of upstate New York, from frontier days to late Victorian times. Costumed interpreters tend to heirloom gardens and livestock; they provide live demonstrations of everyday activities like pottery and barrel making, blacksmithing, baking, and more. A one-room schoolhouse, an opportunity to play nineteenth-century games, and a chance to experience the progression from farming to industry are all part of a day at this living museum.

The Genesee Country Village & Museum (1410 Flint Rd., Mumford; 585–538–6822; gcv.org) is open July through Labor Day, Tues through Sun from 10 a.m. to 5 p.m.; Sept through June, Tues through Fri from 10 a.m. to 4 p.m., and weekends and holidays from 10 a.m. to 5 p.m. Closed Mon except on holidays. A nature center at the village is open all year, and special programs are held year-round. Admission is $18 for adults, $15 for seniors and students (13 to 18) with ID, and $12 for children ages 3 to 12; children under 3 are free.

The city of Rochester's contributions to history, architecture, and American technological advancements cannot be overstated—and visitors have the opportunity to discover them all.

George Eastman, the entrepreneur and inventor whose vision as the founder of Eastman Kodak Company placed an easy-to-use camera in the hands of every consumer, prospered from his innovations and built the stately mansion that stands at 900 East Avenue. Today it's a museum that not only tells the story of Eastman's life and extraordinary philanthropy, but also celebrates the ongoing science and art of photography in the *International Museum of Photography and Film* adjacent to the home. The five-hundred-seat *Dryden Theatre* shows classic films from the museum's massive film and photo archive, which currently holds several million objects. The *George Eastman Museum* (585–327–4800; eastman.org) is open Wed through Sat from 10 a.m. to 5 p.m., Sun from 11 a.m. to 5 p.m. Admission is $15 for adults; $13 for seniors 65+; $5 for students with ID and youth 5 to 17; free to children 4 and under.

On a Pedestal

In 1899 Theodore Roosevelt, governor of New York, came to Rochester to dedicate the country's first public statue to be erected in honor of an African American: Frederick Douglass (1807–95). The escaped slave, abolitionist, consummate orator, and newspaper publisher lived here for seventeen years, and his home on Alexander Street (which no longer stands) was a station on the Underground Railroad. The bronze statue is in *Highland Park* on Highland Avenue. Douglass was interred in *Mt. Hope Cemetery* along with other luminaries, including his friend Susan B. Anthony.

There's no way to miss the *National Museum of Play at the Strong* (1 Manhattan Square Dr.; 585–263–2700; museumofplay.org), a bright, colorful, fun centerpiece of downtown Rochester with its three floors of activities for children and their adult friends, and the home of the *National Toy Hall of Fame*. Go deeper into the city's southwest quadrant, however, and you will find one of Rochester's proudest bragging points: the home of Susan B. Anthony, leading suffragist and abolitionist, friend of Frederick Douglass, and a national leader in the fight for equal rights for women. Anthony's home (17 Madison St.; 585–235–6124; susanb.org) is now the *National Susan B. Anthony Museum & House*, where she published her daily newspaper

An Apple a Day

Drive along upstate New York's highways and byways in spring and you're sure to see apple orchards in bloom. The Empire State produces more than twenty-five million bushels a year, making it number two in the United States (number one is Washington State). The New York State Agricultural Experiment Station (NYSAES) in Geneva, part of Cornell University, has been improving the quality and quantity of apples grown for more than 125 years. In quest of fruit that is drought- and pest-resistant, the NYSAES has developed some of the tastiest hybrids: Cortland, Jonagold, Jonamac, Macoun, and the most popular: the Empire apple, a cross between McIntosh and Red Delicious. Look for the more recently perfected Liberty and Fortune apples in stores, too.

Apple facts: Apples are a good source of vitamin C, fiber, boron, and the polyphenols quercetin and chlorogenic acid, powerful antioxidants that can protect against cancer, heart disease, stroke, and other conditions. Be sure to eat the skin—that's where all the good phytochemicals are. An apple a day won't keep the doctor away—that was a marketing message, not a medical one—but it certainly contributes to a healthier body, and to the continued health of New York State's apple farmers.

and conducted her many initiatives to advance the cause. Here she also was arrested in 1872 for daring to vote in an election, nearly fifty years before women gained the right to vote. Open Tues through Sun; check the website for current hours or tour times. Admission is $15 for adults, $10 for seniors 62+ and active military, and $5 for students.

You can get any kind of ethnic cuisine in Rochester, but here's a tip: Rochester became the home of tens of thousands of Italian immigrants in the early twentieth century, many of whom remained here to found their own businesses; to work for Kodak, Xerox Corporation, and Bausch & Lomb; and to raise their families. This means that the city has more than its fair share of wonderful Italian restaurants. **Ristorante Lucano** (1815 East Ave.; 585–244–3460; ristorantelucano.com), for example, elevates Italian cuisine to an art form with its veal osso buco, gnocchi with lamb sauce, and just about anything the chef decides to do with the day's fresh catch.

If a traditional Italian meal is more to your liking, you can't beat lunch at **Rocky's** (190 Jay St.; 585–232–9717; rockysonjaystreet.com), where the red sauce brings back memories of Nona's Sunday gravy. Moderately priced with large portions, Rocky's makes certain that everyone leaves full, satisfied, and probably carrying a bag of leftovers. Open for lunch Mon to Sat from 11 a.m. to 2 p.m., and dinner Fri from 4 to 7 p.m. Closed Sunday.

Rochester's popularity as a music city comes in part from the **Eastman School of Music**, one of the top-rated music conservatories in the nation, with just nine hundred students annually. One of the city's best-kept secrets is the opportunity to see and hear these students—many of whom will become professionals performing in orchestras and opera companies around the world—for free. On any given day of the academic year, Eastman students give recitals as part of their degree requirements, so Kilbourn Hall, Kodak Hall, and Hatch Hall, the three main recital halls on campus, may host two or three of these concerts every day. All of these performances are open to the general public, and there's no cost to stop in and listen. If you love classical or jazz music, check the daily listings at rochester.edu/eastman/calendar/ and see which students, ensembles, or faculty may be giving a recital that day.

The music emporium with the acronym HOG, which counts among its customers Metallica, Aerosmith, Mötley Crüe, Jon Bon Jovi, and Ozzy Osbourne, is actually a rambling complex of five warehouses jam-packed with an array of "musicana," from guitars to amplifiers to concert T-shirts to a pair of Elvis Presley's leather pants.

Three brothers named Schaubroeck established **The House of Guitars** in 1964, and today the musical mecca calls itself the "World's Largest Music Store" and stocks just about every brand of instrument (if they don't have it, they'll order it), including more than eleven thousand guitars ranging in price from $60 to $50,000. Potential customers are invited to test the merchandise in one of several small rooms set aside for the purpose.

The House of Guitars (645 Titus Ave., Rochester; 585–544–3500; houseof guitars.com) is open Mon through Sat from 10 a.m. to 9 p.m. and Sun from 1 to 5 p.m.

South and east of Rochester is a monument to another important development in the history of American popular culture: the shopping mall. Not a steel-and-glass mall of the 1950s, but a sturdy wooden structure erected in 1879, it was built by Levi Valentine as an all-purpose market and community center. Thus, it lays claim to being the first multistore "shopping center" in the United States. Today it houses the **Valentown Museum**, a collection of nineteenth-century small-town memorabilia that includes a reconstruction of the first railroad station in the Rochester area and a "Scientific Exhibition," which traveled around the country in a covered wagon from 1825 to 1880.

Valentown Hall, as Valentine called his "mall," had front doors opening into a general store, meat market, cobbler shop, barber shop, bakery, and harness shop. The upstairs contained a Grange lodge, rooms where classes in the arts and trades were held, and a community ballroom. The ambitious scheme lasted only thirty years, since the promised railroad connection never materialized (the restored station interior belonged to an earlier rail operation). The building was saved from demolition and restored in 1940 by J. Sheldon Fisher, a member of the Fisher family that gave its name to the town of Fishers, in which the hall is located. Contact the Valentown Museum, at Valentown Square, Fishers (585–924–2645; historicvalentownmuseum.org).

"Ganondagan . . . a city or village of bark, situated at the top of a mountain of earth, to which one rises by three terraces. It appeared to us, from a distance, to be crowned with round towers." This is how M. L'Abbé De Belmont described a major town of the Seneca people, one of the five original Indian nations that have inhabited central New York since prehistoric times. During the French and Iroquois War in the late 1600s, the governor general of New France led an army from Canada against the Seneca in an effort to eliminate them as competitors in the international fur trade.

The story of the Seneca people and the Iroquois (Haudenosaunee) Confederacy to which they belonged is recounted at **Ganondagan State Historic Site**, the location of the state's largest Seneca community in the seventeenth century. The 522-acre National Historic Landmark encompasses the palisaded granary M. L'Abbé De Belmont described, a sacred burial ground, and a system of trails. A reconstructed bark longhouse similar to ones lived in by the Seneca people is one of the site's high points.

The visitor center at Ganondagan State Historic Site (1488 Victor-Holcomb Rd., Victor; 585–924–5848; ganondagan.org) is open Tues through Sun, 9 a.m. to 5 p.m. from May through Oct. Interpretive trails are open year-round from 8 a.m. to sunset, weather permitting. The bark longhouse is open Wed through Sat, 9 a.m. to 4 p.m. The trails are open all year. Admission is $8 for adults, $4 for seniors and students ages 12 through college, $2 for children 5 to 11, and free for children 4 and under.

The early days of vacuum tubes and crystal radios are chronicled in the Antique Wireless Museum south of the thruway in East Bloomfield. The museum's collections have been amassed by Antique Wireless Association (AWA) members throughout the world, and include nineteenth-century telephones (in working order!), some of Marconi's original wireless apparatus, early shipboard wireless equipment, and the crystal radio sets that brought the first broadcast programs into American living rooms. A special attraction is a fully stocked replica of a circa-1925 radio store; another is wireless station W2AN, an actual broadcast operation staffed by AWA members.

The Antique Wireless Museum (6925 Routes 5 & 20, Bloomfield; 585–657–6260; antiquewireless.org/museum) is open Tues from 10 a.m. to 3 p.m., Sat from 1 p.m. to 5 p.m., and closed on New Year's Day, Easter, July 4, and Christmas Day when they fall on a Tues or Sat. Admission is $7 for adults, free to children and teens.

Preserved Americana seems to be the order of the day in this part of upstate New York, and the theme is carried along nicely at the *Granger Homestead and Carriage Museum* in Canandaigua. "Homestead" is actually a bit too homespun a term for this grand Federal mansion, which must have been the talk of Canandaigua and all the farms around when it was built in 1816 by Gideon Granger, a lawyer who had served as postmaster general under Presidents Jefferson and Madison. Granger came here to live the life of a country squire in his retirement, and his descendants lived here until 1930. Nine restored rooms contain the furniture of the nineteenth century, including Federal, Empire, and Victorian styles. Decorative objects, original artworks, and China Trade porcelain are also displayed.

A distinctive attraction of the Granger Homestead, the Carriage Museum exhibits more than fifty horse-drawn vehicles made or used in western New York. An informative exhibit titled "Sleighs and Surreys and Signs and Symbols" explains the sociological implications of the various conveyances on display. The museum offers forty-five-minute horse-drawn antique carriage rides through the town's historic neighborhoods by reservation on Fri at noon, 1, 2, 3 and 4 p.m. through late Oct. Adults are $20; children 4 to 12 are $10; under 3 free. The carriage can hold up to three adults or two adults and three children.

The museum also gives horse-drawn antique sleigh rides on Sun from 1 to 3 p.m., mid-Jan to mid-Mar, weather permitting. Call for conditions, prices, and availability.

The Granger Homestead and Carriage Museum (295 North Main St., Canandaigua; 585–394–1472; grangerhomestead.org) is open late May through early Oct. Guided tours are offered on the hour Tues and Wed from 1 to 5 p.m.; Thurs and Fri from 11 a.m. to 5 p.m. May through Oct. In June, July, and Aug, it is also open on Sat and Sun from 1 to 5 p.m. Admission is $6 for adults, $5 for seniors, and $2 for students.

Sonnenberg Gardens and Mansion State Historical Park—built in 1887 by Frederick Ferris Thompson, who founded the First National Bank of the City of New York—is part of a Gilded Age extravaganza: part Tudor Revival, part Queen Anne. The forty-room mansion is well worth a tour, but even more impressive than the heavily carved Victorian furniture and fine Oriental rugs contained beneath the house's multicolor slate roof are the gardens themselves.

Frederick Thompson died in 1899, and in 1902 his widow, Mary Clark Thompson, began the extensive formal and informal plantings on the estate as a memorial. She worked for the next fourteen years, using just about every major mode of horticultural expression—a Japanese garden, a rock garden, an Italian garden, a sunken parterre display in a Versailles-inspired fleur-de-lis motif, an old-fashioned garden, a garden planted entirely with blue and white flowers, and a rose garden containing more than 2,600 magnificent bushes blossoming in red, white, and pink. After the Roman bath, the greenhouse complex, the fountains, and the statuary, the mansion itself seems like an afterthought. In fact, among the 35,000-plus visitors to the park annually, many never set foot inside the building—so you needn't feel guilty if the gardens captivate you completely.

The High Noon Café, an informal restaurant on the grounds serving savory crêpes, soups, salads, and beverages, is open daily in season from 11 a.m. to 5 p.m. (585–298–2693). An admission fee is not required to visit the café or the Finger Lakes Wine Center (585–394–9016) in Bay House, which sells gourmet foods and offers wine tastings from all over the Finger Lakes region. The tasting room is open May 1 through Oct 31 from noon to 3:30 p.m. Of course, the adjacent gift shop carries a wide variety of Finger Lakes wines.

Sonnenberg Gardens (151 Charlotte St., Canandaigua; 585–394–4922; sonnenberg.org) is open daily mid-May through Oct, 10 a.m. to 4 p.m. In summer, it is open until 5:30 p.m. Walking tours are offered weekdays at 1 p.m. and on weekends at 10 a.m. and 1 p.m. (no tours before Memorial Day or after Labor Day). Admission is $15 for adults, $13 for seniors 60+, $8 for students and military with ID, $3 for children 4 to 12, and free for children 3 and under. A free tram provides transportation around the grounds.

Over the course of thirty years in the 1800s, Mrs. Merle Alling of Rochester amassed the country's largest collection of homespun coverlets. These are now displayed in a 1901 newspaper printing office converted into the **Alling Coverlet Museum**, part of Historic Palmyra. Heirlooms all, they represent both the simple spreads hand-loomed by farmwives and the more sophisticated designs woven on multiple-harness looms by professionals, all crafted between 1820 and 1880. The collection also includes a number of handmade nineteenth-century quilts and antique spinning equipment.

The Alling Coverlet Museum (122 William St., Palmyra; 315–597–6981; historicpalmyrany.com/alling-coverlet-museum) is open daily, June through mid-Sept, 1 to 4 p.m. and by appointment. Admission is free; donations are welcome.

The **William Phelps General Store Museum**, erected in 1825, was purchased by Phelps in 1867 and remained in his family until 1977. Virtually unchanged since then, the store, along with its stock, furnishings, and business records, amounts to a virtual time capsule of Palmyra in the nineteenth and early twentieth centuries. An unusual note: The gaslight fixtures in the store and upstairs residential quarters were used by a Phelps family member until 1976, because electricity had never been installed in the building.

The William Phelps General Store Museum (140 Market St., Palmyra; 315–597–6981) is open June through mid-Sept, Tues through Sat from 1 to 4 p.m. Open Sat only in Oct.

No one should leave Palmyra without visiting **Hill Cumorah**, the sacred site of the Church of Jesus Christ of Latter-Day Saints. Here Joseph Smith, the founder of what became known more colloquially as the Mormon religion, met annually with the angel Moroni from 1823 to 1827 to translate the Book of Mormon from the golden plates Moroni brought for this purpose. No matter what religion you follow, or even if you choose to practice none at all, a visit to the hill and its visitor center provides a fascinating piece of American history. For more than eighty years, Mormons came from all over the world to this hill in July to perform the Hill Cumorah Pageant, a theatrical feat that told stories from the Book of Mormon (the actual book, not the Tony-winning Broadway show). The pageant's final performances were scheduled for 2020 and had to be canceled because of the pandemic, so watch for a future opportunity to see the show in its final season. Hill Cumorah (603 State Route 21, Palmyra; 315–539–2552; hillcumorah.org) is open every day (closed Sun until 1 p.m.): Jan and Feb, 9 a.m. to 5 p.m.; Mar through May, 9 a.m. to 7 p.m.; June through Aug, 9 a.m. to 9 p.m.; Sept through Dec, 9 a.m. to 7 p.m. Free admission.

Eastern Lakes

For a fabulous day of fishing, head for **Sodus Bay** on the shore of Lake Ontario. Many charter boat companies offer their services in-season in this small fishing paradise, where anglers can encounter northern pike, walleye, yellow perch, smallmouth and largemouth bass, pumpkinseed, bluegill, rock bass, crappie, white perch, carp, bullheads, and channel catfish in the bay's relatively shallow (mostly twenty feet deep) waters.

The lighthouse at **Sodus Bay Lighthouse Museum** (7606 N. Ontario St., Sodus Point; 315–483–4936; sodusbaylighthouse.org) was built in 1871 and remained in use until 1901. Museum displays include ship models, dioramas, shipboard equipment, a lens repair shop, and other maritime exhibits, and there's a wonderful view of the lake from the tower. It's open May 15 through Oct 15, Tues through Sun from 10 a.m. to 5 p.m. in June, July, and Aug; noon to 5 p.m. in Sept and Oct. Admission is $6 for adults, $3 for students in grades K to 12, and free for children under 5.

The **1870 Victorian Carriage House Inn** (8375 Wickham Blvd.; 315–483–2100; carriage-house-inn.com) charges from $140 to $190 in season (May through Sept) for rooms and suites with a private bath, TV, and full breakfast. Views overlook the bay, Lake Ontario, and the Sodus Point lighthouse.

Bonnie Castle Farm Bed & Breakfast, on fifty acres of landscaped grounds overlooking Great Sodus Bay, is a three-story Victorian with private balconies and bilevel decks. Each of the five rooms has its own bath; the guesthouse has a kitchen and living room, as well as three bedrooms and four baths.

Bonnie Castle Farm Bed & Breakfast (6603 Bonnie Castle Rd., Wolcott; 315–587–2273) is open year-round. Rates range from $135 to $200 and include a full breakfast with such dishes as orange blossom French toast, frittata, and pumpkin bundt cake. There's also a private beach.

What attracted so many collectors of specialty items to the Finger Lakes is anyone's guess, but museums of such items sprang up all over the region throughout the nineteenth and twentieth centuries. In Newark, for example, the **Hoffman Clock Museum** comprises more than three hundred clocks and watches collected by local jeweler and watchmaker Augustus L. Hoffman. Housed in the Newark Public Library, the collection includes timepieces from Great Britain, Europe, and Japan, although the majority of the clocks and watches are of nineteenth-century American manufacture, with more than a dozen made in New York State. Each summer the museum's curator mounts a special exhibit devoted to a particular aspect of the horologist's art: the development of technology that allows us to keep track of time, or the history of New York State's clockmakers.

No Invaders, Please

If you're planning to put a boat into any of the Finger Lakes, make sure the trailer, hull, and external motor or drive apparatus have been thoroughly cleaned—especially if the vessel has been in the Great Lakes, the St. Lawrence River, Lake Champlain, or connected waters. Zebra mussels and the aquatic weed milfoil are invasive, non-native pests whose spread you can help prevent by scrubbing down hulls, motors, and trailers with hot water.

The Hoffman Clock Museum, Newark Public Library, 121 High Street, Newark (315–331–4370), is open Mon through Thurs from 9:30 a.m. to 8 p.m., Fri 9:30 a.m. to 6 p.m., and Sat 9:30 a.m. to 3 p.m. (closing at 1 p.m. in July and Aug). Admission is free.

If your interest in antiques extends beyond timepieces, head south a few miles to Geneva for a tour of **Rose Hill Mansion**, the Geneva Historical Society's National Historic Landmark property overlooking the east shore of Seneca Lake. Built in 1839, the twenty-six-room mansion is one of the nation's premier examples of the Greek Revival style at its peak of refinement and popularity. Formal, symmetrical, and serene within its boxwood garden, Rose Hill Mansion has been exquisitely restored and furnished with as many pieces original to the house as it has been possible to collect. The twenty-one-room tour highlights the dining room, with its five-foot-long 1815 Portuguese crystal chandelier; the front parlor, containing a seven-piece Rococo rosewood ensemble; and the Green Bedroom, decorated in the Empire style that paralleled the Greek Revival architectural trend. Rose Hill's formality is offset by its airy, spacious character—all of its front windows open from the floor, making a seamless link between ground-floor rooms and the colonnaded front porch.

Rose Hill Mansion (3373 NY 96A, Geneva; 315–789–3848; genevahistorical society.com/visit/rose-hill-mansion/) is open May through Oct, Mon through Sat from 10 a.m. to 4 p.m.; Sun from 1 to 5 p.m. Admission is $10 for adults, $8 for seniors, $6 for students 10 to 18, and free for children 9 and under.

Two of the Finger Lakes' most elegant inn-restaurants overlook its deepest lake, Seneca, in Geneva, the self-proclaimed "Trout Capital of the World."

It took fifty men more than four years to build the turreted red Medina stone **Belhurst Castle**, overlooking Seneca Lake. When it was finally completed in 1889, the cost of construction exceeded $475,000. Today the Richardsonian Romanesque-style inn, on the National Register of Historic Places, appears on *USA Today*'s list of the Top 10 Wine Country Hotels, and *Wine Enthusiast* names it as a "world's best wine hotel" as well.

There are fourteen period mansion rooms in the castle (including one with a private balcony and one in the castle turret, with a widow's walk) and several houses on the grounds behind the castle: the Carriage House, with a four-poster bed and private patio; the Ice House, with a loft bedroom; and the Dwyer Lane House, a three-bedroom ranch house adjacent to Belhurst. Rates range from $195 to $445 in season; off-season rates are available.

Edgar's Restaurant in the Castle offers a range of elegant dishes for dinner nightly, from rack of lamb to stuffed quail, as well as a robust seafood menu and a tempting tray of desserts. A separate prix-fixe menu provides a three-course meal plus dessert. Reservations are strongly recommended; call (315) 781–0201, ext. 3. For lunch and more casual dinners, Stonecutter's Pub combines craft beers, views of Seneca Lake, and pub fare daily from 11 a.m. to 10 p.m.

White Springs Manor, sister property to Belhurst Castle, was once owned by a wealthy lawyer and land baron. The imposing 1806 Georgian Revival mansion, perched on a hilltop in the middle of eighteen acres, affords guests a panoramic view of Seneca Lake and beyond. Each of the twelve guest rooms and the "playhouse" (a detached house) have a private bath, gas fireplace, and queen- or king-size bed. Belhurst's Vinifera Inn, opened in summer 2004, offers rooms with lake views, opulent appointments, fireplaces, and two-person jacuzzis. Rates are $245 to $390.

Belhurst Castle (4069 Lochland Rd., Geneva; 315–781–0201; bclhurst.com) is open year-round.

"An oasis, a little island of beauty, peace, and friendliness in a busy world" is how ***Geneva on the Lake*** describes itself. The inn, with its terra-cotta tile roof, Palladian windows, Ionic columns, classical sculptures, and magnificent formal gardens, was built in 1910 by Byron Nester, who took inspiration from the summer residences around northern Italy's Lakes Garda and Maggiore. Special package rates include wine, fresh fruit and flowers, use of bicycles to explore the town, continental breakfast in the hotel parlor or on the terrace overlooking the gardens and lake (weather permitting), and a credit toward the price of a candlelit dinner in Lancellotti's, the estate's restaurant.

Geneva on the Lake (1001 Lochland Rd., Geneva; 315–789–7190; genevaon thelake.com) is open all year.

"To honor in perpetuity these women, citizens of the United States of America, whose contributions to the arts, athletics, business, education, government, the humanities, philanthropy and science have been the greatest value for the development of their country." Thus were the parameters for entry outlined when the women of Seneca Falls created the ***National Women's Hall of Fame*** in 1969, believing that the contributions of American women deserved a permanent home.

And, indeed, the list of members includes plenty of familiar names: Marian Anderson, Susan B. Anthony, Mary McLeod Bethune, Pearl S. Buck, Rachel Carson, Shirley Chisholm, Hillary Rodham Clinton, Dorothea Dix, Amelia Earhart, Ella Fitzgerald, Betty Friedan, Ruth Bader Ginsburg, Billie Jean King, Coretta Scott King, Nancy Pelosi, Sally Ride, and hundreds of others who have left their mark on American history and the American psyche.

Exhibits, housed in the Seneca Knitting Mill building, include a panel celebrating Elizabeth Cady Stanton, who led the way to rights for women, and artifacts and mementos about the members, events, and activities significant to women's history.

The National Women's Hall of Fame (1 Canal St., Seneca Falls; 315–568–8060; womenofthehall.org) is open from May through Sept, Mon through Sat from 10 a.m. to 5 p.m., and Sun noon to 5 p.m.; Oct through Apr, Wed through Sat, 10 a.m. to 5 p.m. Closed Thanksgiving, Christmas, and the month of Jan. Admission is $7.

Once a stop on the Underground Railroad, the ***Laura Hubbell House Bed & Breakfast*** overlooking Van Cleef Lake was built in the 1850s as a Gothic Revival cottage and later enlarged and remodeled in the Second Empire style. The result is a delightfully eccentric building with scrolled bargeboards, wooden pinnacles, windows of all sizes, and a rear mansard roof with diamond-shaped slate tiles. It's furnished with an eclectic mix of antiques, including an 1860s Eastlake dresser, armchair, and rocker, and has three guest rooms. The wraparound porch overlooks the lake.

Laura Hubbell House Bed & Breakfast (42 Cayuga St., Seneca Falls; 315–712–4382; hubbellbb.com) is open all year. Rates, which include a full breakfast, range from $155 to $175 a night. Guests can swim and use paddleboats from the inn's private dock.

In the village of Waterloo in the summer of 1865 a patriotic businessman named Henry C. Welles put forward the idea of honoring the soldiers who fell in the Civil War by placing flowers on their graves on a specified day of

A Snake in the Grass

Just outside the town of Geneva is ***Bare Hill***, sacred to the Seneca. According to legend, it was here the Creator opened up the earth and allowed their ancestors to enter into the world. But a giant serpent lay in wait, eating the newborns as they appeared. Finally, a warrior, acting upon a dream in which the Creator told him to fear not, slew the snake with a magic arrow, and the snake, in its death throes, disgorged all those he'd eaten.

observance. On May 5 of the following year, thanks to the efforts of Welles and Civil War veteran General John B. Murray, townspeople draped the village in mourning, marched to the local cemeteries and, with appropriate ceremonies, decorated their comrades' graves. Thus, Memorial Day was born.

One hundred years later, in 1966, President Lyndon B. Johnson signed a proclamation officially naming Waterloo the birthplace of Memorial Day. On May 29 of that centennial year, Waterloo's *National Memorial Day Museum* opened in a reclaimed mansion in the heart of town. The once-derelict, twenty-room brick structure is itself a local treasure, especially distinguished by the ornate ironwork on its veranda. The museum's collections cover the Civil War and the lives and era of the originators of the holiday, as well as memorabilia from all other US wars.

The National Memorial Day Museum (35 East Main St., Waterloo; 315–539–9611; wlhs-ny.com/national-memorial-day-museum/) is open Memorial Day weekend through mid-Sept; spring and fall, Tues through Sat from noon to 5 p.m. Admission is by donation.

The Cayuga Museum of History and Art in Auburn is really several museums in one; founded in 1936 in the 1836 Willard-Case Mansion, it tells the rich history of Auburn, "the village that touched the world," and surrounding Cayuga County. On display are business timekeeping devices such as the "Thousand Year Clock," manufactured by Auburn's Bundy brothers, whose Binghamton, New York, operation evolved into IBM, as well as an exhibit on the early history of the now-giant corporation. Other notables from Cayuga County who are highlighted at the museum include abolitionist Harriet Tubman; President Millard Fillmore; E. S. Martin, founder of the original *Life* magazine; prison reformer Thomas M. Osborne; and Ely Parker, the Seneca Native American who penned the Civil War surrender treaty signed at Appomattox.

A Reformer of Women's Fashion

Although Seneca Falls resident Amelia Jenks Bloomer didn't invent "bloomers" (they were invented by Elizabeth Smith Miller), she was instrumental in making them the uniform of nineteenth-century suffragists. The *New York Tribune* described Mrs. Bloomer's outfit: " . . . a kilt descended just below the knees, the skirt of which was trimmed with rows of black velvet. The pantaloons were of the same texture and trimmed in the same style. She wore gaiters." Bloomer made one much greater contribution to the women's movement of the 1850s, however—she introduced Elizabeth Cady Stanton to Susan B. Anthony, setting in motion one of the great partnerships for human rights of the nineteenth century.

The first floor of the mansion features a permanent exhibit about modern medicine in its infancy, while the second floor provides plenty of information about Auburn's landmark penal system of the nineteenth century, in which prisoners worked in silent groups during the day and spent their nights separately in solitary confinement. Striped uniforms, walking in lockstep, and the first use of the electric chair became the hallmarks of this system. Whether the inmates could be considered "rehabilitated" by this treatment became a matter of considerable contention, but in the end—which did not come until the 1930s—more enlightened management threw out the harsh system and replaced it with modern penal rules.

In 1911 Theodore W. Case proved that recording sound on film was possible, and in late 1922, with his assistant Earl I. Sponable, he made talking movies a reality by inventing what later became the Movietone system. The **Case Research Lab Museum** is now a permanent exhibit on the second floor of the Cayuga Museum's carriage house. Displays include the laboratory building, the soundstage, and many examples of the early history and inventions developed to commercialize sound on film.

The Cayuga Museum and the Case Research Lab Museum (203 Genesee St., Auburn; 315–253–8051) are open Feb through Dec, Tues through Sat, 10 a.m. to 3 p.m.; closed Thanksgiving, Christmas, and New Year's Day. Admission is $7 for adults, $6 for seniors and military, and free for students and children.

The "Woman Called Moses" is remembered at the **Harriet Tubman National Historical Park** in Auburn, where Tubman settled after making nineteen trips to the South to rescue more than three hundred enslaved persons. A guided tour includes a visit to the Tubman House, the Home for the Aged, the ruins of the John Brown Infirmary, the former Thompson Memorial A.M.E. Zion Church building, and Mrs. Tubman's grave at Fort Hill Cemetery.

The Harriet Tubman Home (180 South St., Auburn; 315–252–2081; harriet tubmanhome.com) is open Tues through Fri 10 a.m. to 4 p.m., and Sat by appointment. There are extended hours in February, Black History Month. Admission is $5 for adults, $3 for seniors, and $2 for children.

Experts believe that the **Willard Memorial Chapel**—all that remains of the Auburn Theological Seminary campus, which thrived here from 1818 to 1939—is the only extant example of a complete Louis Comfort Tiffany interior. The handsome gray limestone and red sandstone Romanesque Revival building, designed by A. J. Warner of Rochester, has a magnificent interior designed and handcrafted by the Tiffany Glass and Decorating Company. Among the highlights: a three-paneled stained-glass window of "Christ Sustaining Peter on the Water," nine leaded-glass chandeliers, and fourteen opalescent nave windows.

The Willard Memorial Chapel (17 Nelson St., Auburn; 315–252–0339; willard-chapel.org) is open for tours on Fri and Sun at 2 p.m., or by appointment. Admission is $10 per adult, $8 for seniors 62+ and students, and free for children 12 and under.

Patrons and critics agree about *Rosalie's Cucina* in Skaneateles: When you eat at Rosalie's, it's like eating in Italy. The superb, authentic dishes hail primarily from the Tuscan region, and many are family recipes, such as scampi alla Rosalie (shrimp, artichokes, oven-cured tomatoes, candied lemon zest, spinach, and garlic butter over angel hair pasta) and vitello marsala (veal, marsala wine, mushrooms, prosciutto, spinach, and pasta). Entrée prices range from $25 to $44. The restaurant (841 West Genesee St., Skaneateles; 315–685–2200, rosaliescucina.com) is open for dinner nightly; reservations are strongly encouraged.

Classic cars, historic race cars, and racing memorabilia are all exhibited at the *Northeast DIRT Modified Museum & Hall of Fame*. Among the classic cars on display are a 1926 Duesenberg, the 1929 Dodge Roadster that won first place in a cross-country race in 1993, and a 1969 Dodge Charger Hemi 4-speed. For stock car enthusiasts, there's the Buzzie Reutimann "00" coupe, which won the first two Schaefer 100s, and "Batmobile" #112 driven by Gary Balough in 1980. In the Jack Burgess Memorial Video Room, the "Master of the Microphone" recounts exciting racing events of the past. The Northeast Classic Motorsports Extravaganza is held each August.

Northeast DIRT Modified Museum & Hall of Fame (1 Speedway Dr., Weedsport; 315–834–6606) is open Tues and Sun, noon to 5 p.m.; other days by appointment. Admission is $4 for adults and $3 for children and senior citizens.

In England, Americans Victoria and Richard MacKenzie-Childs worked for a small pottery shop, taught art, and designed and made clothing for stage and street wear. When they returned to America, they opened *MacKenzie-Childs, Ltd.*, a multifaceted design studio and factory where more than 150 workers turn out handcrafted, hand-painted giftware, including majolica, glassware, linens, and floorcloths—all done, according to the couple, "within the elegance of a gentlemanly nineteenth-century estate . . . in an atmosphere of ethics, order, and grace."

MacKenzie-Childs, Ltd. (3260 State Route 90, Aurora; 315–364–6118; mackenzie-childs.com), showroom and shop are open year-round, Mon through Sun, 10 a.m. to 5 p.m.

One of the Syracuse area's most satisfying hiking experiences awaits you at *Beaver Lake Nature Center* (8477 East Mud Lake Rd., Baldwinsville; 315–638–2519; onondagacountyparks.com/parks/beaver-lake-nature-center), where careful management provides enough habitat diversity to attract more than two hundred bird species, hundreds of plant species, and all of central New York's most common mammals.

A two-hundred-acre lake forms the centerpiece of this natural space, while hardwood forest, open meadows, and a wetland bog surround the lake. The three-mile Lake Loop hike traverses all of these habitats, bringing you closer to songbirds and waterfowl, squirrels and chipmunks, and a landscape that changes with the seasons, offering wide views in winter and early spring and protecting nesting species in spring and summer.

Beaver Lake Nature Center is open daily all year, from 7:30 a.m. to 7 p.m.; closed Thanksgiving and Christmas. Admission is $5 per car.

As you make your way down the western shore of Cayuga Lake on NY 89, you may choose to stop at one of several wineries along the route, but I highly recommend three places you should not miss. The first, ***Cayuga Lake Creamery*** (8421 NY 89, Interlaken; 607–532–9492; cayugalakecreamery.com) packs more flavor into a dish of ice cream than you will find anywhere else in the Finger Lakes. A little farther south and off to the right, ***Lively Run Goat Dairy Farm and Creamery*** (8978 County Rd. 142, Interlaken; 607–532–4647; livelyrun.com) not only offers samples of all of its goat's milk cheeses and other products, but it gives you the chance to meet the goats—including the kids— which may turn out to be the highlight of your day, if not your whole week.

When you've played with goats and had your ice cream, you're ready for an easy walk to one of the most dramatically stunning places in the Finger Lakes Region: ***Taughannock Falls State Park***. The park provides two different views of this plummeting curtain waterfall: You can see it from a high overlook directly across from the falls, or take the flat, mile-long walk along Taughannock Creek to the falls' plunge pool, where you can feel the spray and hear the thunder of this glorious waterfall from up close.

Ithaca, home to Cornell University, also hosts the ***Museum of the Earth*** with its massive collection of more than seven million fossils, one of the largest in the Western Hemisphere. The museum tells the story of the planet's 4.6-billion-year history, with a focus on the Northeast, through exhibits, hands-on activities, and audiovisual presentations. Among the fossils exhibited are single-celled microfossils, ancient plants, the remains of ancient vertebrates, including dinosaurs, whales, and woolly mammoths, and a magnificent 425-million-year-old trilobite. The Hyde Park Mastodon Fossil skeleton is one of the most complete in the world.

Museum of the Earth, Paleontological Research Institute (1259 Trumansburg Rd., Ithaca; 607–273–6623; museumoftheearth.org) is open Sat through Mon, 10 a.m. to 5 p.m. Admission is $9 for adults, $7 for seniors 65+ and college students with ID, $6 for youths 4 to 17, and free for children 3 and under.

Have you ever wished you could travel from one end of the solar system to another? You can do that, in a way, by taking the **Sagan Planet Walk** at Ithaca's **Sciencenter** (601 1st St., Ithaca; 607–272–0600; sciencenter.org/sagan-walk.html). This outdoor, 1:5 billion–scale model covers three-quarters of a mile in downtown Ithaca, beginning with the sun at Ithaca Commons and ending with Pluto (which was still considered a planet when they built the Planet Walk in 1997) at the Sciencenter. There's a scale model of each planet as you walk from one to the next, with information about that celestial body; recent additions include augmented reality features using a Planet Walk smartphone app, and an audio tour narrated by Bill Nye the Science Guy.

Thanks to a poor boy who grew up to be a wealthy shoe manufacturer and benefactor, 6 of approximately 170 carved wood carousels remaining in this country are located in Broome County. Between 1919 and 1934 George F. Johnson donated to the county six carousels manufactured by the Allan Herschell Companies of North Tonawanda. He placed one stipulation on the gift: Remembering his poor childhood, he felt that everyone should be able to ride and insisted that the municipalities never charge a fee.

Today, gorilla chariots, pigs, horses, and lions hidden in saddle blankets transport riders on their backs to magical realms. And at two of the carousels—Recreation and Ross Parks—the animals twirl to the sounds of the original Wurlitzer band organs. Riders who take a spin on all six merry-go-rounds receive a special button.

The carousels are located at **C. Fred Johnson Park**, Johnson City (607–797–9098); **George W. Johnson Park**, Endicott (607–757–2427); **West Endicott Park**, Endicott (607–754–5595); **Recreation Park**, Binghamton (607–722–9166 or 607–662–7017); **Ross Park**, Binghamton (607–724–5461); and **Highland Park**, Endwell (607–754–5595). They operate from Memorial Day to Labor Day, and annual "Ride the Carousel Circuit" promotions offer buttons or other items to people who ride them all in a single season (check the Broome County website at gobroomecounty.com/community/carousels for details). An exhibit at Ross Park explores the history of carousel making. For general information contact the Broome County Chamber of Commerce at (607) 772–8860.

Places to Stay in the Finger Lakes

AURORA
Aurora Inn
391 Main St.
(315) 364–8888
aurora-inn.com

CORNING
Rosewood Inn
134 E. 1st St.
(607) 962–3253
rosewoodinn.com

GENEVA
Belhurst Castle
4069 Rte. 14 South
(315) 781–0201
belhurst.com

HAMMONDSPORT
Blushing Rose Inn Bed & Breakfast
11 William St.
(607) 569–2687
blushingroseinn.com

ITHACA
Hilton Garden Inn
130 East Seneca St.
(607) 277–8900
ithaca.gardeninn.com

Statler Hotel at Cornell University
130 Statler Dr.
(607) 254–2500
statlerhotel.cornell.edu

SENECA FALLS
Finger Lakes Bed & Breakfast Association
56 Cayuga St.
flbba.org

Laura Hubbell House Bed & Breakfast
42 Cayuga St.
(315) 712–4382
hubbellbb.com

SKANEATELES
Sherwood Inn
26 W. Genesee St.
(315) 685–3405
thesherwoodinn.com

WATKINS GLEN
Idlwilde Inn
1 Lakeview Ave.
(607) 535–3081
idlwildeinn.com

Places to Eat in the Finger Lakes

CANANDAIGUA
Eric's Office
2574 County Rd. 28
(585) 394–8787
ericsofficerestaurant.com

New York Kitchen
800 S. Main St.
(585) 394–7070
nykitchen.com/restaurant/

DUNDEE
Veraisons Restaurant
Glenora Wine Cellars
5435 Rte. 14
(607) 243–9500 or
(800) 243–5513
glenora.com/restaurant/veraisons-restaurant

ELMIRA
Lib's Supper Club
106 W. 5th St.
(607) 733–2752
libssupperclub.net

HAMMONDSPORT
Crooked Lake Ice Cream Company
35 Shether St.
(607) 569–2751
crookedlakeicecream.com

Village Tavern Restaurant & Inn
30 Mechanic St.
(607) 569–2528
villagetaverninn.com

ITHACA
Moosewood Restaurant
215 North Cayuga St.
DeWitt Mall
(607) 273–9610
moosewoodrestaurant.com

LODI
Dano's Heuriger on Seneca
9564 Rte. 414
(607) 582–7555
danosonseneca.com

SKANEATELES

Doug's Fish Fry
8 Jordan St.
(315) 685–3288
dougsfishfry.com

The Krebs 1899
53 West Genesee St.
(315) 685–1800
thekrebs.com

TRUMANSBURG

Inn at Taughannock Falls
2030 Gorge Rd.
(607) 387–7711
t-farms.com

WATKINS GLEN

Jerlando's Ristorante & Pizzeria
400 N. Franklin St.
(607) 535–4254
jerlandospizza.com

OTHER ATTRACTIONS WORTH SEEING IN THE FINGER LAKES

Buttermilk Falls State Park
106 E. Buttermilk Falls Rd.
Ithaca
(607) 273–5761
parks.ny.gov/parks/151

Elizabeth Cady Stanton House
32 Washington St.
Seneca Falls
(315) 568–2991
nps.gov/wori/learn/historyculture/
elizabeth-cady-stanton-house.htm

Memorial Art Gallery
500 University Ave.
Rochester
(585) 276–8900
mag.rochester.edu

Montezuma National Wildlife Refuge
3395 US 20
Seneca Falls
(315) 588–5987
friendsofmontezuma.org

Richardson-Bates House Museum
135 East Third St.
Oswego
(315) 343–1342
rbhousemuseum.org

Seneca Park Zoo
2222 St. Paul St.
Rochester
(585) 336–7200
senecaparkzoo.org

Seward House Museum
33 South St.
Auburn
(315) 252–1283
sewardhouse.org

Watkins Glen International Raceway
Route 16
Watkins Glen
(607) 535–2481
theglen.com

Watkins Glen State Park
1009 N. Franklin St.
Watkins Glen
(607) 535–4511
parks.ny.gov/parks/142/

Women's Rights National Historical Park
136 Fall St.
Seneca Falls
(315) 568–0024
nps.gov/wori

REGIONAL TOURIST INFORMATION IN THE FINGER LAKES

Cayuga County Office of Tourism
25 South St.
Auburn
(800) 499–9615 or
(315) 255–1658
tourcayuga.com

Central Steuben County Chamber of Commerce
47 Liberty St.
Bath
(607) 776–7122
centralsteubenchamber.com

Chemung County Chamber of Commerce
400 East Church St.
Elmira
(607) 734–5137
chemungchamber.org

Corning Area Chamber of Commerce
1 West Market St.
Corning
(607) 936–4686
corningny.com

Finger Lakes Tourism Alliance
309 Lake St.
Penn Yan
(800) 530–7488 or
(315) 536–7488
fingerlakes.org

Finger Lakes Trail Conference
6111 Visitor Center Rd.
Mount Morris
(535) 658–9320
fingerlakestrail.org

Finger Lakes Visitors Connection
19 Susan B. Anthony Ln.
Canandaigua
(585) 394–3915
visitfingerlakes.com

Hammondsport Chamber of Commerce
47 Shethar St.
Hammondsport
(607) 569–2989
hammondsport.org

Ithaca/Tompkins County Convention and Visitors Bureau
904 East Shore Dr.
Ithaca
(800) 284–8422 or
(607) 272–1313
visitithaca.com

Seneca Falls Visitor Center
89 Fall St.
Seneca Falls
(315) 568–1510
senecafalls.com/visitor-center.php

Visit Rochester
45 East Ave. #400
Rochester
(585) 279–8300
visitrochester.com

The Niagara-Allegany Region

Ever since the Erie Canal opened in 1825, New York City and Buffalo have assumed a front door–back door status in New York State. New York City became the Empire State's gateway to the world, a capital of international shipping and finance. The docksides and rail yards of Buffalo, meanwhile, were the portals through which the industrial output and raw materials of the Midwest flowed into the state, and the lumber and coal of the northeast flowed out. Buffalo became an important border city between the East Coast and the new American territories, a center of manufacturing and flour milling whose fortunes have risen and fallen with the state of the nation's heavy industry.

But don't write Buffalo off as an old lunch-bucket town that gets too much snow in the winter. Buffalo has some impressive architecture, from Louis Sullivan's splendid Prudential Building and the art deco City Hall downtown to the Frank Lloyd Wright houses described later in this section. South Park, with its conservatory, and Riverside Park on the Niagara offer welcome open spaces, and culinary treasures like Buffalo chicken wings and beef on 'weck (hot sliced roast beef on a pretzel-salt-topped kimmelweck or kaiser roll) became significant Buffalo imports to the rest of America.

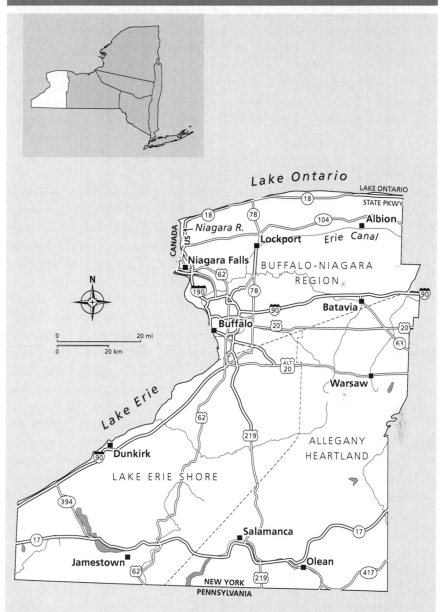

The countryside in the state's southwestern quadrant provides further evidence of why Niagara Falls isn't the only reason to drive to the end of the New York State Thruway. The Pennsylvania border country boasts giant Allegany State Park, a hiking and camping paradise; and the byways along the Lake Erie shore wander through a picture-pretty territory dotted with vineyards, cherry orchards, and roadside stands selling delicious goat's milk fudge. Yes, goat's milk fudge. It's the little serendipities that make traveling fun.

Buffalo-Niagara Region

Just to mix things up a bit, we'll venture into the rolling countryside to begin your tour of western New York. Only forty miles northeast of Buffalo is a pristine tract of some nineteen thousand acres, the core of which (eleven thousand acres) makes up the federal *Iroquois National Wildlife Refuge*, managed by the US Fish and Wildlife Service. On either side of the refuge are the *Oak Orchard* (east) and *Tonawanda* (west) *Wildlife Management Areas*, operated by the State of New York's Department of Environmental Conservation.

Roughly two-thirds of the Iroquois National Wildlife Refuge contains freshwater marshes and hardwood swamps fed by Oak Orchard Creek as it meanders east to west through the refuge. Forests, meadows, and fields slope up gently from the wetland's edge, attracting a wide variety of wildlife. The refuge's scenic overlooks and nature trails are open from sunrise to sunset year-round for self-guided visits and wildlife watching.

Both the Oak Orchard and the Tonawanda areas are primarily wetlands, with some grassland and forest habitat. The dikes surrounding the man-made impoundments, as well as several overlooks and parking areas, provide access that offers superb opportunities not only for hunters (during designated seasons) but for hikers and birders as well.

The best time for birders to visit the area is from early March to mid-May. That's when more than one hundred thousand Canada geese, along with smaller flocks of ducks—American black duck, northern pintail, American wigeon, gadwall, blue-winged and green-winged teal, northern shoveler, and ring-necked duck—pause on their northward migration, with some staying to nest. The transitional habitat along the borders of the marsh attracts shorebirds and wading birds, while the wooded areas fill with migrating spring warblers, vireos, thrushes, and sparrows.

Iroquois National Wildlife Refuge headquarters (1101 Casey Rd., Basom; 585–948–5445; fws.gov/refuge/iroquois/) is open year-round, Mon through Fri from 7:30 a.m. to 4 p.m., except holidays; mid-Mar through May, Sat and Sun, 9 a.m. to 5 p.m. Self-guided exhibits and an observation tower can be found

AUTHOR'S FAVORITES IN THE NIAGARA-ALLEGANY REGION

Anchor Bar and Restaurant

Iroquois National Wildlife Refuge

Jell-O Gallery Museum

National Comedy Center

Old Fort Niagara

Roger Tory Peterson Institute of Natural History

Roycroft Campus and Inn

Theodore Roosevelt Inaugural National Historic Site

Tifft Nature Preserve

at the Oak Orchard Education Center on Knowlesville Road, just north of the town of Oakfield. The center is open daily from sunrise to sunset and is the starting point for four nature trails. For information about Oak Orchard and Tonawanda Wildlife Management Areas, visit dec.ny.gov/outdoor/24442.html, or call (585) 226–2466.

The **Asa Ransom House** is an 1853 farmhouse on the site of one of the country's early gristmills. All but one of the ten guest rooms have fireplaces, and several have private front porches and balconies. The bed-and-breakfast is at 10529 Main St., Clarence (716–759–2315 or 800–841–2340; asaransom.com). A double room, including full breakfast, ranges from $149 to $169 Sun through Fri night and $190 to $225 Sat night.

Thirty Mile Point Lighthouse, more than sixty feet high and constructed in 1875 of hand-carved stone, stands near the mouth of Golden Hill Creek to warn vessels of the sandbar and shoals jutting out into Lake Ontario. Visitors

Stage One

The handsome French Renaissance home at 484 Delaware Avenue in Buffalo was built in 1894 for S. Douglas Cornell, the successful owner of a lead foundry. Cornell, an avid amateur actor, had architect Edward A. Kent install a theater in the attic story of his new mansion. Here he and his prominent Buffalo friends staged frequent performances. Among the amateur players' most enraptured fans was Cornell's little granddaughter, Katherine. Years later, when she became one of the great ladies of the American stage, Katherine Cornell credited those Delaware Avenue theatricals with kindling her ambition to become an actor. Today a theater on the University at Buffalo campus is named in her honor.

can climb the circular steel staircase to the top of the tower for magnificent views of the lake all the way to Canada. The lighthouse, part of **Golden Hill State Park** (Lower Lake Rd., Barker; 716–795–3885; parks.ny.gov/parks/goldenhill/), is free to those who pay a park entrance fee. It's open Fri through Sun and holidays, 2 to 4 p.m.

You won't tick off too many miles in this state without encountering one of the string of forts that once defended the Thirteen Colonies' northwestern frontier, playing a prominent role not only in the struggles between the British and the French for North American supremacy, but in our own Revolutionary War as well. **Old Fort Niagara**, located in Fort Niagara State Park where the Niagara River flows into Lake Ontario, remains the longest continuously occupied military site in the United States and the oldest building in the Great Lakes. Here, the French, who built the fort in 1726, attempted to disguise it as a trading post to convince the Iroquois to allow its construction—but one of the five tribes of the confederacy, the Seneca, were not at the table when the others crafted the agreement. When soldiers arrived as construction drew to a close, the Seneca and the British both took umbrage, and numerous skirmishes resulted in the British taking the fort in 1759. They held it until they lost the Revolutionary War, but in 1813 British troops staged a surprise attack and took it back. Their effort was for naught, however, as the Treaty of Ghent that ended the War of 1812 stated that the fort belonged to the United States.

As recently as World War I, the fort continued to serve as military housing, but after that it fell into disrepair; it underwent a major renovation between 1927 and 1934. Today the private, nonprofit Old Fort Niagara Association maintains the fort's older buildings in cooperation with the State of New York. Beyond the silent military structures, visitors can enjoy broad vistas of Lake Ontario and, in clear weather, the rising mists of Niagara Falls fourteen miles to the south.

Old Fort Niagara, Fort Niagara State Park, Youngstown (716–745–7611; oldfortniagara.org), is open year-round, Wed through Sun, 9 a.m. to 4 p.m. Closed Thanksgiving, Christmas, and New Year's Day. During the summer there are frequent costumed reenactments of military drills, with musket and cannon firings. Admission is $15 for adults, and $10 for children ages 6 to 12; free to children 5 and under.

Scottish émigré Allan Herschell literally carved a place for himself in America's history when, in 1883, he produced the first steam-driven "riding gallery"—known today as a merry-go-round. By 1891, the Herschell-Spillman Company shipped one machine a day to parks and communities around the world and soon became the world's largest producer of carousels and amusement park devices.

The ***Herschell Carrousel Factory Museum***, housed in a historic factory building, traces the history of Herschell, his hand-carved wooden animals, and the finished carousels. Volunteer wood carvers may be at work on the factory's carving floor, and best of all, two antique, hand-carved wooden carousels are there to ride—one for adults and kids, and one just for children. (There are other rides as well.)

Merry-go-rounds need music, so the Wurlitzer Music Roll Department manufactured the paper rolls that produced every carousel's familiar music—and you can see and hear the band organs in the only public display of this kind in the United States.

The Herschell Carrousel Factory Museum (180 Thompson St., North Tonawanda; 716–693–1885; carrouselmuseum.org) is open Wed through Sat, 10 a.m. to 3 p.m.; closed major holidays. Admission is $10 for adults, and $5 for children ages 2 to 16 and seniors 65+; it includes two carousel ride tokens. Extra tokens are $1 each.

Heading upriver (or more likely, down I-190) we come to Buffalo, the Erie Canal's terminus city and gateway to the Midwest. For a quick introduction to this sprawling inland port, head downtown to reconnoiter the city and Lake Erie from the twenty-eighth-floor observatory of City Hall (open weekdays from 9 a.m. to 3 p.m.) and then visit the nearby historic neighborhood of ***Allentown***.

The works of a number of important architects and the homes of several famous people are tucked into the compact Allentown neighborhood. Drive through the neighborhood for a tour of the district's myriad building styles: ***Kleinhans Music Hall*** on Symphony Circle, designed in 1938 by Eliel and Eero Saarinen; the 1869 ***Dorsheimer Mansion*** (434 Delaware Ave.), an early work of the peerless Henry Hobson Richardson; Stanford White's 1899 ***Butler Mansion*** (672 Delaware Ave.) and 1895 ***Pratt Mansion*** (690 Delaware Ave.); and a lovely example of the Flemish Renaissance style at 267 North Street. As for the haunts of the famous, don't miss the childhood home of F. Scott Fitzgerald at 29 Irving Street; the home of artist Charles Burchfield (once a designer for a Buffalo wallpaper company) at 459 Franklin Street; and, at 472 Delaware

The Goats Were Got

According to legend, ***Goat Island*** is named for Old Billy Goat, the only survivor of a herd of livestock left to winter there by settler John Stedman in 1778. Stedman meant to protect his goats from wolves in the area, but the animals could not tolerate the harsh Niagara winter, and they perished in the cold.

Avenue, the carriage house formerly attached to the home of Samuel Langhorne Clemens, who served for eighteen months as the editor and part-owner of the *Buffalo Express*. For information, contact the Allentown Association at (716) 881–1024, or visit allentown.org.

The Greek Revival house at 641 Delaware Avenue presents a fascinating turning point in history: On September 14, 1901, the home of prominent Buffalo lawyer Ansley Wilcox hosted a vigorous forty-two-year-old man who had just rushed in by train from the Adirondacks to take the oath of office as president of the United States. President **William McKinley** had languished in the house for eight days, the victim of an assassin's bullet with the bad luck to be shot before the discovery of antibiotics; he died of infection caused by his wound. The era of Theodore Roosevelt began in this parlor, a presidency that became the catalyst for sweeping changes in the nation's domestic and foreign policy.

Theodore Roosevelt Inaugural National Historic Site tells the story of that fateful day and the tragic event that preceded it. Perhaps the most interesting aspect of the tale concerns the mad dash Vice President Roosevelt made from the Adirondacks to Buffalo. He had gone to the city and stayed for a few days at the Wilcox House after McKinley was shot by an anarchist at the Pan-American Exposition, but after being assured by the president's doctors that his condition had stabilized, he left to join his family at a hunting club in Tahawus, high in a remote mountain area. Notified several days later of McKinley's worsening state, the vice president made an overnight journey by horse and wagon to the nearest train station, where he learned that the president was dead. Roosevelt and his party then raced to Buffalo in a special train. Within two hours of his arrival, he stood in Wilcox's library wearing borrowed formal clothes as he took the oath of office and became the nation's twenty-sixth president.

The Theodore Roosevelt Inaugural National Historic Site (641 Delaware Ave., Buffalo; 716–884–0095; nps.gov/thri) is open Wed through Fri for tours with advance reservation at 10:30 and 11:30 a.m. and 12:30, 1:30, 2:30, and 3:30 p.m.; Sat and Sun at 11:30 a.m. and 12:30, 1:30, 2:30, and 3:30 p.m. Closed New Year's Eve, New Year's Day, Easter, Memorial Day, Independence Day, Labor Day, Thanksgiving, Christmas Eve, and Christmas Day. Admission is $12 for adults; $9 for seniors 62+, college students with ID, and veterans; and $7 for children 6 to 18.

While you're in the Delaware Avenue area, head for the **Buffalo & Erie County Naval & Military Park** (1 Naval Park Cove, Buffalo; 716–847–1773; buffalonavalpark.org), where entirely different kinds of adventures await. Here you can tour the USS *Little Rock*, a Galveston-class guided-missile cruiser used in peacekeeping missions in southern Europe, the Middle East, and Santo Domingo in the 1950s and 1960s. As you approach, you'll see the USS *Croaker*,

Buffalo's Grassy Knoll

On September 6, 1901, President McKinley was in Buffalo attending the Pan-American Exposition. While he shook hands with a long line of waiting admirers, Leon F. Czolgosz waited his turn, walked up to the president, and shot him with a revolver he had hidden under a handkerchief. Today a bronze plaque marks the site where McKinley took the bullet that killed him with gangrene eight days later. It's on the traffic island on Fordham Drive between Elmwood Avenue and Lincoln Parkway. (Czolgosz was put to death the following October.)

a Gato-class submarine that saw action in the Pacific theater during World War II. The USS *The Sullivans*, a Fletcher-class Destroyer DD-537, shot down eight Japanese planes in World War II and bombarded Iwo Jima and Okinawa, playing an important role in the war and, later, in the Korean War as well. Check the website at buffalonavalpark.org/visit/ for this season's tour schedule and pricing.

The waterfront tells another story about Buffalo's history: *Silo City*, the campus of grain silos on the river, represents the last of the city's legacy as a milling and grain storage and shipping port. Some three hundred million bushels of grain passed through here, making the massive grain elevator—which still works—a critically important piece of technology for the pivotal storage operation. Today Silo City has found new life as an arts and cultural district, with gardens, theater, restaurants, and the Buffalo RiverWorks Beer Garden. Learn more about it at Silo City's website, silo.city.

The residential neighborhoods north of downtown Buffalo boast five examples of the work of one of America's greatest architects, *Frank Lloyd Wright*. Most of Wright's residential architecture can be found within the central and upper Midwest, where he brought his "prairie style" to maturity. The fact that a pocket of the master's work exists in Buffalo came about when he designed a house in Oak Park, Illinois, for the brother of John D. Larkin, founder of the Larkin Soap Company of Buffalo. Larkin liked his brother's house enough to bring Wright to Buffalo to design his company's headquarters. The Larkin Building, a light, airy masterpiece of commercial architecture, stood on Seneca Street from 1905 until it was unconscionably demolished in 1950. But five Buffalo houses built for Larkin Soap Company executives remain to this day:

- *William Heath House* (76 Soldiers Pl.), corner of Bird Avenue, completed in 1906 and landscaped by Frederick Law Olmsted. (Private; not open to visitors.)

- **Darwin D. Martin House** (125 Jewett Pkwy.; 716–856–3858; martinhouse.org), corner of Summit Avenue. Also completed in 1906, this expansive home stood vacant for seventeen years prior to the mid-1950s, during which time half of the original Wright windows were lost. The State University of New York at Buffalo restored the home in 1970 and now uses it for offices. Visitors can take a self-guided tour Thurs through Mon; visit martinhouse.org to purchase timed tickets. Self-guided tours are $10 for adults.

- **George Barton House** (118 Summit Ave.) is a smaller brick structure with distinctive top-story casement windows and a broad roof overhang built in 1903–4. The house has been made available as a rental space for small business meetings and gatherings; visit martinhouse.org for information.

- **Gardener's Cottage, Martin Estate** (285 Woodward Ave.): Constructed in 1906, the cottage is one of the few surviving service buildings of the Martin Estate. (Private; not open to visitors.)

- **Walter Davidson House** (57 Tillinghast Pl.): With the exception of Darwin Martin's 1926 summer house, built south of the city on a

ANNUAL EVENTS IN THE NIAGARA-ALLEGANY REGION

MAY

Dyngus Day
Buffalo
(716) 833–5211
dyngusday.com

Falls Fireworks and Concert Series
through mid-Sept
Niagara Falls, Ontario
(877) 642–7275
niagaraparks.com

JUNE

Shakespeare in Delaware Park
through mid-Aug
Buffalo
(716) 856–4533
shakespeareindelawarepark.org

JULY

Fredonia History Days
Fredonia
tourchautauqua.com/events/
fredonia-history-days

AUGUST

Greater Niagara Fish Odyssey
Lake Ontario
fishodyssey.net

bluff above Lake Erie, the 1909 Davidson House is the last of Wright's Buffalo residences. (Private; not open to visitors.)

Just minutes from downtown, the ***Buffalo Museum of Science*** houses an extensive collection of natural science exhibits, anthropology collections, a planetarium, and interactive activities. The museum's main exhibit hall is filled with exciting temporary exhibitions. A visit to the permanent dinosaur exhibit, featuring the skeletons of Seymour the mastodon and Stanley the albertosaurus, provides a fascinating look at some of the favorite prehistoric giants. "Insect World" features insects six times life-size in two vastly different ecosystems—the cloud forest in the coastal Andean highlands of north central Venezuela and the Niagara frontier region of New York State. Two halls of space offer detailed information about our world and the worlds around us, and observatories open the skies to views of stars, planets, and our sun. The museum also features exhibits on endangered species, zoology, flora and fauna, gems and minerals, and technology.

Buffalo Museum of Science (1020 Humboldt Pkwy., Buffalo; 716–896–5200; sciencebuff.org) is open Fri through Sun, 10 a.m. to 4 p.m. Closed Easter, Memorial Day, July 4, Thanksgiving, Christmas Eve, and Christmas Day. Admission is $19 for adults; $16 for seniors 62+, students, and children 2 to 17.

SEPTEMBER

National Buffalo Wing Festival
Buffalo
(716) 565–4141
buffalowing.com

Taste of East Aurora
East Aurora
(716) 652–8444
eanycc.com/
event/8th-annual-taste-of-east-aurora/

NOVEMBER

Winter Festival of Lights
through early Jan
Niagara Falls, Ontario
(905) 356–6061
wfol.com

DECEMBER

Fairgrounds Festival of Lights
Hamburg
(716) 649–3900 ext. 6404
the-fairgrounds.com/festival-lights/

First Night Buffalo
Buffalo
(716) 635–4959
firstnightbuffalo.org

The Buffalo Museum of Science also operates *Tifft Nature Preserve* just three miles from downtown on the Outer Harbor. This 264-acre urban nature sanctuary offers five miles of hiking trails, boardwalks, and a self-guided nature trail, and it's the premier birding spot every spring and fall when warblers, vireos, thrushes, flycatchers, blackbirds, and many other migrating birds crowd the wooded areas. A seventy-five-acre freshwater cattail marsh with blinds provides wonderful viewing of waterfowl, long-legged wading birds, and even bitterns and rails. In winter, owls often roost in the trees by day, and the preserve's flat trails become favorites with cross-country skiers. The Herb and Jane Darling Education Center has some wonderful exhibits on ecology, animals, and plant life.

Tifft Nature Preserve (1200 Fuhrmann Blvd., Buffalo; 716–825–6397; tifft .org) is open daily from dawn to dusk; the Education Center is open Wed through Sat from 10 a.m. to 4 p.m., and Sun from noon to 4 p.m. There is no admission charge, but donations are appreciated.

The *Burchfield Penney Art Center* exhibits the largest and most comprehensive collection of the works of Charles E. Burchfield, one of the country's foremost watercolorists, as well as the works of other western New York artists. The center, which serves the community as a multifaceted cultural and educational institution, also hosts numerous special exhibitions throughout the year.

The Burchfield Penney Art Center, Rockwell Hall, Buffalo State College (1300 Elmwood Ave., Buffalo; 716–878–6011; burchfieldpenney.org) is open Fri through Sun from 11 a.m. to 4 p.m.; closed major holidays. Admission is $10 for adults, $8 for seniors 62+, and $5 for students and children over age 10; free for children under 10 when accompanied by an adult.

You may not think of a cemetery as a place to go for fun, but *Forest Lawn* is more of a city park than a typical cemetery. Forest Lawn became the final resting place of prominent Buffalonians such as Red Jacket, the Seneca orator; Shirley Chisholm, the first Black woman to be elected to the US Congress, and a presidential candidate in 1972; Millard Fillmore, the country's thirteenth president, along with several members of his family; railroad tycoon Charles Goodyear; music legend Rick James; Dr. Roswell Park, a medical pioneer who established the world's first cancer research center, which now bears his name; and famous marine biologist Mary Jane Rathbun, among many others. It also serves as a popular nature sanctuary, with upwards of six thousand trees and sightings of more than two hundred species of birds.

At this cemetery, you'll know for whom the bell tolls: Upon request, attendants will ring the six-foot, three-thousand-pound solid bronze Oishei bell cast in France. Other highlights include the Blocher monument, with life-size figures carved in Italian marble, and numerous unique monuments and mausoleums.

The "Real Thing"?

The Buffalo chicken wings recipe below is reputed to be the genuine Anchor Bar version—but only they know for sure, and they're not talking. In any event, it sure is good:

- 6 tablespoons Durkee's Hot Sauce

- ½ stick margarine

- 1 tablespoon white vinegar

- ⅛ teaspoon celery seed

- ⅛ to ¾ teaspoon cayenne pepper

- ¼ teaspoon Worcestershire sauce

- 1 to 2 teaspoons Tabasco sauce

- dash of black pepper

Mix ingredients in a small saucepan over low heat until margarine melts, stirring occasionally.

Fry wings at 375°F for 12–15 minutes in vegetable oil. Drain for a few minutes on a brown paper bag or paper towels, then put them in a bowl. Pour the sauce over them, cover the bowl, and shake it to coat the wings. (An option here is to put the wings on a baking sheet and bake a few minutes for an extra-crispy coating.) Serve with carrot and celery sticks and blue cheese dressing.

Of course, if you prefer, you can always buy a bottle of the Anchor Bar's authentic wing sauce—bottled at "the source"—to be sure you're getting the genuine article.

Forest Lawn Cemetery (1411 Delaware Ave., Buffalo; 716–288–5999; forest-lawn.com) is open daily, 8 a.m. to 7 p.m., in spring and summer; until 5 p.m. in fall and winter.

Mark Twain aficionados will want to visit the **Buffalo & Erie County Public Library's Grosvenor Rare Book Room**. Among the thousands of manuscripts and first editions dating back to the fifteenth century is the original manuscript of *The Adventures of Huckleberry Finn*. The room also contains other mementos of Twain, who lived in Buffalo from 1869 to 1871. Contact the Buffalo & Erie County Public Library, Lafayette Square, Buffalo, at (716) 858–8900, or visit buffalolib.org; call for hours.

Yes, chicken wings got the name "Buffalo" because they were invented here—at the **Anchor Bar and Restaurant** (1047 Main St., Buffalo; 716–886–8920; anchorbar.com), which has been serving them up with celery and blue cheese dip since 1964. You may wait in line for a table here on weekends, especially during football season, but you'll be glad you did: The Anchor Bar earns its reputation for good food, moderate prices, large portions, and friendly service.

Chicken wings are just one of the culinary specialties associated with Buffalo—don't leave the city without trying "beef on 'weck," a sandwich of thinly sliced roast beef on a kimmelweck roll (that's a hard roll topped with caraway seeds and kosher salt), finished with a dollop of horseradish. Some call the experience life-changing, ruining bland roast beef on white forever. No one knows exactly where the beef on 'weck got its start, but *Schwabl's*, in business since 1837, can produce menus dating back more than one hundred years with the sandwich prominently listed. Try it there at 789 Center Rd., Buffalo (716–675–2333; schwabls.com), or pay a visit to *Charlie the Butcher* (1065 Wehrle Dr., Williamsville; 716–633–8330; charliethebutcher.com), where the sandwich achieves true perfection.

Lake Erie Shore

The southwestern tip of New York State is packed with as eclectic a mix of off-the-beaten-path sights as can be found anywhere. Remember kazoos—those funny little musical instruments you could play just by humming into them? They're still being made in Eden, at *The Original American Kazoo Company Factory, Museum, & Gift Shop*. Established in 1916, it's now the only metal kazoo factory in the world—and it's still making them the same way they were made in 1916. The company used to produce everything from toy flutes and fishing tackle boxes to metal dog beds and peanut vending machines, but in 1965 the demand for kazoos became so great that the firm stopped manufacturing everything else.

The "working museum" at Kazoo Company shows how "America's only original musical instrument" is made, chronicles kazoo history, and even provides the opportunity to make your own kazoo.

The Original American Kazoo Company, Factory, Museum, & Gift Shop (8703 South Main St., Eden; 716–992–3960; edenkazoo.com) is open Mon through Sat, 10 a.m. to 5 p.m. Closed Thanksgiving, Christmas, New Year's, Memorial Day, Easter, Fourth of July, and Labor Day. Admission is free.

Although it's now just a short hop off I-90, it's easy to imagine how isolated the *Dunkirk Historical Lighthouse* must have been when the lantern in the square, sixty-one-foot tower first began guiding ships into Dunkirk Harbor in 1876. Today an automated light in the tower does the job, and the two-story Stick-style keeper's dwelling has been converted into *Veterans' Park Museum*. Displays on the grounds include a forty-five-foot lighthouse buoy tender, a twenty-one-foot rescue boat, and Civil War cannons. Visitors can take a tour of the lighthouse tower. An admission fee is charged for grounds tours and tours of the museum.

Dunkirk Historical Lighthouse and Veterans' Park Museum (1 Lighthouse Point Dr., Dunkirk; 716–366–5050; dunkirklighthouse.com) are open daily, May through June and Sept through Oct, 10 a.m. to 2 p.m., with the last tour at 1 p.m. In July and Aug, the complex is open from 10 a.m. to 4 p.m., with the last tour at 3 p.m. Admission is $10 for adults; $8 for seniors, students, and veterans; and $3 for children ages 4 to 10.

Locals dubbed the sixteen-room mansion completed by James McClurg in 1820 "McClurg's Folly." He designed it, made and baked his own bricks, prepared local timber for the interior woodwork, and landscaped the spacious grounds with ornamental trees and shrubs and a water fountain stocked with goldfish. Today the Chautauqua County Historical Society operates the restored frontier mansion as a museum and library filled with furnishings, fine art, and local artifacts from its collection.

McClurg Museum (20 E. Main St., Westfield; 716–326–2977; mcclurg museum.org) is open Tues through Sat from 10 a.m. to 4 p.m.; winter hours are variable, so call before visiting. Admission is $5 for adults; free for children.

At the northern tip of Chautauqua Lake in Mayville, *Webb's Candies* still makes the same creamy goat's milk fudge it originated in 1942. The staff no longer keep their own goats, but you'll find the confection just as rich and tasty as ever—be sure to ask for a sample of the chocolate fudge with pecans. Webb's makes all its candies by hand, using the old-fashioned copper-kettle method, and has added a host of other treats to its repertoire, including "frogs," hard suckers, chocolate bars, divinity, chocolate clusters, cordial cherries, and all kinds of bark.

Webb's Candies (115 W. Lake Rd., Mayville; 716–753–2161; webbscandies .com) is open daily year-round. In summer the hours are 10 a.m. to 9 p.m.; in winter, noon to 5 p.m. Call for holiday hours.

Chautauqua Lake is also the home of a 133-year-old enterprise that exemplifies the American penchant for self-improvement. The *Chautauqua Institution* gave its name to an endless array of itinerant tent-show lyceums around the turn of the century, but the original institution continues right where it was founded in 1874. Bishop John Heyl Vincent and industrialist (and father-in-law of Thomas Edison) Lewis Miller originally founded Chautauqua with the modest goal of establishing a school for Sunday-school teachers. Chautauqua grew to become a village unto itself, offering not only religious instruction but a program of lectures and adult-education courses as well.

The Chautauqua of today bears little resemblance to the Methodist camp meeting of more than a hundred years ago, although services in the major faiths are held daily. The Chautauqua emphasis on culture and mental and spiritual improvement has led to an extensive annual summer calendar of lectures, classical and popular concerts, dramatic performances, and long- and short-term courses in subjects ranging from foreign languages to tap dancing to creative writing. It even has its own thirty-thousand-volume library.

To put it simply, Chautauqua is a vast summer camp of self-improvement, a place where more than one hundred thousand people every summer can rock (in chairs) on broad verandas, walk tree-lined streets that have no cars, and listen in on a chamber music rehearsal on the way to lunch.

The season at Chautauqua lasts for nine weeks each summer, but admission is available on a daily, weekend, or weekly basis. You will find extensive information on facilities and programs at chq.org; or contact Chautauqua Institution, 1 Ames St., Chautauqua (716–357–6200 or 800–836–ARTS).

One of only six authentic stern-wheel steamboats operating east of the Mississippi, the **Chautauqua Belle** cruises Chautauqua Lake daily from Memorial Day through Labor Day, with departures at 11 a.m., 1:15 p.m., and 3 p.m. and a more limited schedule in May, June, and Sept. The trips last one-and-a-half hours. Fares are $25 for adults, $10 for ages 3 to 12, and free for children under 3. For information, email thechautauquabelle@gmail.com (the staff get ten thousand calls during the season, so you're much more likely to get a response by email) or visit 269belle.com. The boat leaves from the Mayville Dock at 78 Water Street.

Geologists believe that more than three hundred million years ago, *Panama Rocks*—reputed to be the world's most extensive outcropping of glacier-cut, ocean-quartz conglomerate rock—were islands of gravel and sand amid a vast inland sea that extended west toward what is now Utah. As forces deposited layer after layer of these materials, the weight forced the water out, creating a natural form of concrete called quartz conglomerate, or pudding stone.

About 165 million years ago, earthquakes and other geological upheavals raised what became Panama Rocks to its present altitude of 1,650 feet. The layers fractured, and water, carrying minerals such as iron and lead, seeped into the openings. A scant ten thousand years ago, during the last ice age, a passing glacier widened these fractures, creating thousands of crevices and alley passageways.

Today visitors can thread through these passages along a mile-long trail that winds through a world of towering rocks, past cavernous dens and small caves. Most hikers take about an hour and a half to follow the route, although the more adventurous can leave the trail and explore at their own pace.

Because there are no railings, adults must sign a waiver of liability (which you can do online before you visit); the upper part of the trail can be dangerous for children, but the lower trail, which has the most dramatic scenery, is safer. Persons under the age of eighteen must be with an adult to enter the rock area. No pets are allowed.

Panama Rocks Scenic Park (11 Rock Hill Rd., Panama; 716–782–2845; panamarocks.com) is open early May through late Oct, 10 a.m. to 5 p.m. (last admission at 4 p.m.). Admission is $15.50 per person for a season pass; children 5 and under are free, but you can purchase a printed pass for them for 50 cents.

Jamestown, birthplace of one of the country's leading naturalists, celebrates his contribution to the world of nature identification at the **Roger Tory Peterson Institute of Natural History**, housed in a handsome wood and stone building designed by architect Robert A. M. Stern on twenty-seven acres of woods and meadows. The man who introduced the concept of field marks—the distinguishing characteristics of every creature, plant, flower, rock, and shell on the planet—through the Peterson's Field Guides series created a phenomenon of nature exploration he could never have foreseen. This institute stands as a fitting tribute to the world of discovery he opened for millions.

The institute trains educators to help children discover the natural world around them. Part of this program involves changing exhibitions of wildlife art and nature photography at the institute, and the public is invited to visit, hike the surrounding trails, and stop in the Butterfly Garden and gift shop.

The Roger Tory Peterson Institute of Natural History (311 Curtis St., Jamestown; 716–665–2473; rtpi.org) is open Wed through Sat from 10 a.m. to 4 p.m., and Sun from 1 to 5 p.m.; closed all major holidays. Admission is $12 for adults, $10 for seniors and military, $8 for students and children, and $30 for families. The grounds are open daily dawn to dusk.

Lucille Ball made jokes throughout her career about Jamestown, New York, her true-to-life birthplace—but now there's no place funnier than Jamestown, as the **National Comedy Center** opened there in 2018. The 37,000-square-foot facility uses interactive activities, the latest technologies, and more than fifty world-class exhibits to celebrate the work of the true geniuses of comedy. Hailed by *Conde Nast Traveler* as one of the best museums in the country, and by *Time* magazine as one of the top nine things to visit in the United States, and ranked 5/5 on TripAdvisor, this innovative and very, very funny place features exclusive collections of scripts and other memorabilia from comedic giants like Carl Reiner, the Smothers Brothers, and George Carlin, and an inside look at the creative processes that have inspired comedians for generations—as the center's own website says, "from Charlie Chaplin to Dave

Chappelle." And if you've come here expecting to visit the Lucille Ball–Desi Arnaz Museum, you'll find it just down the street at 2 West 3rd Street.

National Comedy Center (203 W. 2nd St., Jamestown; 716–484–2222; comedy center.org) is open Thurs through Mon, 10 a.m. to 5 p.m. Admission $25.50 for adults; $23.50 for seniors 60+; and $18.50 for children ages 6 to 12, active military, and veterans.

Just down the road from Jamestown, Ellington serves as the gateway to New York's **Amish Trail**, a collection of more than two hundred businesses, farms, and other points of interest in Cattaraugus County. The Amish first came here from Ohio in 1949 and formed a community of like-minded families who share a Christian belief system that values unity, faith, and hard work. You will see them traveling in horse-drawn buggies throughout the area (please slow down as you pass them, and respect their desire not to be photographed). Visit amishtrail.com to view an interactive map and choose places you would like to stop during your visit; the Amish make many goods, including quilts, rugs, furniture, baskets, baked goods, candy, fruits and vegetables, and more, and they sell them from their homes. Watch for signs in front yards that let you know they are open. All Amish home businesses are closed on Sundays.

Allegany Heartland

The **Seneca-Iroquois National Museum**, in Salamanca on the Allegany Indian Reservation, traces the cultural and historical heritage of the Seneca, known as "Keepers of the Western Door" of the Iroquois Confederacy. The museum's new home, the Onöhsagwë:de' Cultural Center, presents the continuum of Iroquois history from prehistoric times to the present, with exhibits of archaeological artifacts, decorative and everyday use items, and information about pivotal events in the Iroquois story.

The Seneca-Iroquois National Museum (82 W. Hetzel St., Salamanca; 716–945–1760; senecamuseum.org) is open Nov through Apr, Mon through Sat from 9 a.m. to 5 p.m., and Sun from noon to 5 p.m.; call for hours between Apr and Nov. Admission is $9.50 for adults; $6 for seniors, veterans, and college students; and $5.25 for children 7 and up. Children 6 and under are free.

With 65,000 acres, two 100-acre lakes, and 80 miles of hiking trails, **Allegany State Park**, "the wilderness playground of western New York," is the largest of the state parks. This mecca for both summer and winter outdoor enthusiasts provides lakes for boating and swimming, ballfields, tennis courts, picnic areas, playgrounds, bike paths, and miles of cross-country and snowmobile trails. Hunting is permitted in season for small game, turkey, and deer (archery only); get the permit application on the website. An extensive campground as well as more than 370 cabins—many of them winterized—allow visitors to extend their wilderness experience.

Allegany State Park (2373 ASP, Rte. 1, Salamanca; 716–354–2182; parks .ny.gov/parks/1/) is open daily year-round. From Memorial Day weekend to Columbus Day weekend, an entrance fee may be collected between 9 a.m. and 4:30 p.m.: $7 per car when the lake is open for swimming, and $6 per car when the lake is closed.

Before you leave Salamanca, stop at the **Salamanca Rail Museum**, a fully restored passenger depot constructed in 1912 by the Buffalo, Rochester, and Pittsburgh Railroad. The museum uses exhibits, artifacts, and video presentations to re-create an era when rail was the primary means of transportation from city to city.

Salamanca Rail Museum (170 Main St., Salamanca; 716–945–3133) is open Tues, Thurs, and Sat from 10 a.m. to 4 p.m., Apr through Dec. Admission is free, but donations are welcomed.

It's the pleasant surprises that make traveling off the beaten path rewarding—like discovering that in addition to more than 260 species of rare and unusual trees and herbs and perennial gardens, **Nannen Arboretum** is home to a Japanese stone garden (an abstract garden of stone and sand) and Amano Hashidate Bridge (a Japanese "bridge to heaven"). Find the arboretum (716–699–5046) at 28 Parkside Drive in Ellicottville. Admission is free, and it is open daily from dawn to dusk. Donations are welcomed.

Head north on Route 219 a short distance to Ashford Hollow to see one of the most unconventional sculpture "gardens" ever. Local sculptor Larry Griffis integrated his art with nature, placing his monumental abstract and representational creations throughout a four-hundred-acre woodland setting/nature preserve. **Griffis Sculpture Park** exhibits more than two hundred of his pieces and an additional fifty or so by other international artists, most made of steel and between twenty and thirty feet high. Ten nudes ring a pond, sharing the banks with live swans and ducks. A towering mosquito awaits unwary hikers along one of the ten miles of hiking trails. Giant toadstools grow in a field, waiting for climbers.

Griffis Sculpture Park (6902 Rohr Rd., East Otto; 716–667–2808; griffispark .org) is open daily, May through Oct, from sunup to sundown; closed Nov through Apr. Admission is $5 for adults and $3 for seniors and students.

About 320 million years ago, receding glaciers deposited river and delta sediments on the eroded surface of Devonian shoals in western New York. This erosion exposed crystalline igneous and metamorphic rocks with milky quartz veins, and long transportation of the sediments selectively weathered and eroded the non-quartz minerals throughout the area. This geologic activity

created **Rock City Park**, one of the world's largest exposures of quartz conglomerate (pudding stone), a place where you can wander through crevices
and past towering, colorfully named formations like Fat Man's Squeeze, Tepee
Rock, and Signal Rock, with its one-thousand-square-mile view.

Rock City Park (505A Rocky City Rd., Rte. 16 South, Olean; 716–372–7790;
rockcitypark.com) is open daily, May through Oct, from 9 a.m. to 5 p.m. Admission is $5 for adults, $3 for ages 6 to 12.

Three generations ago, a summer at Chautauqua required visitors to travel
there by rail—specifically by a steam-hauled train of the Erie, Pennsylvania,
or New York Central Railroad. Today the **Arcade and Attica Railroad,**
headquartered just southeast of Buffalo in Arcade, is a real working railroad
with a healthy freight clientele. But the company's passenger operation is an
unabashed throwback, relying for power on a pair of circa-1920 coal burners
pulling old, open-window steel coaches that once belonged to the Delaware,
Lackawanna, and Western. Arcade and Attica passengers enjoy a ride through
some of Upstate's loveliest farm country, or out into wilderness to enjoy New
York's stunning fall foliage display.

The Arcade and Attica Railroad (278 Main St., Arcade; 585–492–3100; aarail
road.com) operates Wed, Sat, and Sun from Memorial Day through the end of
Oct. Special excursions using a diesel engine, including an Easter Bunny run,
a Santa Claus Express, and nature ride/hikes are scheduled off-season. Call for
information. Tickets cost $19; check the website for special prices for holiday
events.

One of the most interesting personalities of turn-of-the-century America
was a self-made philosopher named Elbert Hubbard. In addition to writing a
little "preachment" (as he called it) titled "A Message to Garcia" that dealt with
the themes of loyalty and hard work, and publishing his views in a periodical
called the *Philistine*, Hubbard was famous for importing the design aesthetic
and celebration of handcrafts fostered in England by artist William Morris.
Elbert Hubbard became the chief American proponent of the Arts and Crafts
movement, which touted the virtues of honest craftsmanship in the face of an
increasing tendency in the late nineteenth century toward machine production
of furniture, printed matter, and decorative and utilitarian household objects.

Visually, the style absorbed influences as diverse as art nouveau and Native
American crafts; many homes in the region (including my own) still embrace
the familiar solid, oaken, slat-sided Morris chairs and the mission furniture of
Gustav Stickley. Elbert Hubbard founded a community of craftspeople to build
this furniture, as well as copper and leather items and even printed books.
He called his operation the Roycrofters, headquartered on a "campus" in East
Aurora.

Modern travelers can savor the spirit of Elbert Hubbard today in East Aurora, where the **Roycroft Campus** continues. The campus grounds, now a National Historic Site, feature the **Roycroft Inn**, designed and completely furnished in the Arts and Crafts style, a gift shop filled with handcrafted items, a working pottery studio, an art gallery, and several antiques dealers, all housed in Hubbard-era buildings. The site also includes the **East Aurora Town Museum**, housed in the Town Hall Building—the former Roycroft Campus chapel (31 South Grove St., East Aurora; 716–655–0261; roycroftcampus corporation.com). The campus is open Tues through Sat, 11 a.m. to 5 p.m. Admission is free.

Another window on the Roycroft era is the **Elbert Hubbard–Roycroft Museum**, located in a 1910 bungalow built by Roycroft craftsmen and now on the National Register of Historic Places. Part of the furnishings, including the superb Arts and Crafts dining room, are original and were the property of centenarian Grace ScheideMantel when she turned the house over to the museum in 1985. (ScheideMantel's husband, George, once headed the Roycroft leather department.) Other Roycroft products on display at the house include a magnificent stained-glass lamp by Roycroft designer Dard Hunter and a saddle custom-made for Hubbard just prior to his death on the torpedoed *Lusitania* in 1915.

There is also a wonderful period garden, complete with a sundial and a "gazing ball," maintained by "The Master Gardeners" of the Erie County Cooperative Extension Service.

The Elbert Hubbard–Roycroft Museum (ScheideMantel House, 363 Oakwood Ave., East Aurora; 716–652–4735; roycrofter.com/museum), is open Tues through Sat, 11 a.m. to 5 p.m. Admission is $10 adults, $5 students and military with ID, and free for active-duty military from Armed Forces Day through Labor Day.

Elbert Hubbard opened the Roycroft Inn in 1903 to accommodate the people who came to visit his community of craftsmen. When Hubbard and his wife died in 1915, their son, Elbert II, assumed leadership of the Roycroft enterprises. Beginning in 1938, the ownership of the inn passed from the Hubbard family through a series of owners. In 1986 the inn received National Historic Landmark status, and it reopened in 1995 after extensive restorations by the Margaret L. Wendt Foundation.

All of the inn's charm and history have been preserved. Although the suites have all of the modern-day amenities, each has been meticulously restored and furnished with historically accurate elements, including Stickley furniture, Roycroft lamps and wall sconces, and wallpaper in the style of William Morris.

The Roycroft Inn (40 South Grove St., East Aurora; 716–652–5552 for reservations only, 877–652–5552; roycroftinn.com) rents three-, four-, and five-room suites starting at $165 a night, including continental breakfast. The restaurant is open for lunch Mon through Sat, for dinner nightly, and for Sunday brunch.

Before taking leave of East Aurora, stop in at the home of one of our least-discussed presidents, Millard Fillmore. Born in the Finger Lakes town of Genoa in 1800, Fillmore came to East Aurora to work as a lawyer in 1825. He built his house on Main Street with his own hands, the only presidential residence to make that claim. He moved it to its present Shearer Avenue location the same year and lived there with his wife until 1830. Restored by previous owners and the Aurora Historical Society, the **Millard Fillmore House National Landmark** contains country furnishings of Fillmore's era, as well as more refined pieces in the Greek Revival or Empire style of the president's early years. A high standing desk graced Fillmore's law office; the rear parlor, added in 1930, showcases furniture owned by the Fillmores in later years, when they lived in a Buffalo mansion. Fillmore took the large bookcase with him to the White House during his presidency.

The Millard Fillmore House National Landmark (24 Shearer Ave., East Aurora; 716–652–8875; aurorahistoricalsociety.com/pages/millard-fillmore-presidential-site) is open June through Oct on Wed, Sat, and Sun, with tours at 1, 2, and 3 p.m. Admission is $10 adults, $5 children 13 to 18, and free for children 12 and under.

We know everyone loves Jell-O, but we bet you didn't know it was invented in the village of Le Roy, where there is a museum dedicated to it, and housed in the oldest house in town. In 1897 Le Roy had earned a reputation as the Patent Medicine Capital of the world—not a moniker any town would strive to retain. Instead, it was the gelatinous creation of P. B. Waite, which his wife named Jell-O, that earned the town a place in history. Waite sold his recipe to the Genesee Pure Food Company for $450, but it was not until 1964, when Jell-O was sold to the Postum Company (which later became General Foods), that Jell-O ceased being made in Le Roy.

Today, the **Jell-O Gallery Museum**, in the Historic Society's Le Roy House, documents the creation and rise of America's favorite dessert. Here you can find answers to pressing trivia questions: Who eats the most Jell-O? What is the best-selling flavor? How many flavors have been introduced over the years? Which fruits float in Jello-O, and which ones sink?

The Jell-O Gallery Museum, in the Le Roy House (23 East Main St., Le Roy; 585–768–7433; jellogallery.org), is open Apr through Dec, Mon through Sat, 10 a.m. to 4 p.m.; Jan through Mar, Mon through Fri, 10 a.m. to 4 p.m. Admission is $5 for adults and children 12 years of age and older, and $1.50 for children 6 through 11; free for children 5 and under.

Places to Stay in the Niagara-Allegany Region

ALBION

Fair Haven Inn
14369 Ridge Rd.
(585) 589–9151
tillmansvillageinn.com

BUFFALO

The Mansion on Delaware Avenue
414 Delaware Ave.
(716) 886–3300
mansionondelaware.com

CHAUTAUQUA

Athenaeum Hotel
3 S. Lake Dr.
(716) 357–4444
chq.org/athenaeum-hotel

The Spencer Hotel & Spa
25 Palestine Ave.
(800) 398–1306 or
(716) 357–3785
thespencer.com

DUNKIRK

Clarion Hotel Marina and Conference Center
30 Lake Shore Dr. East
(800) 525–8350 or
(716) 366–8350
clariondunkirk.com

NIAGARA FALLS

Red Coach Inn
2 Buffalo Ave.
(716) 282–1459
redcoach.com

WESTFIELD

Brick House B&B
7573 East Rte. 20
(716) 326–6262
brickhousebnb.com

Places to Eat in the Niagara-Allegany Region

ALBION

Tillman's Historic Village Inn
14369 Ridge Rd.
(585) 589–9151
tillmansvillageinn.com

BUFFALO

Bacchus Wine Bar & Restaurant
54 W. Chippewa St.
(716) 854–9463
bacchusbuffalo.com

Chef's Restaurant
291 Seneca St.
(716) 856–9187
ilovechefs.com

REGIONAL TOURIST INFORMATION IN THE NIAGARA-ALLEGANY REGION

Destination Niagara USA
10 Rainbow Blvd.
Niagara Falls
(877) FALLS–US
niagarafallsusa.com

Go Wyoming County Chamber & Tourism
36 Center St., Ste. A
Warsaw
(800) 839–3919
gowyomingcountyny.com

Visit Buffalo Niagara
403 Main St.
Buffalo
(716) 852–0511
visitbuffaloniagara.com

OTHER ATTRACTIONS WORTH SEEING IN THE NIAGARA-ALLEGANY REGION

Artpark
450 S. Fourth St.
Lewiston
(716) 754–9000
artpark.net

The Broadway Market
999 Broadway
Buffalo
(716) 893–0705
broadwaymarket.com

Buffalo Niagara Heritage Village
3755 Tonawanda Creek Rd.
Amherst
(716) 689–1440
bnhv.org

Colonel William Bond–Jesse Hawley House
143 Ontario St.
Lockport
(716) 434–7433
niagarahistory.org/bond-house/

1891 Fredonia Opera House
9 Church St.
Fredonia
(716) 679–0891
fredopera.org

Lily Dale Assembly
5 Melrose Park
Lily Dale
(716) 595–8721
lilydaleassembly.com

Lockport Cave & Underground Boat Ride
5 Gooding St.
Lockport
(716) 438–0174
lockportcave.com

Niagara Falls State Park *Maid of the Mist* **Boat Tour**
151 Buffalo Ave.
Niagara Falls
(716) 284–8897
maidofthemist.com

Left Bank
511 Rhode Island St.
(716) 882–3509
leftbankrestaurant.com

KENMORE

Lombardo Ristorante
1198 Hertel Ave.
(716) 873–4291
ristorantelombardo.com

NIAGARA FALLS

The Griffon Brewery and Gastropub
2470 Military Rd.
(716) 236–7474
griffongastropub.com

Red Coach Inn
2 Buffalo Ave.
(800) 282–1459 or
(716) 282–1459
redcoach.com

Wine on Third
501 Third St.
(716) 589–9463
wineonthird.com

TONAWANDA

Saigon Bangkok
512 Niagara Falls Blvd.
(716) 837–2115
saigon-bangkok.com

WILLIAMSVILLE

Trattoria Aroma
5229 Main St.
(716) 631–2687
aromamainst.com

The Catskills

To generations of Jewish New Yorkers heading north to escape summers without air-conditioning in Manhattan, Brooklyn, and the Bronx, the Catskills once meant languid days filled with shuffleboard and table tennis at sprawling vacation colonies like the Nevele, Grossinger's, and the Concord. The resort era represented so vividly in the movie *Dirty Dancing* and the Amazon Prime series *The Marvelous Mrs. Maisel* has long since passed, but the spectacular scenery and fresh air remain, without the crowds that once jammed towns like Liberty, Monticello, and Roscoe.

We can thank the state for this, and its foresight in creating ***Catskill Park and Forest Preserve***, seven hundred thousand acres of mountains and valleys, forests and farms, rivers, streams, and waterfalls. Today the region serves not only as ground zero for fly-fishing, but as a vital watershed, supplying half the state, including New York City, with clean drinking water. Reservoirs and flowing rivers throughout the region provide recreational opportunities as well as water sources, with the sound of moving water one of the hallmarks of any wilderness hike or stroll through a town anywhere in the preserve.

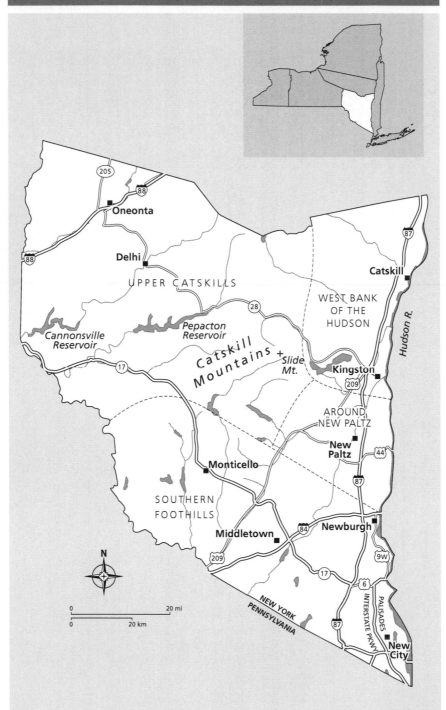

With thirty-five peaks topping out at more than 3,500 feet, the Catskills have long attracted skiers, and they have become a haven for mountain bikers and rock climbers as well. More casual day-hikers will find all kinds of trails leading to expansive views of foliage-covered peaks and slopes, while extreme sports enthusiasts know that the Catskills also provide some ice-climbing adventures that rival the Rocky Mountains.

Today, towns along the New York State Thruway, like Kingston, New Paltz, Woodstock, Hudson, and Saugerties, brim with chic shops and fine dining, food co-ops, inns, and spas—not to mention farm markets, wineries, and distilleries. It's time to rediscover the Catskills, an enduringly charming region of the state.

In this chapter, we'll start in the southeast and expand our horizons to the north and west.

Southern Foothills

During World War II, more than 1.3 million soldiers shipped out from Camp Shanks to fight in North Africa and Europe. They lived and trained in 2,500 buildings sprawled across 1,300 acres; today a small exhibit, vintage training films, and memorabilia at **Camp Shanks World War II Museum** tell the story of the men and women who passed through here on their way to the front. The museum, at 20 Greenbush Road, Orangeburg (845–359–5100; hudsonriver valley.com/sites/Camp-Shanks-World-War-II-Museum-/details), is open June through Aug, Sat and Sun, noon to 4 p.m.

The **Edward Hopper House**, birthplace and boyhood home of the realist painter famous for works such as *Nighthawks*, is now a New York State Historic Site. One room of the home, built in 1858, documents his life and work in Nyack. Three other rooms exhibit works by local artists. Jazz concerts are

AUTHOR'S FAVORITES IN THE CATSKILLS

Harriman State Park	Opus 40
Historic Huguenot Street	Pratt Rock Park
Kaaterskill Falls	Rondout Reservoir
Kaleidoscraper	Sam's Point Preserve
Minnewaska State Park Preserve	Saugerties Lighthouse
Museum at Bethel Woods	

presented in the restored garden in the summer. The house and gallery (82 North Broadway, Nyack; 845–358–0774; edwardhopperhouse.org) is open year-round, Thurs through Sun from noon to 5 p.m., and closed New Year's Day, Presidents' Day, July 4, Thanksgiving, and Christmas. Admission is $8 for adults, $6 for seniors, $3 for students 17 and older, and free for children 16 and under.

The town of Harriman and **Harriman State Park**, a unit of the Palisades Interstate Park system, are now just names on the map to most travelers, though some New Yorkers may remember the late diplomat and one-time New York governor W. Averell Harriman. But the town and the park were named for the governor's father, E. H. Harriman, at one time the most powerful railroad baron in the United States. Edward Henry Harriman (1848–1909) controlled some sixty thousand miles of American railways, including the Union Pacific. The present-day park represents much of the twenty-thousand-acre estate he acquired northwest of New York City, and which he left to his wife with the intention that it would one day be transferred to state ownership.

Today Harriman State Park offers some of the most challenging and exciting hiking on the west side of the Hudson River Valley, as well as secluded beaches and picnic sites on tranquil mountain lakes. Visit parks.ny.gov/parks/145 for maps, campsite reservations, and information about openings, closures, black bear sightings, and everything else you need to know to make the most of your visit.

Just about everyone knows where West Point is, but how many Hudson Valley travelers or military buffs can locate **Constitution Island**? Though it's practically on the east shore of the Hudson, separated from the mainland only by marshes, we include it here because visitors have to take a boat to get to the island, and the boat leaves from West Point.

Constitution Island served no further military purpose after the Revolutionary War, but it had an important part to play in General Washington's strategy for keeping British naval traffic out of the upper Hudson River. During the earlier part of the war, the fortifications on the island did not succeed in keeping the British out—in fact, construction of Fort Constitution had not reached completion when the Redcoats captured it in 1777.

West Point Washouts

Not everyone is cut out for the rigors of cadet life at West Point. In 1831, after eight months, Edgar Allan Poe was dismissed for insubordination. Artist James A. McNeill Whistler washed out in his third year when he failed chemistry. He later commented, "Had silicon been a gas, I would have been a major general."

By the following year, however, the Americans recaptured the island and made the most of its position opposite the new American defenses at West Point. Here ingenious American barricades could stop British ships dead in the water: Troops stretched an immense iron chain across the river from West Point to Constitution Island. The chain, forged of stout New Jersey iron (a portion of it can be seen at the state reservation at Ringwood, New Jersey), floated across the river on rafts of logs, and soldiers anchored it securely at either shore and built three redoubts and a battery on the island to protect the chain's eastern end. The chain did its job, and Constitution Island saw no further hostilities throughout the remaining three years of the war. Tours leave from West Point's South Dock, and admission is $15 for adults, $10 for seniors and children 6 to 16, and free for children under 6, as well as cadets, active-duty military, and personnel of the Department of Defense. For ferry and tour dates and times, visit constitutionisland.org/tours.

The island gained fame in the nineteenth century as the home of the Warner sisters, Susan (1819–85) and Anna (1824–1915). Under pseudonyms Elizabeth Wetherell (Susan) and Amy Lothrop (Anna), the two sisters wrote a total of 106 books, collaborating on 18 of them; in one of them, Anna wrote the words to what became a universally sung hymn, "Jesus Loves Me." Susan's book *The Wide, Wide World* remains in print today, a bestseller when it was released in 1850, with more than 225,000 copies sold in its first decade. Part of the present-day tour of the island is a visit to the ***Warner House***, fifteen rooms of which are furnished in the Victorian style of the Warner sisters' heyday. Learn more about the Warners at constitutionisland.org/warner-family.

Manitoga, Algonquin for "Place of the Great Spirit," was the home of Russel Wright, one of the country's foremost designers of home furnishings and a proponent of American design. His designs reflected his love of natural, organic shapes, and he extended this respect for the earth and nature to the grounds where he built his home, Dragon Rock.

When he bought the property for his home in 1942, 150 years of logging and quarrying had taken their toll. Over the next thirty years, Wright worked to restore the land, designing a living theater—a carefully cultivated backdrop of native trees, ferns, mosses, and wildflowers that appears as if it grew there naturally.

A year before he died, the designer-naturalist opened his land to the public, and today programs at Manitoga teach ecology, science, art, and design. Visitors can wander several one-way paths that Wright designed as journeys into the secrets of the forest, the result of his studies of the landscape and its natural contours to determine the direction of each route. The main path passes by his home, designed to blend into the landscape of the quarry.

The grounds of Manitoga (584 Route 9D, Garrison; 845–424–3812 ext. 105, weekends 845–422–2380; visitmanitoga.org/) are open from mid-May through mid-Nov, Fri through Mon for tours at 11 a.m. and 1:30 p.m., with an additional 3:30 p.m. tour on Sat. The grounds are open the rest of the year on weekdays only. A donation is requested if visitors hike the grounds. Tour prices are based on the number of people in your party; go to visitmanitoga.org for reservations and details.

In the 1830s John Jaques emigrated from Europe to the small town of Washingtonville. Trained as a shoe- and bootmaker, he planned to support himself with his trade, but to augment his income he purchased ten acres of land on Main Street and planted grapes in the rich, loamy Hudson Valley soil

ANNUAL EVENTS IN THE CATSKILLS

JANUARY

Hudson Valley Rail Trail Winterfest
New Paltz
(845) 691–6313
ulstercountyalive.com/calendar/
hudson-valley-rail-trail-winterfest-3

MAY

East Durham Irish Festival
(800) 434–FEST
eastdurhamirishfestival.com/festival/
schedule/

Hudson Valley Mayfaire
New Paltz
(845) 338–3468
facebook.com/HudsonvalleyMayFaire/

Mountain Jam
Bethel
mountainjam.com

Woodstock-New Paltz Arts and Crafts Fair
New Paltz
festivalnet.com/18948/New-Paltz-New-
York/Craft-Shows/Woodstock-New-
Paltz-Art-and-Crafts-Fair-Spring-Show

JULY

Bard SummerScape
Annandale-on-Hudson
fishercenter.bard.edu/summerscape/

Belleayre Music Festival
Highmount
(800) 254–5600
facebook.com/BelleayreMusicFestival

Hurley Stone House Day
Hurley
(845) 331–4121
stonehouseday.org

AUGUST

Annual Daniel Nimham Intertribal Pow Wow
Carmel
(800) 808–1994
facebook.com/Annual-Daniel-Nimham-
Pow-Wow-198172383539508/

Dutchess County Fair
Rhinebeck
dutchessfair.com

to sell at market. When he became a church elder, he used some of his grapes to make sacramental wine.

Today **Brotherhood** is America's oldest winery, and the church where Jaques's wine was first served is the winery's gift shop. Brotherhood has made wine continuously since 1839, surviving Prohibition by selling "sacramental" wine and asking no questions. Its vast underground cellars, the largest in the country and comparable to those of famous European wineries, now house many varieties of specialty, table, dessert, and premium vintage wines, including Grand Monarque champagne. A tour of the winery includes a visit to the underground cellars and a sampling of a half dozen wines.

Brotherhood (100 Brotherhood Plaza, Washingtonville; 845–496–3661; brotherhoodwinery.net) is open Wed through Fri from 11 a.m. to 6 p.m.; Sat

Maverick Concert Series
Woodstock
(646) 965–2365
maverickconcerts.org

SEPTEMBER
Esopus Apple Festival
Port Ewan
facebook.com/
events/423385365191410/

The Great Catskill Mountain Quilt Show
Windham
(518) 263–2000
catskillmtn.org/events/mountain-culture-festival/2007/quilt-show.html

Hudson River Valley Ramble
Various locations
(518) 473–3835
hudsonrivervalleyramble.com/ramble

OCTOBER
Hunter Mountain Oktoberfest
Hunter
(518) 263–4223
greatnortherncatskills.com/events/
oktoberfest-weekends-hunter-mountain

NOVEMBER
Annual Greek Festival
Kingston
(613) 777–6380
greekcommunityofkingston.com/events

Rosendale International Pickle Festival
Rosendale
rosendalepicklefestival.org

11 a.m. to 7 p.m.; and Sun 11 a.m. to 5 p.m. Tastings are $15 per person. Visit the website for a calendar of events.

Orange County is known for its fine standardbred horses—the horses of the harness track. Hambletonian, sire of virtually all of today's trotters, was born here. The *Harness Racing Museum & Hall of Fame* tells the stories of many of the horses and humans who made the sport so exciting for so many. Whether or not you have a passion for racing, you certainly will delight in the original Currier & Ives prints always on display here, with themed exhibits from the museum's vast collection of the artists' work.

The Harness Racing Museum & Hall of Fame (240 Main St., Goshen; 845–294–6330; harnessmuseum.com) is open daily from 10 a.m. to 6 p.m.; Nov to Mar it closes at 5 p.m. Admission is $7.50 for adults, $5.50 for seniors, and $3.50 for children 6 to 12.

Across the way at 44 Park Place is *Goshen Historic Track*, the oldest active harness track in the country and the first sporting site in the nation to be designated a National Registered Historic Landmark by the National Park Service. Catch a racing day here by visiting goshenhistorictrack.com for the schedule.

The hamlet of Sugar Loaf has enjoyed a reputation as a crafts community for more than 250 years. Today more than twenty artisans live and work in the original barns and buildings, creating a variety of goods ranging from stained glass to pottery to hand-tooled leather products. Visitors are invited to watch the artists at work in their studios and browse through a variety of specialty and gift shops peppered throughout the town.

In addition, *Sugar Loaf Art and Craft Village* offers an extensive program of concerts, festivals, and special events throughout the year. The seven-hundred-seat theater, Lycian Center (lycian.com/centre), offers a venue for performances by national and international touring companies in Broadway musicals, drama, dance, concerts, and children's shows.

Sugar Loaf Art and Craft Village (Sugar Loaf Chamber of Commerce, Inc., 1371 Kings Hwy., Chester; 845–469–9181; sugarloafnewyork.com) is open year-round. Days and hours vary from shop to shop; click on "Sugar Loaf Shops" on the website for complete information.

The next time you eat an onion, consider this: It might well have been grown in black dirt formed twelve thousand years ago in a glacial lake, in an area now known as Pine Island. As the glaciers melted and the climate warmed, vegetation grew, died, and sank to the bottom of the lake. The lake area earned the nickname "the drowned lands" and remained a swamp until the early 1900s, when immigrants came, bought the land cheap, drained the lake by hand, built drainage ditches, and then planted onions in the rich black

Black Tie, No Tails

Toward the end of the nineteenth century, in the gated community of millionaires' estates called *Tuxedo Park*, in the Ramapo Mountains near the New Jersey border, daring young fashion plates scandalized their elders by abandoning traditional full evening dress with its cutaway tailcoats in favor of a shorter black jacket cut like a daytime suit coat. Despite initial resistance, the new style caught on, and the new semiformal men's uniform came to be known as the tuxedo.

soil. Today, with thousands of acres planted, the "black dirt" region is one of the country's leading producers of onions.

Pine Island onions go into every bowl of onion soup gratineé at *The Jolly Onion* (625 Glenwood Rd., Pine Island; 845–981–7272; thejollyonion.com), Pine Island's signature restaurant. The same can be said for the Pine Island onion ring tower, the handmade potato-onion pierogies, and the onion riding atop the country fried chicken sandwich. After a visit to the "black dirt" region and the Jolly Onion, you'll never again think lightly of the humble bulb.

A Victorian country estate high in the Catskill Mountains, *the Inn at Lake Joseph* nestles against a 250-acre lake surrounded by thousands of acres of forest and wildlife preserve. Built by Thomas Hunt Talmadge in the latter part of the nineteenth century, the estate served as a retreat for the Dominican Sisters, as a vacation home for Cardinals Hayes and Spellman of New York, and finally as a sumptuous inn.

Choose from seventeen rooms and suites with whirlpool tubs, fireplaces, and private sundecks. Every room includes a full country breakfast each morning, and amenities include a heated swimming pool, trails for hiking, birding, or cross-country skiing through the surrounding woodland, and a billiard room and library. Lake Joseph also has a reputation as one of the finest largemouth bass lakes in the state.

The Inn at Lake Joseph (162 St. Joseph Rd., Forestburgh; 845–791–9506; lakejoseph.com) is open year-round. Weekend rates range from $215 to $595. There is a $20-per-day fee for pets.

From December through March (eagle time), Sullivan County becomes home to a large concentration of migrant bald eagles—mostly from Canada. A few of their favorite nesting places include *Mongaup Falls Reservoir and Rio Reservoir* in Forestburgh and the *Rondout Reservoir* in Grahamsville (look for the eagle watch area on Route 55A). For an update and complete list of sites, contact the Audubon Society of New York State, Eldred (845–557–8025; ny.audubon.org).

Many devotees of fly-fishing believe that, in North America, the sport began in the Catskills. Seeing the streams that run along the Beaverkill and Willowemoc Valleys, it's hard to imagine a more suitable location for a center devoted to preserving the heritage and protecting the future of fly-fishing in the United States. That's the mission of the **Catskill Fly Fishing Center and Museum**, on the shores of the Willowemoc River between Roscoe and Livingston Manor.

Founded in 1891, the facility illuminates the contributions and lives of the great names associated with the Catskill area—Gordon and Hewitt, Dette and Darbee, LaBranche and Flick—as well as Lee Wulff, Poul Jorgensen, and others from the world of fly-fishing. Interpretive exhibits on the evolution of the sport, as well as hundreds of meticulously crafted rods, flies, and reels, are on display. Special guest fly tying experts demonstrate their craft every Saturday afternoon throughout the season. The center offers a variety of educational and recreational programs year-round, including courses in stream ecology and angling, fly tying, and rod building.

The Catskill Fly Fishing Center and Museum (1031 Old Route 17, Livingston Manor; 845–439–4810; cffcm.com) is open Fri through Mon, 10 a.m. to 4 p.m. Closed holidays.

Feeling stressed? Consider escaping for a peaceful weekend at **Dai Bosatsu Zendo Kongo-ji**, a Zen Buddhist monastery on fourteen hundred acres in the Catskill Mountain Forest Preserve. All are welcome here, whether it be for a three-day weekend for novices who want to learn basics, such as sitting, breathing, and chanting; a longer stay for those steeped in the way of Rinzai Zen Buddhism; or even those just looking for an overnight retreat. The grounds are open to day visitors who call in advance March through November.

As expected, accommodations are simple but comfortable and include three vegetarian meals a day. Rooms with private and shared baths are available. Rates begin at $75 per night; you can also reserve a cottage for $200 per night.

Dai Bosatsu Zendo Kongo-ji (223 Beecher Lake Rd., Livingston Manor; 845–439–4566; zenstudies.org) requests that guests reserve at least two weeks in advance.

Around New Paltz

You will pass a wall of quartz conglomerate cliffs on your way to **Minnewaska State Park Preserve**, one unlike anything else you've seen in New York State. The **Shawangunk Mountain Ridge**—"the Gunks" to people in the know—is one of the premier rock-climbing destinations in the United States.

Look closely as you approach to see if people in technical climbing gear are working to scale these cliffs on the day of your visit. Many lifelong New Yorkers have no idea that this fascinating rock formation exists in their state, nor have they discovered the park just beyond it—one that rivals the Berkshire Mountains and even Acadia National Park for fragrant forests, clear "sky lakes," and gorgeous waterfalls.

Minnewaska State Park Preserve, high in the Shawangunk Mountains, presents an outdoor paradise of hiking trails, waterfalls, and scenic vistas. A network of wide carriage roads, created by wealthy landowners who admired the scenery from horse-drawn vehicles, today provide access for bicyclists, hikers, and horseback riders to many of the park's major highlights. A 5.4-mile out-and-back hike brings you to one of the park's greatest draws: Rainbow Falls, a challenge to reach but with a tremendous reward. For the less ambitious, there's swimming at the more accessible Lake Minnewaska, nestled amid white sandstone cliffs (it's easy to see why the indigenous people named it "floating waters").

Minnewaska State Park Preserve (5281 Rte. 44/55, Kerhonkson; 845–255–0752; parks.ny.gov/parks/Minnewaska/) is open year-round, 9 a.m. to 7 p.m.; admission is $10 per vehicle.

Not far from the main park, **Sam's Point Preserve** (400 Sam's Point Rd., Cragsmoor; 845–647–7989; parks.ny.gov/parks/193), a unit of Minnewaska, contains one of the world's best examples of ridgetop dwarf pine barrens. Here energetic hikers can visit the Ice Cave, a naturally chilled cave with a network of staircases, corridors, squeezes, icy spots, and climbs that can be just the thing in the middle of July. The trail to the cave passes Sam's Point, a ledge that furnishes a 270-degree view of the countryside—a particularly magnificent one when autumn turns the leaves crimson and gold. Open year-round, dawn to dusk; $10 per vehicle. Snowshoe rental is available at the visitor center.

In 1714 Luis Moses Gomez, a refugee from the Spanish Inquisition and a community leader in New York City, purchased twelve hundred acres of land along the Hudson highlands and another 3,000 acres with his sons over the next several years. They built a fieldstone blockhouse on Jews Creek, used the creek's power for mills and lime kilns, and ran a thriving enterprise. Today the **Gomez Mill House** is the oldest surviving Jewish residence in North America. Over the ensuing years, subsequent owners of the house made changes to the original structure: Wolvert Ecker, a patriot during the Revolutionary War, built a second floor and hosted meetings in the house with fellow revolutionaries. In the twentieth century, Craftsman-era designer Dard Hunter rebuilt the old gristmill into a paper mill and made paper by hand, cut and cast type, and handprinted his own books. Today the Gomez

Foundation for Mill House preserves the home as a museum, which is listed on the National Register of Historic Places.

The Gomez Mill House (11 Mill House Rd., Marlboro; 845–236–3126; gomez.org) is open Sat and Sun with tours at 10:30 a.m., 1:30 p.m., and 3 p.m. Admission is $10 for adults, $7 for seniors 62+, and $4 for children 7 to 17 and students with ID; children under 7 are free.

The sophisticated **Buttermilk Falls Inn & Spa** (220 North Rd., Milton; 845–795–1500; buttermilkfallsinn.com), a seventy-acre estate overlooking the Hudson River, features thirteen rooms, three carriage houses, the North Cottage, and a two-story, 3,500-square-foot spa. Guests unwind with a stroll on the estate's tranquil grounds, past cascading waterfalls, winding brooks, flowering terraces, a peacock and chicken rookery, and a pre-Revolutionary cemetery. The spa offers deep-tissue and hot-stone massages and purifying facials using organic skin care products. Buttermilk Spa's couples massage and spine-realigning "raindrop technique" are two of its signature treatments. Various sixty-minute sessions are priced at $120 and up. Four spacious massage rooms even have river views. Henry's at the Farm, the on-site restaurant, is open daily from 2 to 8 p.m.

Persecuted by the Catholic majority in their native France, many Huguenots came to New York in pursuit of freedom and tolerance. In 1677, twelve of their number purchased the lands around present-day New Paltz from the Esopus Munsee people and built log huts as their first habitations.

As the twelve pioneers and their families prospered, they decided to build more permanent dwellings. Here are seven perfectly preserved houses, with additions that were built by the settlers' descendants over the years. Today the Huguenot Historical Society (81 Huguenot St., New Paltz; 845–255–1660 or 845–255–1889; huguenotstreet.org) maintains these homes as museums, along with a reconstructed 1717 French church and a replica of an Esopus Munsee wigwam, to tell the stories of all the people—including Dutch settlers, enslaved Africans, and Native cultures—who shared residency on this land. You can take a self-led walking tour anytime (there's an app for that: search for **Historic Huguenot Street** in your smartphone's app store), or a guided tour that is $12 for adults, $10 for students and seniors, and free for children 12 and under.

Just north of New Paltz, at High Falls, is a museum dedicated to a great work of engineering born from an energy crisis—a disruption in coal supply brought about by America's 1812–14 war with Great Britain. Two brothers, Maurice and William Wurts, envisioned a canal to bring Pennsylvania anthracite (hard coal) from the mines to New York City and the vicinity. In 1825, they formed the Delaware and Hudson Canal Company to link Honesdale, Pennsylvania, with the Hudson River port of Eddyville, New York.

Benjamin Wright, chief engineer of the Erie Canal, handled the surveying and engineering of the 108-mile route. The first canal reached completion in 1828, and between 1847 and 1852, crews enlarged and deepened it to accommodate heavier traffic. In 1829, the company also began to work its gravity-operated rail line between Honesdale and Carbondale, Pennsylvania, with a new English steam locomotive. Nothing of the original canal remains but a few weedy stretches, but the Delaware and Hudson Railroad survives to this day as the oldest transportation company in the United States.

The **Delaware and Hudson Canal Museum** tells the story of the old canal, not merely through glassed-in exhibits but by preserving the extant structures, channel, and locks in the High Falls vicinity. Visitors learn about the canal through sophisticated dioramas, photos, and technological exhibits, including models of a working lock and gravity railroad. Self-guided tours and trails take in five locks and nearby canal segments, as well as the remains of John Roebling's suspension aqueduct.

The Delaware and Hudson Canal Museum (23 Mohonk Rd., High Falls; 845–687–2000; canalmuseum.org) is open May through Oct, Sat and Sun, 10 a.m. to 4:30 p.m. Admission is by donation.

Even as canals and railroads changed the face of America, the first conservationists started speaking out against the dangers of the Industrial Revolution. Among them was John Burroughs, a native New Yorker who wrote twenty-five books on natural history and the philosophy of conservation. In 1895 Burroughs built a rustic log hideaway in the woods outside the village of West Park, barely two miles from the west bank of the Hudson. He called it **Slabsides**, a National Historic Landmark today.

Burroughs, whose permanent home was only a mile and a half away, came to his little retreat to write and to observe his natural surroundings. John Muir came here to talk with Burroughs, as did Theodore Roosevelt and Thomas Edison. They sat around the fire on log furniture of Burroughs's own manufacture, much of which still resides in the cabin.

Slabsides, which was deeded to the John Burroughs Association after the author's death in 1921, now stands within the 191-acre John Burroughs Sanctuary, a pleasant woodland tract that forms a most fitting living monument to his memory. The sanctuary's 2½ miles of trails are open daily from dawn to dusk year-round; on the third Sat in May and the first Sat in Oct, the John Burroughs Association (261 Floyd Ackert Rd., West Park; 845–384–6320; johnburroughsassociation.org) holds an open house with tours of the cabin from 11 a.m. to 4 p.m. In addition to an opportunity to see the cabin, the special days include informal talks and nature walks. Admission is free.

Nestled in the heart of a 24,000-acre natural area in the Shawangunk Mountains, overlooking Lake Mohonk, you'll find the **Mohonk Mountain House**, a sprawling Victorian castle resort built in 1869 and now a National Historic Landmark, as well as a member of Historic Hotels of America. Its 251 guest rooms, 5 guest cottages, 150 working fireplaces, and 200 balconies make this a choice location for anyone seeking a peak experience in the Catskills and Hudson Valley. Above the Mohonk Mountain House stands Sky Top Tower, an observation tower built in 1923 of Shawangunk conglomerate quarried at its base, and from the top on a clear day, you can see forever—or at least as far as the Rondout and Wallkill Valleys, New Jersey, Connecticut, Vermont, Pennsylvania, and Massachusetts. (The tower is also known as the Albert K. Smiley Memorial Tower in tribute to the cofounder of the Mohonk Mountain House.)

Guests, of course, have use of the resort's spacious grounds, greenhouse, gardens, and many amenities, but even if you're not an overnight guest, you can pay a day-visitor fee ($15 per person, $20 if you're on a bicycle or horse, or if you plan to rock climb) that will give you access to the tower; eighty-five miles of hiking trails, paths, and carriage roads; and the lovely landscaped grounds with their formal show gardens, herb garden, and Victorian maze.

Day visitors are also invited to visit the **Barn Museum**, in one of the largest barns in the Northeast. Built in 1888, it houses many nineteenth-century horse-drawn vehicles and working tools made more than 150 years ago. The Barn Museum (845–255–1000, ext. 2447), is open daily from Memorial Day through Oct and Sat and Sun in winter, 10 a.m. to 4 p.m. In the winter, day visitors can cross-country ski on more than thirty-five miles of marked, maintained ski trails.

Mohonk Mountain House (1000 Mountain Rest Rd., New Paltz; 845–255–1000; mohonk.com; for reservations, 855–883–3798). Overnight rates vary according to view and decor, but all include three meals. They range from $732 a night for a double in one of the traditional-style rooms to $2,488 for a suite.

West Bank of the Hudson

Emile Brunel Studio and Sculpture Garden, also known as **Totem Indian Trading Post**, showcases more than a dozen megalithic sculptures by Emile Brunel, founder of the New York Institute of Photography, who died in Boiceville in 1944. One of these pieces, *The Great White Spirit*, may actually contain the ashes of the artist. The man who perfected the one-hour film-developing process—making it possible for moviemakers to see "rushes" of the film they shot the same day—also owned and ran one of the most popular hotels in the

Catskills, the Chalet Indian. His enthusiasm for the outdoors and for art infuses this unusual garden.

Totem Indian Trading Post (Route 28 and Desilva Road, Boiceville; 845–205–3839; brunelpark.org) is open daily for self-guided tours from 1 to 5 p.m. Admission is free.

Floating down Esopus Creek on a lazy afternoon as it winds through the Catskill Mountains is the ultimate vacation: relaxing, scenic, and fun. **The Town Tinker** rents tubes, helps chart your course, provides instruction as needed, and arranges transportation. The creek can kick up class II rapids with one- to three-foot waves, so some ability to maneuver around rocks and other obstacles is required. The route takes approximately two hours, and Town Tinker Tube Taxis provides transportation.

The Town Tinker (10 Bridge St., Phoenicia; 845–688–5553; towntinker .com) is open daily mid-May through Sept from 9 a.m. to 6 p.m. (last rentals are at 4 p.m.). Basic inner tubes rent for $25 a day. A full-gear package for $50 includes a tube with seat, life vest, wetsuit, and helmet as well as one-time transportation. Children must be 12 years old and good swimmers. Taxi transportation is $5 per trip.

If you'd rather tour Esopus Creek by rail, **Catskill Mountain Railroad** offers a six-mile round-trip ride, stopping at Phoenicia at a circa-1900 train depot. Catskill Mountain Railroad Company (Westbrook Lane Station, 55 Plaza Rd., Kingston; 845–332–4854; catskillmountainrailroad.com) operates weekends and holidays Memorial Day weekend through late Oct, with trains running hourly 11 a.m. to 5 p.m. Fare is $21 round-trip for adults; $19 for seniors, military, and veterans; $13 for children ages 2 to 12; children under 2 are free. Call ahead to verify schedules.

Back in the summer of 1969, more than four hundred thousand music fans gathered for three days at Max Yasgur's farm in Bethel to hear Jimi Hendrix, Janis Joplin, Bob Dylan, Joni Mitchell, Joan Baez, Arlo Guthrie, the Grateful Dead, and dozens of other voices that defined a generation. Today visitors can share that experience at the **Museum at Bethel Woods** (200 Hurd Rd., Bethel; bethelwoodscenter.org), a tribute not only to the concert itself, but to the times that made such a phenomenon possible. It captures the cultural transformations at work at the time—from the rise of the civil rights movement to the moon landing—and even provides an augmented reality tour that lets you become one of the 450,000 people on the ground at the farm. Bethel Woods Center for the Arts is open daily May through Nov from 10 a.m. to 5 p.m.; Nov 2 through Dec 23, Thurs through Sun from 10 a.m. to 5 p.m.; closed Thanksgiving, Christmas Eve, and Christmas Day. Admission for adults is $19.69, $15 for seniors 65+, $10 for children 6 to 18, and free for children 5 and under. Discounts are available for ordering tickets online in advance; there is an additional fee for the augmented reality experience.

Perhaps it's no surprise that the area forever associated with psychedelics should spawn the world's largest kaleidoscope. Down the road in Mount Tremper, the **Emerson Resort & Spa** features an attraction you will find nowhere else: the **Kaleidoscraper**, built in an old farm silo and more than 60 feet high with three 38-foot mirrors. Constructed in 1996 by Charles Karadimos, a well-known name in the multi-prism vision field, the scope features three specially designed seasonal shows conceived by 1960s artist Isaac Abrams and his son and scored by Gary Burke: "America, the House We Live In," presents a slice of history in music and light; "Hexagon Holiday," a winter wonder shown from Christmas through Presidents' Day weekend; and "Metamorphosis," which opens in early spring, just as the buds are popping, and traces the progress of the seasons through the Catskills. Entry is $7 per person; children under 12 get in free. Visit emersonresort.com/worlds-largest-kaleidoscope/ for more details.

Emerson Place also has a country store and other shops, including the Kaleidostore, where handmade, one-of-a-kind kaleidoscopes are on sale. The recently rebuilt Emerson Resort & Spa now has twenty-five new suites in addition to the Adirondack-style accommodations at the old Lodge at Emerson Place. Rates for a standard double start at $355 a night; call (845) 688–2828 or go to emersonresort.com for particulars.

If you're looking for a different dining experience, **Catskill Rose** is an excellent option. How about appetizers such as sauteed shrimp with saffron tomato risotto cake and entrées like smoked pork shank with bourbon sauce? The restaurant, at 5355 Route 212 in Mt. Tremper (845–688–7100), begins serving dinner at 5 p.m. Thurs through Sun. Reservations are appreciated; see the current menu at catskillrose.com.

One of the country's first art colonies was founded in Woodstock in 1903, and today Ulster County is still a haven for artists. **The Woodstock Byrdcliffe Guild** (34 Tinker St., Woodstock; 845–679–2079; woodstockguild.org), a multiarts center, displays and sells works of some of the area's best. It's open Fri through Sun from noon to 5 p.m.; closed Jan and Feb.

The baguette is a work of art at **Bread Alone** (22 Mill Hill Rd., Woodstock; 845–679–2108). Workers at the European-style bakery shape the breads by hand and then bake the loaves in wood-fired ovens. Among the house specialties: brioche, challah, and sourdough currant buns. The bakery is open daily from 7 a.m. to 5 p.m.; see breadalone.com for locations in Boiceville, Rhinebeck, and Kingston.

For almost forty years until his death in 1976, Harvey Fite created a monumental environmental sculpture out of an abandoned Saugerties bluestone quarry. **Opus 40**, made of hundreds of thousands of tons of finely fitted stone, covers more than six acres. Visitors can walk along its recessed lower pathways, around the pools and fountains, and up to the nine-ton monolith at the summit. To create his Opus, Fite worked with traditional tools that were used by quarrymen here. **The Quarryman's Museum** houses his collection of tools and artifacts.

Opus 40 and Quarryman's Museum (50 Fite Rd., Saugerties; 845–246–3400; opus40.org) is open Memorial Day weekend through Columbus Day weekend, Fri, Sat, and Sun and most Monday holidays (call in advance), noon to 5 p.m. Admission is $11 for adults, $8 for students and senior citizens, and free for children under 5.

If you've ever looked longingly at a distant lighthouse, wishing you could escape social media for a bit, check in to the **Saugerties Lighthouse**, an 1869 stone structure at the mouth of Esopus Creek on the Hudson River. Deactivated by the US Coast Guard in 1954, the lighthouse has since been restored by the Saugerties Lighthouse Conservancy, which operates it as a museum and inn. In 1990 the Coast Guard installed a fourth-order solar-powered light, and the lighthouse once again aids mariners.

Two second-floor bedrooms can be rented for Thurs through Sun nights year-round at $250 per room with a two-night minimum on weekends. All guests share a kitchen and a first-floor bathroom. The lighthouse is surrounded by water, so to reach it, you will walk a half-mile nature trail (at low tide only), so keep this in mind when you pack. Reservations are essential.

The museum at Saugerties Lighthouse Conservancy (168 Lighthouse Dr., Saugerties; 845–247–0656; saugertieslighthouse.com) is open Sun from noon to 3 p.m., Memorial Day through Labor Day. There is a suggested donation of $5 for adults and $3 for children.

You may assume that Niagara Falls takes the record as the highest waterfall in New York State, but the falls that wins the title actually flows deep in the Catskills. (From the town of Catskill, take NY 23A West for 13.2 miles to the bend in the road at Bastion Falls. Pass the falls and turn in to the parking area on the left side of the road, about 0.2 miles after Bastion Falls.) **Kaaterskill Falls** leaps from a rock ledge as a narrow curtain of white water, plunging past a natural grotto to a second scooped-out shelf at which it gathers force to finish its plunge toward the floor of Kaaterskill Clove.

The falls attracts all kinds of adventurers to hike the well-maintained 0.6-mile trail to see it, thanks to Thomas Cole, founder of the Hudson River School of Art, who immortalized the falls in his painting *View of Kaaterskill Falls* in the early 1800s. Washington Irving described the cove as "wild, lonely, and shagged, the bottom filled with fragments from impending cliffs, and scarcely lighted by the reflected rays of the setting sun."

The path to the base of the falls is not particularly difficult, for which we must thank the Adirondack Mountain Club for their careful maintenance and for building stairs out of solid rock. In spring, when its snow cover melts and refreezes into glare ice, you will want ice-gripping footwear; we highly recommend a walking stick to give you a third point of contact with the ground.

Now let's go to the Bronck's. No, it's not the wrong chapter—or the wrong spelling. Bronck was the family name of one of the original clans of Swedish settlers in New Amsterdam and the Hudson Valley. Pieter Bronck settled on the west bank of the Hudson near what is now Coxsackie, and his seventeenth-century house farmstead has become the **Bronck Museum**, where eight generations of Broncks lived. Leonard Bronck Lampman willed the acreage and buildings to the Greene County Historical Society, along with the entire farm settled in those early years. Thus, we get to appreciate not only the oldest of the farm buildings but also all of the barns, utility buildings, and furnishings acquired over two centuries of prosperity and familial expansion. What it all amounts to is an object lesson in the changes in style, taste, and sophistication that took place between the seventeenth and nineteenth centuries.

The Bronck Museum (90 County Road 42, Coxsackie; 518–731–6490; gchistory.org/projects) is open Memorial Day until mid-Oct, Thurs and Fri for tours at 11 a.m. and 2 p.m. Admission is $8 per person.

Upper Catskills

If you're heading west from the Hudson Valley into the upper Catskills, a stop at the **Durham Center Museum** in East Durham provides an instructive look at the things a small community finds important. In many ways this museum is an archetype of the "village attics" that dot the land, and travelers could do worse than to take an occasional poke into one of these institutions. At the museum, housed in a circa-1825 one-room schoolhouse and several newer adjacent buildings, the collections run from Native American artifacts and portions of local petrified trees to old farm tools and mementos of the 1800 Susquehanna Turnpike and the 1832–40 Canajoharie-Catskill Railroad, both of which passed this way. Visitors can also see a collection of Rogers Groups, those plaster statuette tableaux that decorated Victorian parlors and played on bourgeois heartstrings before Norman Rockwell was born. Finally, don't miss the collection of bottled sand specimens from around the world, sent by friends of the museum. If you're planning a trip to some far-off spot not represented on these shelves, don't hesitate to send some sand.

The Bridges of Delaware County

Six historic covered bridges are among the rural attractions of Delaware County. The Hamden and Fitches Bridges span the west branch of the Delaware River, while the Downsville Bridge, crossing the Delaware's east branch, is the longest covered bridge still in use in New York State at 174 feet. Two smaller bridges can be a little trickier to find: The Lower Shaverton Bridge crosses Trout Brook in Hancock; the Erpf Bridge crosses over a pond outlet on private property. (There's a sixth one, but it originated in another part of the state in 1870, and its owner moved it to this area in 2012—this, plus some modern upgrades, keeps it off the county's official list.)

The Durham Center Museum (3006 Route 145, East Durham; 518–239–8461; greatnortherncatskills.com/arts-culture/durham-center-museum) is open Memorial Day through Columbus Day (call for hours). Admission is $2.50 for adults and $1 for children under 12. Groups are welcome by appointment. Genealogical researchers are welcome year-round by appointment.

Two 1876 Queen Anne boardinghouses were restored and joined to create **Albergo Allegria** (43 Route 296, Windham; 518–734–5560; albergousa.com), a luxurious sixteen-room inn and carriage house with an elegant Victorian flavor and modern-day amenities. Rates, which start at $179/night, include afternoon tea (served alfresco on warm days) and a gourmet breakfast, with treats such as stuffed French toast, Belgian waffles, and honey-cured bacon.

In 1824 a young man named Zadock Pratt came to a settlement called Schoharie Kill to establish a tannery. He bought some land, surveyed it, and set up his factory. Over the next twenty years, more than thirty thousand employees, using hides imported from South America, tanned a million sides of sole leather, which were shipped down the Hudson River to New York City—and in the meantime Pratt established Prattsville, one of the earliest planned communities in New York State.

Pratt went on to become a member of US Congress, elected in 1836 and again in 1842, and he sponsored the bill that created the Smithsonian Institution. Equally enduring may be the legacy he left behind here in the town that bears his name: **Pratt Rock Park** (518–299–3395; greatnortherncatskills.com/outdoors/pratt-rock-new-yorks-mount-rushmore), on Main Street, which he commissioned a team of stone workers to complete between 1842 and 1862. Carved into the park's cliffs are symbols of Mr. Pratt's life, including a huge bust of his son who was killed in the Civil War, a horse, a hemlock tree, an uplifted hand, his tannery, a wreath with the names of his children, and an unfinished tomb where Pratt was to be buried overlooking the village (he was buried in a

The Long Good Night

The town of *Palenville* made the decision that it must be the home of Washington Irving's greatest fictional snoozer, Rip Van Winkle. The mild-mannered Winkle took his twenty-year nap in a ravine somewhere in these parts, halfway up a Catskill mountain. Hikers still search for the spot where Rip sat, drank from a keg offered to him by an old man with thick, bushy hair and a grizzled beard, and watched odd-looking fellows playing ninepins before he drifted off. As Irving had never visited the Catskills before he wrote the story, Palenville certainly is as good a guess as any for the origin of this very sleepy character.

conventional grave at the other end of town). There's also a grave site with a stone bearing the names of his favorite dogs and horses. Pratt donated the finished sculpture to the town in a gesture of unparalleled magnanimity and ego, and *Ripley's Believe It or Not* later dubbed it "New York's Mount Rushmore." A planned restoration is in the works to make the monument more accessible to the public.

If a hike to Pratt Rock hasn't told you enough about Zadock Pratt, take time to visit the **Zadock Pratt Museum** (14540 Main St., Prattsville; 518–299–3395; zadockprattmuseum.org) located in Zadock Pratt's restored homestead in the center of town. The museum, on the National Register of Historic Places, is just a half mile from the rocks. It focuses on the history and culture of the northern Catskills in the mid-nineteenth century and is open Memorial Day to Columbus Day, Sat and Sun, 10 a.m. to 5 p.m. There is an admission fee.

Nearby, the National Register Reformed Dutch Church, with its handsome three-tiered tower, was built in 1804.

In Roxbury, New York, we again come into contact with the naturalist John Burroughs. He may have spent much of the last decades of his life at Slabsides, down on the Hudson, but here in Roxbury he was born in 1837, and he spent the last ten summers of his life at Woodchuck Lodge. He was buried here, in a field adjacent to the lodge, on April 2, 1921. The grave site and the nearby "Boyhood Rock" that he cherished as a lad are now part of *John Burroughs Memorial State Historic Site*.

Unique among historic sites in this region, the Burroughs Memorial's chief feature (apart from the grave and the rock) is simply a field surrounded by forests and the rolling Catskill hills—as fine a memorial as one could possibly imagine for a man who once said about the Catskills, "Those hills comfort me as no other place in the world does—it is home there."

John Burroughs Memorial State Historic Site (1067 Burroughs Memorial Rd., Roxbury) is open during daylight hours. Admission is free. For information call (518) 827–6111 or see parks.ny.gov/historic-sites/3/.

Many of John Burroughs's modern-day spiritual descendants use the term "appropriate technology" to refer to renewable, nonpolluting sources of energy. Over in the northwestern Catskills town of East Meredith, the *Hanford Mills Museum* celebrates one of the oldest of these alternative-energy sources, the power of running water harnessed to a wheel. Kortright Creek at East Meredith has been the site of water-powered mills since the beginning of the nineteenth century, and the main building on the museum site today was built in 1846.

The old mill became the Hanford Mills in 1860, when David Josiah Hanford bought the operation. During the eighty-five years in which they owned the mill, the Hanford family expanded its output to include feed milling and the manufacture of utilitarian woodenware for farms and small industries. The mill complex grew to incorporate more than ten buildings on ten acres, all clustered around the millpond. The mill continued operation until 1967.

Much of the original nineteenth-century equipment at Hanford Mills is still in place and in good working order. Today's visitors can watch lumber being cut on a big circular saw and shaped with smaller tools, all powered by the waters of Kortright Creek. At the heart of the operation is a 10-by-12-foot waterwheel, doing what waterwheels have done for more than two thousand years. Visitors may explore at their leisure or take a guided tour.

The Hanford Mills Museum (51 County Hwy. 12, East Meredith; 607–278–5744; hanfordmills.org) is open daily, May 1 to Oct 31, from 10 a.m. to 5 p.m. Admission is $9 for adults; $7 for seniors 65+ and teachers; and $4.50 for active-duty military, veterans, and first responders; free for children 12 and under. Group rates are available.

Breaking "Legs"

The tiny town of *Acra* was once home to one of Prohibition's most infamous criminals. *Jack "Legs" Diamond* heard about a potent applejack that the locals made from cider, and he decided to move in and "organize" the stills. He bought a farmhouse just north of the village for his gang headquarters and began calling on the mountain bootleggers. Unfortunately for Legs, the locals didn't want to be organized, and they gunned him down. Wounded, he had the trunks of the trees around his house painted white to hinder a possible ambush, but he could only hold off the inevitable for so long: The night after a court acquitted him on a kidnapping charge, two gunmen entered his room in an Albany rooming house and shot him in the head.

Places to Stay in the Catskills

GREENVILLE

Greenville Arms 1889 Inn
11135 NY 32
(518) 966–5219
greenvillearms.com

HIGH FALLS

Camp and Stream Coach House
913 Route 213
(845) 687–7946
cscoachhouse.com

NEWBURGH

Goldsmith Denniston House
227 Montgomery St.
(845) 562–8076
facebook.com/
DennistonBB/

PINE BUSH

Harvest Inn Hotel
95 Boniface Dr.
(845) 744–5700
harvest-inn.com

SAUGERTIES

Saugerties Bed and Breakfast at B&B Tamayo
89 Partition St.
(845) 246–9371
saugertiesbedandbreakfast
.net

The Villa at Saugerties
159 Fawn Rd.
(845) 246–0682
thevillaatsaugerties.com

WALKILL

Audrey's Farmhouse
2187 Bruynswick Rd.
(845) 895–3440
audreysfarmhouse.com

WINDHAM

Hotel Vienna
105 NY 296
(518) 734–5300
thehotelvienna.com

Places to Eat in the Catskills

DELHI

Quarter Moon Cafe
53 Main St.
(607) 746–8886
quartermooncafe.com

HIGH FALLS

Egg's Nest
1300 NY 213
(845) 687–7255
theeggsnest.com

REGIONAL TOURIST INFORMATION IN THE CATSKILLS

Delaware County Chamber of Commerce
5½ Main St.
Delhi
(607) 756–2281
delawarecounty.org

Great Northern Catskills of Greene County
700 County Route 23B
Catskill
(518) 943–3223
greatnortherncatskills.com

Sullivan Catskills Visitors Association
15 Sullivan Ave.
Liberty
(800) 882–2287 or
(845) 747–4449
scva.net

OTHER ATTRACTIONS WORTH SEEING IN THE CATSKILLS

Byrdcliffe Historic District
Glasgow Turnpike and Lark's Nest Road
Woodstock
(845) 679–2079
woodstockguild.org/about-byrdcliffe/
byrdcliffe-history/

Fort Delaware Museum of Colonial History
6615 NY 97
Narrowsburg
(845) 252–6660
sullivancatskills.com/business/fort-
delaware-museum-of-colonial-history/

Hudson River Cruises
1 East Strand St.
Kingston
(845) 253–4951 or
(800) 843–7472
hudsonrivercruises.com

Hudson River Maritime Museum
50 Rondout Landing
Kingston
(845) 338–0071
hrmm.org

Hunter Mountain Skyride
64 Klein Ave.
Hunter
(800) 486–8376
huntermtn.com/explore-the-resort/
activities-and-events/summer-activities/
scenic-skyride.aspx

Knox's Headquarters State Historic Site
289 Old Forge Hill Rd.
New Windsor
(845) 561–5498
parks.ny.gov/historic-sites/5/

Museum Village of Old Smith's Clove
1010 NY 17M
Monroe
(845) 782–8248
museumvillage.org

New Windsor Cantonment State Historic Site
374 Temple Hill Rd.
New Windsor
(845) 561–1765
parks.ny.gov/historic-sites/newwindsor/

Rondout Lighthouse
One Rondout Landing/Hudson River
Kingston
(845) 338–0071
hrmm.org/rondout-lighthouse.html

Thomas Cole National Historic Site
218 Spring St.
Catskill
(518) 943–7465
thomascole.org

Trolley Museum of New York
89 East Strand St.
Kingston
(845) 331–3399
tmny.org

Washington's Headquarters State Historic Site
84 Liberty St.
Newburgh
(845) 562–1195
parks.ny.gov/historic-sites/17/details
.aspx

West Point Museum
2110 New South Post Rd.
West Point
(845) 938–3590
history.army.mil/museums/IMCOM/
westPoint/index.html

HIGHLAND

The Would Restaurant
120 North Rd.
(845) 691–9883
thewould.com

KINGSTON

Armadillo Bar and Grill
97 Abeel St.
(845) 339–1550
armadillokingston.com

Le Canard Enchaine
276 Fair St.
(845) 339–2003
le-canardenchaine.com

Ship to Shore
15 West Strand St.
(845) 334–8887
shiptoshorehudsonvalley
.com

PHOENICIA

**Brio's Pizzeria &
Restaurant**
68 Main St.
(845) 688–5370
brios.net

WALTON

The Rainbow Lodge
440 Rainbow Lodge Rd.
(607) 865–7534
facebook.com/
The-Rainbow-
Lodge-173123309371229/

WOODSTOCK

The Little Bear
295 Tinker St. B
(845) 679–8899
the-little-bear.business.site

**Mountain Gate Indian
Restaurant**
4 Deming St.
(845) 679–5100
mountaingateny.com

New York City

What qualifies as "off the beaten path" in New York City? There are so many things to see and do—the Empire State Building, the Statue of Liberty, the Museum of Modern Art, the Metropolitan Museum of Art, Carnegie Hall, the Metropolitan Opera, Broadway shows, the shops on Fifth Avenue. It's clear that unless your time, energy, and budget are unlimited, you can't do it all; just consider that the city has some two hundred museums and roughly twenty-five thousand restaurants on its eight-thousand-plus miles of streets.

I hope that *New York Off the Beaten Path* helps you discover some of my favorite places, the places that most tourists would struggle to find—the independent bookstores, the neighborhood pizzerias, the neighborhoods themselves.

The fast-paced capital of finance and culture, New York City is also a place with more than four hundred years of history, a place where Dutch farmers and great writers and poets and presidents have lived. The Broadway show *Hamilton* calls 1776 New York "the greatest city in the world," and it remains one of the largest and most diverse metropolitan areas on the planet 250 years after that show's story takes place.

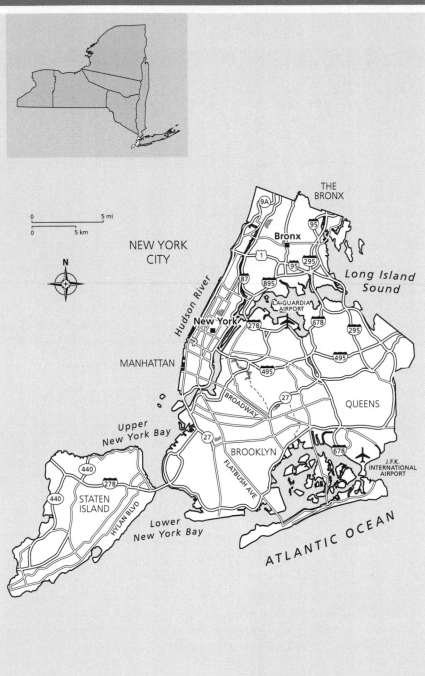

THE
BRONX

9A

Bronx

95

1

87   895   295

Hudson River

LA-GUARDIA
AIRPORT

Long Island
Sound

New York

278

295

678

NEW YORK
CITY

N

0   5 mi
0   5 km

MANHATTAN

495

BROADWAY

495

27

QUEENS

Upper
New York Bay

27

BROOKLYN

678

J.F.K.
INTERNATIONAL
AIRPORT

STATEN
ISLAND

440

278

440

HYLAN BLVD

FLATBUSH AVE

Lower
New York Bay

ATLANTIC OCEAN

Manhattan

Big Onion Walking Tours offers a number of interesting walks led by educators and graduate students of history and culture (212–439–1090; bigonion .com). Priced at $30, the tours cover many areas of the city, from Harlem to the Lower East Side to Greenwich Village, and beyond to Brooklyn, including a walk across the Brooklyn Bridge.

The Central Park Conservancy (212–360–2726; centralparknyc.org) offers walking tours daily, some of which are free. You'll see gardens, woodlands, monuments, and meadows, and you'll learn about the park's history and the visionary design work achieved by the partnership between Frederick Law Olmsted and Calvert Vaux.

Sandemans Tours (212–606–4064; neweuropetours.eu/sandemans-tours/new-york/free-tour-of-new-york/) provides a two-and-a-half-hour walking tour of downtown New York that meets on the steps of the National Museum of the American Indian every Thursday at noon; reservations required. While touted as "free," you will pay for the tour—whatever you feel your tour guide deserves as a tip. The tour includes the Charging Bull statue, Wall Street, the 9/11 Memorial, and many other highlights.

Where to stay in Manhattan can be an issue. The respectable places (and I'm not talking about luxury digs, where the prices are astronomical) are priced considerably higher than comparable accommodations in smaller cities. Many hotels, especially the chains, offer discounts to members of AAA or AARP; inquire about such discounts when you check for rates. Always ask for the best possible rate or current promotions, as this information generally will not be volunteered. Using hotel booking apps like Hotels.com, Priceline, Booking .com, and others may help you find lower rates, especially on short notice, when some hotels drop their rates to book unused rooms.

AUTHOR'S FAVORITES IN NEW YORK CITY

Chinatown	New York Botanical Garden
Economy Candy	Strand Bookstore
Hamilton Grange	Studio Museum in Harlem
Katz's Delicatessen	Theodore Roosevelt Birthplace National Historic Site
Lower East Side Tenement Museum	
Museum of Chinese in America	Una Pizza Napoletana

Bed-and-breakfast inns often can cost less than a hotel room, and for that reason I include a booking service listing at the end of this chapter. Airbnb does tremendous business in the five boroughs, with many property owners renting out their apartments or condos as overnight accommodations, often at reasonable rates. Check there, but check the reviews carefully before you book—you want to be sure the place you choose gets cleaned after every guest, and that you're getting an actual room and not sacking out on someone's living room couch.

One of the more attractive options among Manhattan's boutique hotels is **The Shoreham** (33 West 55th St.; 212–247–6700; shorehamhotel.com). The Shoreham provides guests convenient access to a number of attractions, designer boutiques, department stores, jewelers, and some of the city's best restaurants. The rooms have a European style; they are functional and well laid out, with marble and slate bathrooms and a nice selection of Aveda toiletries. The pillow-top beds are excellent, as are the high-end linens, flat-screen televisions, and superior music systems in select rooms. The hotel has an intimate bar, a superior restaurant, and a fitness room. Especially appealing: the free Internet access for up to three devices. (Most NYC hotels add significant charges for this.) In-room spa services are available. Depending on the time of year, rooms start as low as $134 for a standard queen.

When you're in the Times Square area, stop by the Official NYC Information Center between West 44th and West 45th Streets for free brochures, maps, coupons, discounts, and citywide information from the bilingual staff. For more information check nycgo.com.

Museum-hopping in Manhattan can take you from beyond Battery Park at the island's southern tip all the way up to Washington Heights. In the process, you can get a crash course in the exquisite diversity of this great city, from its

The Big Apple

The city's nickname was first coined in the 1920s, when John J. Fitz Gerald, a sportswriter for the *Morning Telegraph*, overheard stable hands in New Orleans refer to New York City's racetracks as the Big Apple. "The Big Apple," he wrote in his column in 1924. "The dream of every lad that ever threw a leg over a thoroughbred and the goal of all horsemen. There's only one Big Apple. That's New York."

A decade later, jazz musicians, who used the slang word "apple" for any city they were touring, adopted the term to refer to New York City, and especially Harlem, as the jazz capital of the world. The meaning: There are many apples on the tree of success, but when you pick New York City, you pick the Big Apple.

Eat New York—It's a Bargain!

Twice a year, once in winter and once in summer, scores of the city's restaurants—
including many fine-dining (and expensive) places—participate in Restaurant Week.
For two weeks only, they offer three-course lunches and dinners at bargain prices.
(In 2020 it was $26 for lunch, $42 for dinner.) Check nycgo.com/restaurantweek for
details.

Native American roots to the recent influx of Central and South American residents, and the vast wave of immigration of the 1800s and early 1900s, supplying the workforce that built New York's bridges, skyscrapers, and infrastructure.

Of the first-rank museums in the city of New York, the Smithsonian Institution's **George Gustav Heye Center of the National Museum of the American Indian**, at the Alexander Hamilton US Custom House, is the only one devoted entirely to the culture of New York's indigenous people. George Heye, heir to an oil fortune, worked as a railroad construction engineer in the Southwest. In 1897 he bought the first of his Native American artifacts, a contemporary Navajo buckskin shirt, and from that point he went on to develop a collection that encompassed all things Native, from Alaska to Tierra del Fuego. He bought items that had just been made (including, it is said, the clothes off Native Americans' backs) and archaeological finds dating from long before the European discovery of America. Heye founded his museum in 1916, and it opened to the public six years later. At that stage the collector had owned some four hundred thousand objects; today the museum has more than a million individual items.

Throughout the year Native American musicians, dancers, artists, and elders present both formal and informal programs designed to help visitors better understand Native American cultures.

The National Museum of the American Indian, George Gustav Heye Center, Smithsonian Institution, Alexander Hamilton US Custom House (One Bowling Green; 212–514–3700; americanindian.si.edu) is open daily except Christmas from 10 a.m. to 5 p.m. and Thurs until 8 p.m. Admission is free.

More than two thousand photographs, a large collection of artifacts, original documentary films, and individual narratives create a picture of Jewish life and culture from the late 1880s to the present at the **Museum of Jewish Heritage: A Living Memorial to the Holocaust**. The museum is in Battery Park City overlooking the Statue of Liberty and Ellis Island. The museum (36 Battery Place; 646–437–4200; mjhnyc.org) is open Wed, Thurs, and Sun, 10 a.m. to 5 p.m.; it is closed on Jewish holidays and Thanksgiving. Admission is $16 for adults, $12 for seniors and people with disabilities, and $10 for students and veterans. Admission is free for all Holocaust survivors, active members of the military, first responders, and students and teachers through grade 12 in schools in New York, New Jersey, and Connecticut with valid ID.

In the mid-1800s Lucas Glockner, a German-born tailor, bought a lot at 97 Orchard Street on the Lower East Side that measured 25 by 100 feet. The lot was originally intended for single-family town houses, but Glockner erected a six-story tenement with apartments for twenty-two families, as well as two storefronts in the basement. Each floor featured four three-room apartments with a total of 325 square feet each. Only one of the three rooms had windows.

Although 1,100 people have been documented as living at 97 Orchard Street between 1863 and 1935, a more realistic estimate suggests that 7,000 people from more than twenty-five nations lived there during its seventy-two-year residential service—120 people at any given time.

The building at 97 Orchard Street is the first tenement to be preserved in America, now known as the *Lower East Side Tenement Museum*. The meticulous restoration brings the cramped, gritty conditions into sharp focus, and skilled tour guides can answer any question about how people managed to survive (and how many of them didn't) with the bare minimum accommodations for sanitation, food storage and preparation, and other necessities most of us take for granted today.

The museum also hosts a series of weekend walks through the historic Orchard Street area to help visitors learn how different immigrant groups shaped, and continue to shape, the Lower East Side.

All programs at the Lower East Side Tenement Museum (212–431–0233; tenement.org) begin at the Visitor Center, 90 Orchard St., at the corner of Broome Street. Public tours are offered Tues through Fri from 1:20 to 4:45 p.m., Sat and Sun from 11 a.m. to 4 p.m. Tickets are $15 for adults; $11 for students and seniors.

Among the Earliest Arrivals

The country's oldest Jewish congregation, *Congregation Shearith Israel* ("Remnant of Israel"), dates to September 12, 1654, when a group of newly arrived Jews from Spain and Portugal held a Rosh Hashanah service in New Amsterdam. The oldest gravestone in the congregation's first cemetery, at 55–57 St. James Place off of Chatham Square, bears the date 1683. The remains of many Colonial-era Jews interred here had to be moved to newer cemeteries in Manhattan to make room for road construction.

Taxi Tips

If you're looking for the traditional New York taxi experience, skip the Uber or Lyft apps and hail one of the more than twelve thousand yellow medallion cabs in the city, driven by cabbies from some eighty-five different nations. If the cab's center roof light is not lit, it's not available.

One fare covers all passengers. The fare starts at $2.50 for the first 1/5 mile, 50 cents for each 1/5 mile thereafter, and 50 cents for each minute in slow traffic or not in motion. A $1 surcharge is added to rides begun between 4 and 8 p.m., and a 50-cent surcharge is added between 8 p.m. and 6 a.m. Bridge or tunnel tolls are paid by the passenger. Cabs can issue printed receipts, which are especially helpful if you leave something behind. There's a flat rate of $52 plus tolls, rush-hour surcharges, and tip (generally 15 to 20 percent) to transport passengers between Manhattan and John F. Kennedy Airport.

If you've wondered how New York's cabs came to be yellow, it's because John Herz, who founded the Yellow Cab Company in 1907, chose the color after he read a study by the University of Chicago indicating that it was the easiest to spot.

What may be the world's best pastrami sandwich—and a little New York history—can be found at *Katz's Delicatessen* (105 East Houston St.; 212–254–2246), making it a must stop for any carnivorous tourist. Not only are the sandwiches terrific, but the huge dining room also evokes memories of the neighborhood's good old days, when egg creams cost a nickel. You can sit at the table where Meg Ryan and Billy Crystal sat for the climactic scene in *When Harry Met Sally* (you know the one) and enjoy chicken soup with matzo balls, potato latkes, noodle kugel, or just about any other Jewish dish you like.

Do you miss Pixy Stix? How about Teaberry gum? These and hundreds of other candies that have become a distant memory are still available at *Economy Candy* (108 Rivington St. at Essex St.; economycandy.com). Candies stacked to the ceiling, including every Pez dispenser you can remember (and some you never knew existed), gift baskets, sugar-free varieties, seasonal items, and even hamantaschen and fresh halvah make a visit to this crazy candy store one you will never forget. Open Mon, 2 to 5 p.m.; Tues and Thurs, 1 to 5 p.m.; Fri, 2 to 5:45 p.m.; Sat and Sun, 1 to 5:45 p.m. To order for curbside pickup or to check on the availability of a specific candy, email help@economycandy.com.

Before you leave the Lower East Side, be sure to explore as many of its different cultural treasures as your schedule allows. Nowhere in the country is the nation's melting pot more prevalent than it is here in the oldest section of New York City—especially in the growth of the Asian American community center we know as *Chinatown*. About 40 percent of Lower Manhattan's residents are of Chinese descent, and this neighborhood's explosive growth over the last several decades speaks to the strength of this population in New York. For visitors, the treats come in the form of fascinating shopping—often revealing foods and items found rarely in other parts of the country—and the restaurants, where every Asian delicacy you can imagine gets an authentic treatment, based on the traditions of all eight of China's distinctive regions. Outdoor carts and produce stands offer heaps of fruit and vegetables in season,

ANNUAL EVENTS IN NEW YORK CITY

JANUARY

Three Kings Day Parade
Spanish Harlem
(212) 831–7272
elmuseo.org

Winter Show at the Park Avenue Armory
(718) 292–7392
thewintershow.org

FEBRUARY

Chinatown Lunar New Year Parade
Mott and Canal Streets
betterchinatown.com

Westminster Kennel Club Dog Show
(212) 213–3165
westminsterkennelclub.org

MARCH

St. Patrick's Day Parade
(718) 231–4400
nycstpatricksparade.org

APRIL

Macy's Flower Show
macys.com/s/flower-show/

MAY

Five Boro Bike Tour
(212) 870-2080
bike.nyc/events/td-five-boro-bike-tour/

Fleet Week
(212) 245–0072
militarynews.com/app/fleetweeknewyork/

9th Avenue International Food Festival
(212) 581–7029
ninthavenuefoodfestival.com

Washington Square Outdoor Art Exhibit
(212) 982–6255
wsoae.org

JUNE

The Metropolitan Opera Summer Recital Series
(212) 362–6000
centralpark.com/things-to-do/concerts/
the-metropolitan-opera-summer-recital-series/

Museum Mile Festival
(212) 606–2296
mcny.org/museummile

National Puerto Rican Day Parade
nprdpinc.org

NYC Pride Week and March
(212) 807–7433
nycpride.org

Shakespeare in the Park
(212) 967–7555
publictheater.org/programs/
shakespeare-in-the-park

and exotic grocery stores hang herbs, roots, and other natural elements used in Eastern medicine. Find the information you need to begin your Chinatown experience at chinatown-online.com. (If you're in the area but you don't have time to visit the Lower East Side, new Chinatowns have sprung up in Flushing, Queens, and Sunset Park, Brooklyn.)

To learn the detailed and complex story of Chinese immigration, and to gain a sense of the experience of being Chinese in America over the course of

Tribeca Film Festival
(212) 941–2400
tribecafilm.com/festival

JULY
Macy's Annual Fourth of July Fireworks
macys.com/social/fireworks/

AUGUST
Harlem Week
harlemweek.com

US Open Tennis Championships
(718) 760–6200
usopen.org

SEPTEMBER
African American Day Parade
(917) 294–8107
africanamericandayparade.org

The Feast of San Gennaro
(212) 764–6330
sangennaronyc.org

New York Film Festival
(212) 875–5050
filmlinc.org/nyff2020/

Pulaski Day Parade
pulaskiparade.org

West Indian American Day Parade
(718) 467–1797
wiadcacarnival.org

OCTOBER
Columbus Day Parade
(212) 249–9923
columbuscitizensfd.org/parade

Village Halloween Parade
halloween-nyc.com

NOVEMBER
Macy's Thanksgiving Day Parade
macys.com/social/parade/

New York City Marathon
(212) 860–4455
nyrr.org/tcsnycmarathon

DECEMBER
New Year's Eve in Times Square
(212) 768–1560 or
(212) 484–1222
timessquarenyc.org/
times-square-new-years-eve

Radio City Music Hall's Christmas Spectacular
(212) 247–4777
radiocity.com

Rockefeller Center Tree-Lighting Ceremony
(800) NYC–ROCK or
(212) 588–8601
rockefellercenter.com/holidays/
rockefeller-center-christmas-tree-lighting/

many decades, visit the **Museum of Chinese in America** (MOCA) at 211–215 Centre Street (212–619–4785; mocanyc.org). This fourteen-thousand-square-foot space houses many exhibition galleries and interactive kiosks, all clustered around a traditional Chinese courtyard with a permanent exhibition about the experiences of Chinese immigrants. Maya Lin, the designer of the Vietnam Veterans Memorial in Washington, DC, designed the museum, making it as moving and dramatic an experience as visiting the iconic wall in the nation's capital. Open Tues, Wed, Fri, Sat, and Sun, 11 a.m. to 9 p.m.; Thurs 11 a.m. to 9 p.m. Admission is $12 for adults; $8 for seniors 65+, military, educators, and students with ID; and free for children under 2 and visitors with disabilities and one caretaker.

The **Lesbian, Gay, Bisexual & Transgender Community Center**, located in Greenwich Village, is the largest of its kind on the East Coast and the second largest in the world. Among the services offered are a free welcome packet with maps and community information; an information and referral staff on duty throughout the center's open hours; and Internet access at the David Bohnett Cyber Center. The center also runs social service, public policy, educational, and cultural/recreational programs. The **National Archive of Lesbian, Gay, Bisexual & Transgender History** (gaycenter.org/archives/), also located at the center, sponsors regular exhibits, publications, and scholarly research activities, and the center regularly offers arts, culture, and entertainment events, ranging from book readings to comedy shows, theater, dance, and music.

The Lesbian, Gay, Bisexual & Transgender Community Center (208 West 13th St.; 212–620–7310; gaycenter.org) is open daily Mon through Fri from 9 a.m. to 10 p.m.

Back in Buffalo, we saw the house where Theodore Roosevelt was inaugurated president of the United States. Here in the city, you can see where his life began, at the **Theodore Roosevelt Birthplace National Historic Site**. The building that stands here today is a faithful reconstruction of the brownstone row house in which T. R. was born on October 27, 1858. It was built following the former president's death in 1919, replacing a nondescript commercial building that had gone up only three years before, when the original Roosevelt home was torn down.

Open to the public since 1923, and a National Historic Site since 1963, the reconstructed Roosevelt home is furnished in the same style—and with many of the same articles—familiar to the sickly lad who lived here for the first fourteen years of his life. The president's widow and his two sisters supervised the reconstruction, recalling room layouts, furniture placement, and even interior color schemes. The result is a careful study not only of the environment that produced the scholar and improbable athlete who would become a rancher, police commissioner, Rough Rider, New York governor, and president, but also of the lifestyle of New York's more comfortable burghers in the middle of the nineteenth century.

The "new" Roosevelt house stands in stubborn contrast to the modern buildings that surround it, reminding us of just how completely the neighborhoods of New York have changed over the years. The Theodore Roosevelt Birthplace National Historic Site (28 East 20th St.; 212–260–1616; nps.gov/thrb/) is open Tues through Sat 9 a.m. to 5 p.m.; closed on federal holidays. Admission is free.

Book lovers will find bliss at the **Strand Bookstore** (888 Broadway and 12th St.; 212–473–1452; strandbooks.com). With an inventory that includes "18 miles of books" (their count, not mine), the Strand stocks everything from bestsellers to dollar books to rare editions that sell for thousands of dollars. (You can also visit a Strand Annex at 95 Fulton Street and a Central Park kiosk at 60th Street and Fifth Avenue, across the street from the Pierre Hotel.)

Whatever you may expect based on the name, Manhattan's **Museum of Sex** actually dedicates its exhibits to the "history, evolution, and cultural

Over and Underground

When not exploring New York on foot (or splurging on a taxi), you will use the services of the **Metro Transit Authority** (MTA), the most efficient and economical way to get around. This vast transportation network, the largest in North America, includes 665 miles of subway tracks, 6,418 subway cars, 472 rail and subway stations, and 5,725 buses—and provides some 1.84 billion rides a year. People with disabilities can ride the buses comfortably using wheelchair lifts located near the middle of the vehicles.

The subway network does not service Staten Island, but a ferry runs between Whitehall Street in lower Manhattan and St. George on Staten Island. Though the ferry exists to transport commuters, it offers visitors a five-mile, twenty-five-minute ride with majestic views of New York Harbor—free! Visit siferry.com for details.

As of 2021, a single ride on a bus or subway was $2.75; no drivers take cash, so buy a MetroCard at any subway station for a minimum of $5.50 or more. If you're going to be in New York for a few days or longer, buy a timed card to save some cash: A seven-day card for $33 gives you unlimited swipes for those seven days. Children under forty-four inches ride free when accompanied by an adult. For other options, visit new.mta.info/fares. Seniors age 65 and over may also apply for a card that allows them to buy rides at half price; without the card it is necessary to show the red, white, and blue Medicare card as identification.

significance of human sexuality." Its holdings include the Ralph Whittington collection of erotica, assembled by a distinguished former curator of a prestigious museum, and artifacts from the nearby Harmony Theater, formerly known as the Melody Burlesque. Recent special exhibitions have included offerings such as "Superfunland: Journey into the Erotic Carnival," and "Cam Life: An Introduction to Webcam Culture," an exploration of the blurred lines between public and private life. Few museums provide such compelling insights into activities relevant to just about everyone who visits.

The Museum of Sex (233 Fifth Ave. at 27th St.; 212–689–6337; mosex.com) is open Sun, Mon, Wed, and Thurs, 2 to 9 p.m.; Fri 2 p.m. to 10:40 p.m.; and Sat noon to 10:40 p.m.; closed Tuesdays, Thanksgiving, and Christmas. Admission is $14.50. There's a shop, of course . . . and a bar, so leave yourself some extra time beyond the ninety minutes the museum recommends for your visit.

The Search for the Perfect Pizza

With confidence that every visitor to New York might crave a mouth-watering "tomato pie" at least once, here is a guide to the most legendary makers. To many pizza aficionados, the very best is to be found at *Una Pizza Napoletana* (646–692–3475; unapizza.com) at 175 Orchard Street in the East Village, where master pizzaolo Anthony Mangieri makes his dough by hand with no yeast and allows it to rise for three days. After topping his pizza with the finest ingredients, including fresh buffalo mozzarella, fresh basil, and San Marzano tomatoes, he bakes it in a wood-burning oven. The result is a pie that's both rich and light, bursting with the tang of Sicilian sea salt. As Master Mangieri is a purist, you will find only the Neapolitan classics here: marinara, margherita, bianca (white), and filetti (with cherry tomatoes).

The thin-crust pies at *Totonno's*, a Coney Island establishment dating back to 1924 and still run by the namesake family, led Zagat, the *New York Times*, and even the James Beard Foundation to proclaim this pizzeria as the best in New York City. Find it at 1524 Neptune Avenue in Brooklyn (718–372–8606; totonnosconeyisland.com).

Lombardi's Little Italy (32 Spring St.; 212–941–7994; firstpizza.com) lays claim to being the first pizzeria in America, opening here in 1905. Its second location in Chelsea serves up the same Neapolitan, chewy-crust goodness at 290 Eighth Avenue (212–256–1973).

Brooklyn has a pizzeria on just about every block, but *Di Fara*, established in 1965 (1424 Avenue J; 718–258–1367; difarapizzany.com), makes some of the most celebrated pies in New York, according to *USA Today*, CNN Travel, and the *New York Post*, to name a few—and you can buy it by the slice if you're on a sampling tour. Bronx favorites include *Full Moon* (600 East 187th St.; 718–584–3451; fullmoonpizza .com); Staten Islanders are fortunate to have *Denino's Pizzeria* (718–442–9401; deninossi.com) at 524 Port Richmond Ave.

An Act of God

In 1870 the American actor Joseph Jefferson went to a church near the spot where the Empire State Building now stands to arrange for a friend's burial service. Upon learning that the deceased was an actor, the rector suggested that Jefferson make arrangements at a church around the corner. Jefferson is said to have replied, "Thank God for the little church around the corner," and that's how the **Church of the Transfiguration** at 1 East Twenty-Ninth Street got its nicknames, "Little Church around the Corner" and the "Actors' Church." Over the years, grateful thespians, including Sarah Bernhardt, have worshiped here, and there are memorial windows to actors such as John Drew, Edwin Booth, and Richard Mansfield.

While midtown Manhattan may seem like it's all glass and steel, the ***American Folk Art Museum*** cherishes the homey and handmade, too. Founded by a group of collectors in 1961, the museum is devoted to preserving the country's rich folk heritage. Its expansive collection includes paintings, drawings, sculpture, textiles, furniture, functional and decorative arts, photographs, and contemporary environmental works. With pieces dating from the mid-eighteenth century to the present, the collection reflects the museum's increasingly broad definition of the field of folk art. The museum presents special exhibitions and events throughout the year.

The American Folk Art Museum at 2 Lincoln Square (Columbus Avenue between 65th and 66th Streets; 212–595–9533; folkartmuseum.org) is open Wed through Sun, 11:30 a.m. to 6 p.m. Closed Mon and Tues, Christmas Day, New Year's Day, and Thanksgiving, and closes early on July 4. Admission is free.

When "the Hamiltons moved uptown," as the song goes in the Broadway show, they moved to ***Hamilton Grange*** (414 W. 141st St.; 646–548–2310; nps .gov/hagr), now a National Memorial managed by the National Park Service. America's first secretary of the treasury under George Washington lived his final days here with his wife, Elizabeth Schuyler Hamilton, and their children. Take the ranger-led tour of the upstairs rooms above the visitor center to see the city through their eyes, and to understand how the privileged class lived on what was, at the time, a thirty-two-acre estate. Hamilton, a poor orphan from the Caribbean island of Nevis, gained his social status by serving as General George Washington's most trusted aide-de-camp during the Revolutionary War, commanding some of the forces at the Battle of Yorktown, and writing most of the Federalist Papers, a compelling argument for the tenets of the US Constitution. Open Wed through Sun, 10 a.m. to 4 p.m.; guided tours at 10 and 11 a.m. and

2 p.m., and self-guided tours at noon and 3 p.m. Closed Thanksgiving Day and Christmas Day. Admission is free.

Dedicated to highlighting the art and culture of Puerto Rico and Latin America, *El Museo del Barrio*'s collection includes more than eight thousand works of art, from pre-Columbian vessels to contemporary pieces. Among the holdings are the second-largest collection of Taino objects in the country, remnants of an extinct culture from the Greater Antilles; secular and religious pieces, including an outstanding collection of 360 santos de palo (carved wooden saints used for household devotions); and an exhibit documenting the history of print- and poster-making in Puerto Rico from the 1940s to the present.

El Museo del Barrio (Heckscher Building, 1230 Fifth Ave. at 104th St.; 212–831–7272; elmuseo.org) is open Sat and Sun from noon to 5 p.m.; closed New Year's Day, July 4, Thanksgiving Day, and Christmas Day. Suggested donation is $9 for adults and $5 for seniors and students.

Rich in history, tradition, music, and food, Harlem is enjoying yet another renaissance, reflected in strong property prices and the influx of new businesses. A number of companies now offer specialized tours of the area; among the options offered by *Harlem Spirituals* (690 Eighth Ave., 1st fl.; 212–391–0900; harlemspirituals.com) are "Harlem Gospel on Sunday," which includes a church service and a soul-food brunch, and "Soul Food and Jazz." Multilingual tours are available; reservations are required.

For information on some of the lodging options in Harlem, as well as events and tours, visit harlemonestop.com. For dining options in the area, check whatseatingharlem.com.

The *Studio Museum* in Harlem was founded in 1967 as a working and exhibition space for Black artists. Today, its building at 144 West 125th Street is undergoing a major redesign and renovation, which should be completed in late 2021 or early 2022. The country's first accredited African American fine arts museum already housed an extensive collection of nineteenth- and twentieth-century African American art, twentieth-century Caribbean and African art, and traditional African art and artifacts. But this building is more than a museum;

Free for all

Though New York may be one of the world's most expensive cities, a great many fine things are free. Visit nycgo.com/maps-guides/free-in-nyc-things-to-do-in-nyc-today/ and you will find how to get tickets to tapings of live TV shows, free museums, tours, art galleries, park activities, and more.

Key to the City

The first-time visitor may wish to see some of the city's most popular attractions, and for this we recommend the *CityPass*, a $235 value priced at $136 (ages 6 to 17, $112). The pass includes admission to the American Museum of Natural History and the Space Show in the Hayden Planetarium, the Metropolitan Museum of Art, the Empire State Building Observatory, the Guggenheim Museum, either the Circle Line Sightseeing Cruise or ferry access to the Statue of Liberty and Ellis Island, and the 9/11 Memorial Museum. For more information call (888) 330–5008 or visit citypass .com and click on New York City.

it's a center for interpreting its contents to both children and adults. In addition to an artists-in-residence program and an outreach program for Harlem's public schools, the museum hosts numerous workshops, arts and humanities programs, and special exhibits throughout the year. Call or check the website before planning your visit to be sure the museum has reopened in its new space: (212) 864–4500; studiomuseum.org.

Manhattan's only lighthouse—nestled underneath the George Washington Bridge in Fort Washington Park on Jeffrey's Hook—served as a beacon to ships for twenty-six years on Sandy Hook, New Jersey. As the US Coast Guard better understood the dangers at Jeffrey's Hook, where shipwrecks happened regularly, they moved the forty-foot-tall **Little Red Lighthouse** there in 1921, where it continued to operate until 1947. The lighthouse became famous in the 1942 children's book *The Little Red Lighthouse and the Great Gray Bridge* by Hildegarde Swift and Lynd Ward. In 1951, the Coast Guard intended to dismantle it, but supporters (mainly fans of the book) rallied to save it.

Today the lighthouse, with its forty-eight brightly painted cast-iron plates, is a part of the Historic House Trust of New York City. Visitors can climb the spiral staircase to an observation deck that looks out across the river at the Palisades. Exhibition panels at the base provide information about the river. The

Wherefore the Egg Cream?

There are no eggs or cream in the egg cream, though some sources say that the original fountain drink, still beloved by New Yorkers, used a syrup made with eggs and mixed with cream to give a richer taste. But the egg cream as we know it today is a mixture of milk, chocolate syrup, and seltzer—and costs more than the nickel originally charged.

Little Red Lighthouse, in Fort Washington Park at 178th Street (212–304–2365; nycgovparks.org/parks/fort-washington-park/highlights/11044) is no longer open for tours, but you can see it when you visit the park.

The Bronx

Now we come to the only borough of the City of New York not located on an island: the Bronx. In 1639, Swedish commercial sea captain Jonas Bronck became the first European settler to establish himself in this area, and he named the river that runs through this borough, forever connecting his own surname with the land around it.

Today, with a population of 1.4 million, the Bronx claims an impressive number of famous people who have lived here: performers Anne Bancroft, Tony Curtis, Robert Klein, Hal Linden, Penny and Gary Marshall, Rita Moreno, Chaz Palminteri, Roberta Peters, Regis Philbin, and Carl Reiner; athletes Lou Gehrig and Jake La Motta; authors E. L. Doctorow, Theodore Dreiser, Edgar Allan Poe, Mark Twain, and Herman Wouk; statesmen John Adams, John F. Kennedy, and Colin Powell; designers Calvin Klein and Ralph Lauren; and orchestra conductor Arturo Toscanini. Just as many luminaries are buried here, by the way—a visit to *Ferncliff Cemetery* in Hartsdale includes the graves of Ed Sullivan, Basil Rathbone, Judy Garland, Jerome Kern, Joan Crawford, Jam Master Jay, Heavy D, Aaliyah, Oscar Hammerstein, Thelonious Monk, Paul Robeson, and Malcolm X. Tom Carvelas, founder of Carvel Ice Cream, also found his last resting place here, just a few blocks from his first ice-cream stand.

The Bronx's golden age in the 1920s saw the building of the "El," an elevated subway line; Yankee Stadium; the mile-long Grand Concourse (which many likened to the Champs Elysées); and a population boom. Artifacts of that history—and earlier, all the way back to the eighteenth century—can be found in the *Museum of Bronx History*, in a 1758 fieldstone house that looks as if it would be more at home on a farm in Bucks County, Pennsylvania, than in the borough of endless row houses and apartment buildings.

The Museum of Bronx History (3266 Bainbridge Ave. at 208th St., Bronx; 718–881–8900; bronxhistoricalsociety.org/museum-of-bronx-history/valentine-varian-house-history/) is open Sat from 10 a.m. to 4 p.m.; Sun from 1 to 5 p.m.; and weekdays by appointment. Admission is $5 for adults and $3 for students, children, and seniors. The Bronx County Historical Society, which administers the museum and the Poe Cottage, offers tours of the Bronx as well as a lecture series. Visit bronxhistoricalsociety.org for the schedule.

Bronx history contains a chapter with relevance to the history of literature: the home of a thirty-seven-year-old poet, short-story writer, and critic named

Edgar Allan Poe. In 1846 Poe rented a small wooden cottage in what is now ***Poe Park***—East Kingsbridge Road and the Grand Concourse, not far from the campus of Fordham University. (In Poe's day the school was known as St. John's College.) Poe's wife was in fragile health, and the Bronx was a healthier environment than the couple's former home in New York City. But Virginia Clemm Poe died of tuberculosis early in 1847 anyway, leaving Poe in the state of despondency reflected in his poem "Annabel Lee" and other melancholy verse.

Poe maintained his residence in the Bronx after his wife's death, drinking heavily and trying to keep up with his bills by delivering an occasional lecture. While returning from one of his lecture trips, he died in Baltimore in 1849.

Sometimes the world takes better care of dead poets' residences than it does the poets while they are alive, and such was the case with Edgar Allan Poe. Though the rapidly growing Bronx enveloped the ***Poe Cottage*** during the latter half of the nineteenth century, in 1902 the city dedicated a park in his honor across the street from the house and moved the cottage there eleven years later, where it became a museum in 1917.

The Edgar Allan Poe Cottage (Grand Concourse and East Kingsbridge Rd., Bronx; 718–881–8900; bronxhistoricalsociety.org/poe-cottage/) is open Thurs and Fri, 10 a.m. to 3 p.m.; Sat 10 a.m. to 4 p.m.; and Sun 1 to 5 p.m. throughout the year. Admission is $5 for adults and $3 for students, seniors, and children.

Not all of the Bronx was gobbled up by developers, though; today, 24 percent of its forty-two square miles is still green space. Discover some of the borough's six thousand open acres at the ***New York Botanical Garden*** (2900 Southern Blvd.; 718–817–8700; nybg.org). Open Tues through Sun, 10 a.m. to 6 p.m., featuring more than one million plants in fifty separate gardens and collections—a welcome respite from pavement and brownstones. Just down the road at 2300 Southern Boulevard, the ***Bronx Zoo*** (718–220–5100; bronxzoo .com) is the largest metropolitan zoo in the United States, a 265-acre park with more than eight thousand exotic animals, from aardvark to zebra—including a Madagascar exhibit with plenty of lemurs. Open daily 10 a.m., Apr to Oct, until 5 p.m. Mon through Fri, and 5:30 p.m. on weekends and holidays. Admission is $34.95 for adults, $24.95 for children 3 to 12, and free for children 2 and under.

A visit to the borough should also include a stop at ***Wave Hill***, a twenty-eight-acre preserve in the Riverdale neighborhood at the northwest corner of the Bronx. Wave Hill is not wilderness, but a section of the borough that remained in its natural state until the middle of the last century, when it was first acquired as a country estate. Today, it's the only one of the great Hudson River estates within the city limits preserved for public use.

In 1836 New York lawyer William Morris bought fifteen acres of riverbank real estate and built Wave Hill House, one of the two mansions that today grace the property, as a summer retreat. Thirty years later, publisher William Appleton acquired the Morris tract, remodeled the house, and began developing the gardens and conservatories for which the property would become famous. When financier George Perkins bought the estate in 1893, he increased its size to eighty acres, bringing the gardens to their apogee. He added a scattering of six fine houses, including not only Wave Hill but also Glyndor, which had been built by Oliver Harriman. Glyndor burned in 1927, and Perkins's widow had it rebuilt; Glyndor II, as it is known, is still a part of the Wave Hill property.

Today, the attractions of Wave Hill include art exhibits, concert series, outdoor dance performances, and special events. But the star is still the landscape, with 350 varieties of trees and shrubs, plus the wild and cultivated flowers planted in three greenhouses, in formal and informal gardens, and along the pathways of the estate. A ten-acre section of woods has been restored as a native Bronx forest environment, complete with elderberries, witch hazel, and native grasses.

Wave Hill (249th St. and Independence Ave., Bronx; 718–549–3200; wave hill.org) is open Wed through Sun, 10 a.m. to 5:30 p.m. It is closed Christmas and New Year's Day. Admission is $10 for adults, $6 for seniors 65+ and students, $4 for children 6 to 18, and free for children under 6. Admission is free on Thurs.

While Manhattan's museums boast grand collections of artists from days gone by, the permanent collection at the ***Bronx Museum of the Arts*** focuses on the work of contemporary artists of African, Asian, and Latin American descent. It has presented hundreds of critically acclaimed exhibitions featuring works by culturally diverse and under-recognized artists.

The Bronx Museum of the Arts (1040 Grand Concourse, at 165th St., Bronx; 718–681–6000; bronxmuseum.org) is open Wed through Sun from 2 to 6 p.m. Admission is free.

A City of Islands

Look at a map and you'll see that Manhattan and Staten Island are islands; Queens and Brooklyn are on the western tip of Long Island. That means that of New York City's five boroughs, only the Bronx is part of the mainland. However, there is an island that's part of the Bronx: City Island, a marine-based community that feels like a New England fishing village. In 1898 the five boroughs were incorporated into a single entity, known as Greater New York.

And since man does not live by culture alone, the Bronx's Little Italy, Belmont and Arthur Avenues, offers a feast for the eyes and the stomach. You'll find colorful and delicious food in markets overflowing with fruits, vegetables, salamis and sausages, homemade mozzarella, a rainbow of olives, luscious pastries, and breads. Our personal favorite: the mouthwatering sandwiches—the Michelangelo made of mozzarella and prosciutto, for example—at *Mike's Deli* at 2344 Arthur Avenue, Bronx (718–295–5033; arthuravenue.com).

Brooklyn

Not so long ago, few tourists would have put Brooklyn on their to-do list; today, with new hotels and ten restaurants listed in the Michelin Guide to fine dining, the borough prides itself on being a destination.

You can get a postcard view of Brooklyn if you travel there on foot from lower Manhattan, walking across the iconic 1883 *Brooklyn Bridge*, which ranks as one of the world's great suspension bridges. You'll arrive in Brooklyn Heights, an upscale and quite beautiful fifty-block historic district that has been seen in such films as *Moonstruck* and *Prizzi's Honor*. Among the famous people who have lived here are Truman Capote, Walt Whitman, Arthur Miller, Benjamin Britten, and Gypsy Rose Lee.

If you're traveling with children between the ages of two and ten, head over to the *Brooklyn Children's Museum*, founded in 1899, the first museum in the world designed expressly for youngsters. The museum offers all kinds of hands-on experiences in child-scaled spaces like World Brooklyn, where kids play in shops and businesses sized just for them and take on the role of baker, grocer, manager, shopkeeper, or builder. Live animals like turtles and snakes live in the Science Inquiry Center, and in Neighborhood Nature, children get up close to the kinds of plants, animals, and ecosystems they encounter in their own backyards.

The Brooklyn Children's Museum (145 Brooklyn Ave., Brooklyn; 718–735–4400; brooklynkids.org) is open during the school year Tues, Wed, and Fri, 10 a.m. to 5 p.m.; Thurs, 10 a.m. to 6 p.m.; Sat and Sun, 10 a.m. to 7 p.m. (Open longer hours during school vacations.) Closed Mondays, Memorial Day, July 4, Labor Day, Thanksgiving, Christmas Day, and New Year's Day. General admission is $13; on Thurs from 2 to 4 p.m. and Sun 4 to 7 p.m., patrons can pay whatever they wish.

The country's first public Japanese garden provides an exotic refuge in the middle of Brooklyn. Designed in 1915 by Takeo Shiota, the Japanese Hill-and-Pond Garden at the *Brooklyn Botanic Garden* is an urban retreat like no other in the metropolitan area. Visitors enter through an orange-red Torii gate to a magical world of azaleas, pines, and weeping cherry trees, where dwarf bamboo and irises edge a pond inhabited by bronze cranes, and waterfalls cascade gently from recessed grottoes.

Beyond the Japanese garden, Brooklyn Botanic presents fourteen themed and landscaped areas, including the Shakespeare garden, a lily pool terrace, a fragrance garden, an herb garden, and a landscape of native plants and flowers for those looking to learn about what grows best in Brooklyn. Six conservatories house bonsai, aquatic plants, orchids, desert plants, and a tropical paradise, and specialized collections draw visitors to the flowering cherries in mid-spring, the lilac collection in May, and the rose gardens when they bloom in June.

The Brooklyn Botanic Garden (1000 Washington Ave., Brooklyn; 718–623–7200; bbg.org) is open in spring and summer, Tues, Wed, and Sun, 10 a.m. to 6 p.m.; Thurs, Fri, and Sat, 10 a.m. to 8 p.m. Closed Mon, except on holiday Mondays, and closed major holidays. Admission is $18 for adults, $12 for seniors 65+ and students 12 and up with ID, and free for children under 12. Community tickets are available for free for people facing financial hardship.

Explore a different kind of green space in Sunset Park's **Green-Wood Cemetery** (500 25th St., Brooklyn; 718–728–7300; green-wood.com). Not only is it one of the world's most beautiful cemeteries, with a harbor view and 478 acres rich with flowering shrubs, trees, and lakes, but Green-Wood is a cemetery with star power. "It is the ambition of the New Yorker to live upon Fifth Avenue, to take his airings in [Central] park, and to sleep with his fathers in Green-Wood," the *New York Times* quipped in 1866. Among some six hundred thousand people buried here (nearly double the population of Pittsburgh) are Leonard Bernstein; Samuel Morse; Louis Comfort Tiffany; F.A.O. Schwarz; Tammany Hall leader William "Boss" Tweed; Susan Smith McKinney-Steward, the first Black female doctor in New York State; and mob boss Joey Gallo. Guided tours are offered during the Halloween season and at other times during the year. You can explore at your leisure any day of the year: The cemetery's main entrance opens daily at 7 a.m. and remains open until 7 p.m. Admission is free.

At the **Brooklyn Museum** (200 Eastern Pkwy., Brooklyn; 718–638–5000; brooklynmuseum.org), where the third floor holds one of the finest Egyptian collections in the world, the first-floor Steinberg Family Sculpture Garden showcases artwork and architectural details removed from vanished New York City buildings. Here you'll find Adolph Weinmann's *Night*, an allegorical female figure carved from pink granite. Along with a companion named *Day*, she once drowsed against a massive clock at one of the entrances to McKim, Mead, and White's magnificent Pennsylvania Station, built in 1910 and lost to developers in 1963. Five floors of art, including a collection from Asia and the Islamic culture, a center for feminist art, and the work of contemporary artists, provides more than enough viewing for several visits. Museum hours are Wed, Thurs, and Sun, 11 a.m. to 6 p.m.; Fri and Sat, 11 a.m. to 8 p.m. Admission is $20 for adults, $12 for seniors 65+ and students 13+ with ID, $8 for children 4 to 8, and free for children 3 and under.

If you're looking for lunch in the vicinity of the museum, restaurants and shops on Atlantic Avenue serve up some of the best Middle Eastern food in the city. Try the fresh-baked pita bread and baklava from ***Damascus Bread & Pastry Shop*** (195 Atlantic Ave., Brooklyn; 718–625–7070), and olives, hummus, spanakopita, and all sorts of prepared delicacies from ***Sahadi's*** (187 Atlantic Ave.; 718–624–4550; sahadis.com). Then it's lunch or dinner at the ***Tripoli Restaurant*** (156 Atlantic Ave.; 718–596–5800; tripolirestaurant.com), where authentic Lebanese dishes are modestly priced; entrées start at under $12, and the traditional meza, consisting of twenty scrumptious dishes, is $44.50.

The New York Aquarium, on Coney Island, houses more than ten thousand animals, including sea otters, harbor seals, California sea lion, and black-footed penguin, as well as zebra sharks, rays, plenty of tropical fish, and invertebrates like jellyfish and octopus. Exhibits in Conservation Hall focus on the society's efforts to protect marine species around the world, replicating habitats in areas such as the Belize Barrier Reef, the Amazon River, the coral reef, and Lake Victoria. The Aquatheater features a two-hundred-thousand-gallon pool where the animal demonstrations receive rave reviews from thousands of guests.

The New York Aquarium (602 Surf Ave. at West 8th St., Brooklyn; 718–220–5100, nyaquarium.com) is open daily at 10 a.m.; it closes at 6 p.m. Apr through mid-Sept, at 5 p.m. from late Sept through Oct, and at 4:30 p.m. Nov through Mar. Admission is $26.95 for adults, $24.95 for seniors 65+, and $22.95 for children ages 3 to 12; children 2 and under are free. Parking fees start at $18 per car for up to 3 hours.

For a real change of pace on a summer's day, take the subway to Coney Island Station and visit ***Luna Park***, the amusement park filled with rides and attractions to rival the original Coney Island. Opened in 2010, the park features innovative new rides, food kiosks (including good ol' Nathan's hot dogs), games, and even the Cyclone, the wooden roller coaster that delighted fans of

Trees Grow in Brooklyn

The ***Brooklyn Botanic Garden*** was founded in 1910 on the site of an ash dump. It now features twelve thousand plant species from throughout the world.

Coney Island back in the day. For the price of admission, guests get a Luna Card with 140 credits on it to use for rides, games, and even dining any day that season; the credits are good through Nov 1. Check the website at lunaparknyc .com/plan/ for this year's fees. Open hours and days vary with the season and the weather, so be sure to check before you travel.

The *Coney Island Museum* retains the memories of the legendary amusement park. It contains a growing collection of engaging Coney Island memorabilia, as well as temporary exhibits that showcase different perspectives on the fun of the old days. Admission is $5 for adults and $3 for seniors, children under 12, and local residents. The museum is open Sat from noon to 5 p.m. and Sun 2 to 5 p.m., with longer hours in summer. For information call (718) 372–5159 or visit coneyisland.com/programs/coney-island-museum.

Queens

Queens may well be the most ethnically diverse 115 square miles on earth, with the number seven subway line nicknamed "The International Express" and designated a National Millennium Trail by the 1999 White House for its representation of the immigrant experience.

Dine on superb Greek food in Astoria, or Indian food and Peruvian grilled chicken in Jackson Heights. Asian restaurants in Flushing reflect the large Chinese and Korean population, while Sunnyside offers visitors nightlife at a Spanish theater or a Romanian nightclub. In Woodside, you can rent a Thai video or hear traditional music at an Irish pub. Add a population of Italians, Japanese, Colombians, Puerto Ricans, Israelis, Maltese, Asian Indians, and more—and there you have Queens.

Thanks to this fascinating level of diversity, the borough has become an important cultural destination. Some of the metropolitan area's most exciting international art exhibits are hosted at the Museum of Modern Art's *PS1 Contemporary Art Center* (22–25 Jackson Ave., Long Island City; 718–784–2084; moma.org/ps1) in Long Island City (where most of the borough's cultural

A Kind Cut, Indeed

The first tree to be designated an official landmark by the New York City Landmarks Preservation Commission was the weeping beech tree now in *Weeping Beech Park*, 37th Avenue between Parson Boulevard and Bowne Street, in Flushing. It grew from a cutting taken from a tree at an estate in Beersal, Belgium.

OTHER ATTRACTIONS WORTH SEEING IN NEW YORK CITY

American Museum of Natural History
200 Central Park West at 79th St.
(212) 769–5100
amnh.org

Central Park
Between Fifth Avenue and Central Park West
from 59th St. to 110th St.
centralpark.com

The Cloisters (Met)
99 Margaret Corbin Dr.
Fort Tryon Park
(212) 535–7710
metmuseum.org/visit/plan-your-visit/met-cloisters

Empire State Building
350 Fifth Ave.
(212) 736–3100
esbnyc.com

Hispanic Society of America Museum & Library
613 West 155th St.
(212) 926–2234
hispanicsociety.org

Jewish Museum
1109 Fifth Ave.
(212) 423–3200
thejewishmuseum.org

Metropolitan Museum of Art
1000 Fifth Ave.
(212) 535–7710
metmuseum.org

Museum of Modern Art
11 West 53rd St.
(212) 708–9400
moma.org

Museum of the City of New York
1220 Fifth Ave.
(212) 534–1672
mcny.org

Neue Gallerie
1048 Fifth Ave.
(212) 994–9493
neuegallerie.org

New York Public Library
Fifth Ave. and 42nd St.
nypl.org

St. Patrick's Cathedral
Fifth Ave. at 50th St.
(212) 753–2261
saintpatrickscathedral.org

attractions are located). Known for avant-garde exhibits and art that makes people think, the facility includes permanent collections, galleries with traveling exhibitions, a theater, and many modern installations. During exhibition openings, artists who receive free workspace in the buildings open their studios to the public, and in summer, DJs spin tunes on the roof. Open Thurs through Mon, noon to 8 p.m. Check the website for current ticket prices.

"It is said that stone is the affection of old men," said Japanese American sculptor Isamu Noguchi, explaining his own obsession with the medium. View the smooth, cold stone of his pieces, and perhaps you'll understand. They're at the *Isamu Noguchi Garden Museum*, a brick factory building the artist converted for his use in the 1970s. Prior to the museum's opening, he added a dramatic open-air addition and an outdoor sculpture garden. Today more than 250 of his works are exhibited in twelve galleries in the building. They include stone, bronze, and wood sculptures; models for public projects and gardens; elements of dance sets designed for choreographer Martha Graham; and Noguchi's Akari lanterns.

Noguchi's major granite and basalt sculptures are displayed in the garden, as is his tombstone, under which half of his ashes are interred. The other half are buried in his garden studio in Japan.

The Isamu Noguchi Garden Museum (9–01 33rd Rd. at Vernon Blvd., Long Island City; 718–204–7088; noguchi.org) is open Wed through Fri from 10 a.m. to 1 p.m. and 2 to 5 p.m., Sat and Sun from 11 a.m. to 2 p.m. and 3 to 6 p.m. Admission is $10 for adults, $5 for seniors 65+ and students, and free for children under 12. On the first Friday of every month, admission is free.

Balanced on the border between Brooklyn and Queens, *Jamaica Bay Wildlife Refuge* (175–10 Cross Bay Blvd., Queens; 718–318–4340; nps.gov/gate/learn/historyculture/jamaica-bay-wildlife-refuge.htm) has the distinction of being a wide-open saltmarsh and open space in the most congested city in the country. As part of Gateway National Recreation Area, it preserves 12,600 acres, including several islands in Jamaica Bay not far from John F. Kennedy International Airport. The refuge provides critically important habitat to diamondback terrapin and horseshoe crab, which lay their eggs on its beaches. It's also one of the best birding locations in all of New York City, perhaps second only to Central Park. A visitor center on-site has trail maps, bird lists, and other items to help broaden your experience of this remarkable place. Trails are open daily dawn to dusk. Admission is free.

Since the 1920s, hundreds of jazz musicians have made their homes in Queens, including such icons as Dizzy Gillespie, Fats Waller, Billie Holiday, Ella Fitzgerald, and the late, great Louis Armstrong. Armstrong trumpeted and sang his way out of New Orleans as a young man, traveling the world to perform in just about every jazz venue around the globe. For nearly thirty years, however, "Satchmo" did have a quiet place here where he rested, rehearsed, and spent time with friends and family between recording sessions, club gigs, and concert tours.

The *Louis Armstrong House* in Corona preserves the legend's modest, two-story home at 34–56 107th Street in Corona. He and his wife, Lucille, bought the house in 1943, and he lived there until his death in 1971. (Lucille passed away in 1983.)

Long before Flushing Was Flushing

Dutch settlers named this town Vissingen back in 1645; when the English took control of the area in 1683, they quickly changed the name to the Town of Flushing because of its position on the banks of Flushing Creek. Not until the introduction of flush toilets in the 1880s, however, did this name become the least bit amusing—and even then, the new contraptions were known as water closets, and flushing did not immediately enter the lexicon. In 1906, inventor William Elvis Sloan introduced his improvement on the toilet design, the Flushometer . . . sealing the town of Flushing's fate as the butt of countless jokes.

Now completely restored and open to visitors, the 1910 house holds a collection of Armstrong memorabilia, including scrapbooks, photos, and gold-plated trumpets. The home's furnishings remain much as they were during Louis and Lucille's lifetime. A gift shop on the premises sells Armstrong CDs, books, postcards, T-shirts, red beans and rice, and other items.

The Louis Armstrong House (34–56 107th St., Corona; 718–478–8274; satchmo.net) is open Wed through Fri from 10 a.m. to 5 p.m., Sat and Sun from noon to 5 p.m. (last tour at 4 p.m. each day). Admission is $12 for adults; $8 for students, seniors 65+, active-duty military, and children; free for children under 5.

Home of the New York Mets and the US Open Tennis Championships, not to mention two World's Fairs (1939 and 1964), Flushing (a neighborhood of Queens) plays an important role in providing homes to hundreds of thousands of immigrants. Among the earliest was John Bowne, who built ***Bowne House*** in 1661. To get some idea of what the future outlying boroughs of New York were like in those days, consider that two years after the Bowne House was built, the town meeting of nearby Jamaica offered a bounty of seven bushels of corn for every wolf shot or otherwise eliminated from the area. Wolves weren't the only threat John Bowne faced: A Quaker, he openly challenged Governor Peter Stuyvesant's edict banning his religion by holding meetings of the Society of Friends in his own kitchen. He was arrested and sent back to Europe in 1662, but he returned to New York two years later, after he was exonerated by the Dutch West India Company, manager of the New Amsterdam colony.

Now the oldest house in Queens, the Bowne House reflects not only the Dutch/English Colonial style in which it was originally built, but also all of the vernacular styles with which it was modified over the years. Everything here belonged to the Bownes, making this property a unique documentation of one family's experience in New York virtually from the time of its founding to the beginning of the modern era.

In 1694 the Friends of Flushing Village moved their meeting out of Bowne's house to a newly erected **Quaker Meeting House**. By 1717 the membership had grown so large that the Quakers built an addition onto the Meeting House, doubling the size of the original structure. Since then, the house has remained virtually unchanged—a perfectly preserved early American structure still used as its builders intended.

The Quaker Meeting House (137–16 Northern Blvd., Flushing; 929–251–4301; flushingfriends.org) is open for worship every Sun from 11 a.m. to noon. All are invited to attend. Tours are conducted at noon on Sun, or by appointment scheduled two weeks in advance.

Staten Island

A seventeenth-century Quaker attending a clandestine meeting at the Bowne House might seem to have little in common with a twentieth-century Tibetan Buddhist, but the two shared a bond of persecution on opposite sides of the world.

One of the uglier aspects of the Maoist period in China was the annexation of Tibet and the suppression of its ancient culture and religion. Despite some recent liberalization on the part of the Chinese occupiers, Tibet remains an extremely difficult place to visit; and ironically, Westerners interested in Tibetan art and religious artifacts have learned to rely on foreign rather than native Tibetan collections.

One such collection is the **Jacques Marchais Museum of Tibetan Art**. The museum houses more than a thousand examples of Tibetan religious art—paintings, carved and cast statues, altars, ritual objects, and musical instruments—each of which was created to aid in the meditation that is such an important part of Buddhism, especially as practiced in Tibet.

And who was Jacques Marchais? "He" was a woman named Jacqueline Coblentz Klauber who operated a Manhattan art gallery under the masculine French pseudonym. Klauber/Marchais had a lifelong interest in things Tibetan, a fascination that she said originated in her childhood, when she would play with Tibetan figures her great-grandfather brought back from the Orient. She never traveled to Tibet, but she added to her collection carefully until her death in 1947.

With its terraced gardens, lily pond, and air of detachment and serenity, the Marchais Museum creates a sublime setting for the religious objects that make up the collection, representing centuries of Tibetan culture.

The Jacques Marchais Museum of Tibetan Art (338 Lighthouse Ave., Staten Island; 718–987–3500; tibetanmuseum.org) is open Feb through Dec, 1 to 5 p.m. Wed through Sun; Sat only in Jan, 1 to 5 p.m. Admission is $6 for adults, $4 for senior citizens and students, and free for children under 6.

Within walking distance of the Marchais Museum lives ***Historic Richmond Town***, a Colonial Williamsburg–like living history restoration, complete with a general store, an old county courthouse, and America's oldest elementary school. Many of the buildings are staffed by craftspeople working with period equipment. White clapboard farmhouses dot the property's one hundred acres, and a central museum houses exhibits of Staten Island–made products that reveal the history and diversity of New York's least-populous borough.

Historic Richmond Town (441 Clark Ave., Staten Island; 718–351–1611; historicrichmondtown.org) is open Wed through Sun, 1 to 5 p.m., from the day after Labor Day to June 30, with guided tours given at 2:30 p.m. on weekdays and at 2 and 3:30 p.m. on weekends (visitors must be on tours to enter buildings). From July 1 through Labor Day, hours are Wed through Fri, 10 a.m. to 5 p.m.; Sat and Sun, 1 to 5 p.m. In summer, tours are self-guided, with costumed interpreters along the way. Closed major holidays. Admission is $10 for adults, $8 for seniors and students 12 to 17, and $6 for children ages 4 to 11. Children 3 and under are free.

An authentic Chinese Scholar's Garden is one of the highlights at the lovely eighty-acre ***Snug Harbor Cultural Center & Botanical Garden***. It's an environment of wood, rocks, water, a variety of plants, and nineteenth-century furniture in the style of the Ming Period, all carefully composed to create an air of quiet meditation. Other displays include a Pond Garden; Heritage Rose, White, and Perennial Gardens; and a Sensory Garden designed to provide physically challenged persons with a garden experience. The garden, at 1000 Richmond Terrace, Staten Island (718–273–8200; snug-harbor.org/botanical-garden/new-york-chinese-scholars-garden/), has hours that change with the seasons; visit the website for the latest schedule. Admission to all facilities, including the Newhouse Galleries, is $5 for adults; $4 for seniors and students with ID; free for children 5 and under.

The 260-acre ***Clay Pit Ponds State Park Preserve*** allows visitors to step back in time to a Staten Island of two hundred years ago, when epochs of geological history lay exposed here. Maintained because of its unique natural and historical significance, the preserve contains sands and clays deposited here during the Cretaceous period nearly seventy million years ago. These, along with glacial deposits left behind twelve thousand years ago, provide a soil that supports a fascinating assemblage of plants, such as black jack oaks, American chestnuts, and a variety of ferns in numerous habitats, including ponds, bogs, sandy barrens, freshwater wetlands, and fields. The park provides a home to more than 180 species of birds, including fifty-seven different migratory songbirds, broad-winged hawk, yellow-billed and black-billed cuckoo, wood thrush, veery, Swainson's thrush, and eastern whip-poor-will, a species of special concern.

During the 1800s a man named Abraham Ellis and his partner, Balthaser Kreischer, mined clay here, digging it out of a huge pit with shovels and pick-axes. Donkeys hauled it on rails to the brickworks to the southwest, where it was used to make products like paints, dyes, and laundry bluing. When the mines closed, the pit filled with water and marsh plants began to appear, until the area filled with flora and fauna. Today, Ellis Swamp is home to cattails and yellow pond lilies, and it serves as a mecca for wildlife like box turtles, raccoons, spring peepers, and overwintering waterfowl.

The preserve has an excellent printed trail guide, which outlines several short walks beginning at the picnic area behind the preserve headquarters. The preserve (83 Nielsen Ave., Staten Island; 718–967–1976; parks.ny.gov/parks/claypitponds/) is open daily from dawn to dusk. Educational programs, such as nature walks, pond ecology, bird-watching, and tree and flower identification, are offered at the interpretive center, which is open Tues through Sat, 9 a.m. to 4:30 p.m. Fees may be charged in busy seasons.

Fort Wadsworth, first used during the American Revolution, played a key role in the New York Harbor defense system until the early 1970s. It became a National Park site and **Lighthouse Center and Museum** in 1995. Start your visit by viewing the introductory video at the visitor center before heading out on the 1½-mile trail around the site.

The visitor center at Fort Wadsworth (120 New York Ave., Staten Island; 718–354–4500) is open Wed through Sun, 9 a.m. to 5 p.m. Call for information on ranger-led tours. Admission is free.

In 1857, while Alexander Graham Bell was a ten-year-old boy living in Scotland, Antonio Meucci developed the first working telephone, transmitting a human voice over a copper wire charged with electricity. While he was busy inventing, he played host to his friend, the great Italian patriot Giuseppe Garibaldi. The globe-trotting Garibaldi, who not only campaigned to drive foreign powers from his beloved Italy but had also fought on behalf of Uruguay in its struggle for independence from Argentina, worked as a candlemaker on Staten Island. Later he would achieve his greatest victory, as the leader of the "red shirts" who liberated Sicily and southern Italy from Bourbon dynastic rule; this set the stage for the ultimate defeat of the pope's temporal power and the incorporation of the Papal States into a secular Kingdom of Italy under the House of Savoy.

The *Garibaldi Meucci Museum* (420 Tompkins Ave., Staten Island; 718–442–1608; garibaldimeuccimuseum.com) explains all this and more. The museum, owned and operated by the Order of the Sons of Italy in America, the oldest organization of Italian American men and women in the United States and Canada, is open year-round, Wed through Sun, 1 to 5 p.m. General admission is $10.

The oldest cultural institution on Staten Island is the *Staten Island Museum*, founded in 1881 and headquartered in the small community of St. George, just two blocks from the Staten Island Ferry Terminal. Exhibits focus on the art, natural science, and cultural history of Staten Island and its people, drawing from the institute's collections of more than two million artifacts and specimens.

The art collection includes many fine works from ancient to contemporary periods, including works by Staten Island artists such as Jasper Cropsey, Guy Pène du Bois, and Cecil Bell. Also included are pieces by internationally acclaimed talents such as Marc Chagall, Reginald Marsh, and Robert Henri, as well as decorative arts, furniture, clothing, and more. The natural history collections include five hundred thousand insects, twenty-five thousand plant specimens, and geologic, shell, and archaeological specimens. The archives and library comprise the largest holdings of Staten Island history and science you'll find anywhere.

The Staten Island Museum (Staten Island Institute of Arts and Sciences, 1000 Richmond Terrace, Staten Island; 718–727–1135; statenislandmuseum.org) is open Sat and Sun, noon to 4 p.m. Suggested admission is $8 for adults, $5 for students and senior citizens, and $2 for children 2 to 12.

On the south shore of Staten Island is a little-known but historically important community called *Sandy Ground*—the oldest continuously inhabited free Black settlement in the nation. It was founded in the early nineteenth century by freed Black men from New York who started a farming community; in the middle of the century, free Black oyster fishermen from Maryland and Delaware joined them. Descendants of the original settlers still live on Sandy

Nickels Add Up

In 1810 a sixteen-year-old Staten Island farm boy named Cornelius Vanderbilt borrowed $100 from his mother to buy a small boat to ferry passengers and freight across the Narrows to Manhattan. By the time of his death in 1877, "Commodore" Vanderbilt had parlayed that initial investment into a steamship and railroad fortune of $100 million—not bad, even by the standards of twenty-first-century capitalism.

Ground, and the Sandy Ground Historical Society runs a museum and library that examines the life and history of the freed Blacks who settled in the area prior to the Civil War, including its place on the Underground Railroad. Highlights of the collection include letters, photographs, film, art, rare books, quilts, a letter from W. E. B. Du Bois, and other artifacts, such as a can of Tettersalve, a beauty product manufactured by Harlem businesswoman Madame C. J. Walker.

The **Sandy Ground Historical Museum** is located at 1538 Woodrow Road, Staten Island (929–314–4395; sandyground.wordpress.com). Admission is $6. Spring and summer hours are Tues through Thurs, and Sun from 1 to 4 p.m.

Clear Comfort, one of the picturesque suburban "cottages" that dotted the shoreline of nineteenth-century Staten Island, was the home of Alice Austen (1866–1952), one of the country's first female photographers. Her father, John, completed an extensive renovation of the house over a period of twenty-five years. By the time he finished, he had transformed the run-down eighteenth-century Dutch farmhouse into a magnificently landscaped Carpenter Gothic cottage.

Alice lived in the house until illness and financial problems forced her to move in 1945. In the 1960s a group of citizens launched a successful effort to save Clear Comfort, and in 1985, they completed an exact restoration based on hundreds of Austen's photographs. The home became a National Historic Landmark in 1993.

Today the gingerbread-gabled home overlooking the Narrows—the shipping channel for the Port of New York—serves as a gallery for Austen's photographs documenting life in turn-of-the-twentieth-century America. Changing exhibitions exploring themes inspired by her work and times often use images

Overnight in the Big Apple

According to data compiled by Smith Travel Research in 2017, New York City's five boroughs contain more than 115,500 hotel rooms in more than 630 properties.

How can you find the best deals on comfortable rooms?

Your best bet will be to use one or more of the many smartphone apps or websites that offer hotel room choices and reviews. For the best deals, we suggest apps like Hotels.com, Booking.com, and HotelTonight.com or lastminutetravel.com, which collect offers for rooms that remain available on short notice.

Often the later you wait to book a New York hotel room, the better the price. However, this requires a taste for risk-taking and probably shouldn't be attempted at peak tourist periods—between Thanksgiving and New Year's, for example—when many hotels sell out completely.

There's an App for That

Clever developers have created apps that will help you choose the perfect meal for your tastes. Try ChefsFeed or the Scoop (developed by the *New York Times*) to help you sort through the more than six thousand restaurants in the Big Apple.

from the Staten Island Historical Society's Alice Austen Collection of nearly three thousand negatives. A video narrated by Helen Hayes tells the story of "Alice's World."

The **Alice Austen House** (2 Hylan Blvd., Staten Island; 718–816–4506; aliceausten.org/museum) is open Thurs through Fri from noon to 4 p.m. and closed Thanksgiving, the day after Thanksgiving, Christmas Day, New Year's Day, and the months of Jan and Feb. General admission is $5.

Places to Eat in New York City

THE BRONX

Crab Shanty
361 City Island Ave.
(718) 885–1810
originalcrabshanty.com

Dominick's Restaurant
2335 Arthur Ave.
(718) 733–2807
facebook.com/
Dominicks-Restaurant

Jake's Steakhouse
6031 Brdwy.
(718) 581–0182
jakessteakhouse.com

Rambling House
4292 Katonah Ave.
(718) 798–4510
ramblinghousenyc.com

Roberto's
603 Crescent Ave.
(718) 733–9503
robertosbronx.com

BROOKLYN

Convivium Osteria
68 Fifth Ave.
(718) 857–1833
convivium-osteria.com

Frankie's 457 Spuntino
457 Court St.
(718) 403–0033
frankiesspuntino.com

Junior's Restaurant and Bakery
386 Flatbush Ave.
(718) 852–5257
juniorscheesecake.com

Peter Luger Steakhouse
178 Brdwy.
(718) 387–7400
peterluger.com

Queen
84 Court St.
(718) 596–5955
queenrestaurant.com

MANHATTAN

Becco
355 West 46th St.
(212) 397–7597
becco-nyc.com

Buddha Bodai Vegetarian
5 Mott St.
Chatham Square
(212) 566–8388
chinatownvegetarian.com

Chez Josephine
414 West 42nd St.
(212) 594–1925
chezjosephine.com

Distilled New York
211 West Brdwy.
(646) 809–9490
distilledny.com

Gotham Bar and Grill
12 East 12th St.
(212) 380–8660
gothambarandgrill.com

Grotta Azzurra
177 Mulberry St.
(212) 925–8775
bluegrotta.com

Il Cortile
125 Mulberry St.
(212) 226–6060
ilcortile.com

Joe's Shanghai
9 Pell St.
(212) 233–8888
joesshanghairestaurants
.com

Le Pain Quotidien
multiple locations
painquotidien.com

**McSorley's Old Ale
House**
15 E. 7th St.
(212) 474–9148
mcsorleysoldalehouse.nyc

Montebello
120 East 56th St.
(212) 753–1447
montebellonyc.com

Shun Lee Palace
155 East 55th St.
(212) 371–8844
shunleerestaurants.com/
location/shun-lee-palace/

Sylvia's
328 Malcolm X Blvd.
Harlem
(212) 996–0660
sylviasrestaurant.com

Tavern on the Green
67th St. and Central Park
West
(212) 877–8684
tavernonthegreen.com

Turkish Cuisine
631 Ninth Ave.
(212) 397–9650
turkishcuisinenyc.com

Veselka
144 2nd Ave.
(212) 228–9682
veselka.com

**Yonah Schimmel Knish
Bakery**
137 E. Houston St.
(212) 477–2858
knishery.com

QUEENS

Bahari Estiatorio
3114 Brdwy.
Astoria
(718) 204–8968
bahariestiatorio.com

Bella Via
47–46 Vernon Blvd.
Long Island City
(718) 361–7510
bellavialic.com

Casa Enrique
548 49th Ave.
Long Island City
(347) 448–6040
henrinyc.com/casa-enrique/

Park Side
107–01 Corona Ave.
(718) 271–9871
parksiderestaurantny.com

Stamatis
2909 23rd Ave.
Astoria
(718) 932–8596
facebook.com/
AnnaStamatisBilillis

STATEN ISLAND

Bayou
1072 Bay St.
(718) 273–4383
bayounyc.com

Beso
11 Schuyler St.
(718) 816–8162
besonyc.com

Fushimi
2110 Richmond Rd.
(718) 980–5300
fushimigroup.com/
statenisland/

Giuliana's Ristorante
4105 Hylan Blvd.
(718) 317–8507
giulianassi.com

**Killmeyer's Old
Bavaria Inn**
4254 Arthur Kill Rd.
(718) 984–1202
killmeyers.com

Steiny's Pub
3 Hyatt St.
(718) 442–9526
steinyspub.com

REGIONAL TOURIST INFORMATION
FOR NEW YORK CITY

Bloomingdale's International Visitors Center
Lexington Avenue, 1st floor (at 59th Street)
(212) 705–2098
nyc-arts.org/organizations/434/
bloomingdale-s-international-visitors-
center

Bronx Tourism Council
ilovethebronx.com

Central Park Dairy Visitor Center
Central Park West near 65th Street
(212) 794–6564
centralpark.com/things-to-do/attractions/
dairy-visitor-center-gift-shop/

Chinatown Information Kiosk
Canal and Baxter Streets
(646) 998–5520

Fashion Center Information Kiosk
553 Seventh Ave. (at 39th Street)
(212) 398–7943
nyc-arts.org/organizations/437/
fashion-center-information-kiosk

Grand Central Partnership
Grand Central Terminal, South Side,
Main Concourse
(directly across from Main Information
Kiosk)
grandcentralpartnership.com

Javits Convention Center
655 West 34th St., Concierge Desk
Eleventh Avenue (between 35th and
36th Streets)
(212) 216–2100

Lincoln Square Business Improvement District Kiosk
1841 Broadway (at 60th Street)
(212) 581–3774
lincolnsquarebid.org

Metro Transit Authority (MTA)
mta.info/nyct

New York City Parks
nycgovparks.org

New York State Division of Tourism
Albany
(800) CALL–NYS
info@iloveny.com
iloveny.com

New York State Office of Parks, Recreation, and Historic Preservation
Albany
(518) 474–0456
parks.ny.gov

NYC & Company
810 Seventh Ave.
(212) 484–1200
nycvisit.com
This is the official tourism organization
for New York City. It distributes
hundreds of free maps, brochures, and
discount coupons for many attractions.
The organization offers multilingual
guidance and a free copy of the Official
NYC Guide, which is filled with money-
saving coupons for hotels, restaurants,
sightseeing, and shopping.

NYC & Company and I Love NY Times Square Information Center
Plaza between Seventh Avenue,
Broadway, 44th, and 45th Streets

NYC & Company and I Love NY Visitors Information Kiosk
City Hall Park
(Barclay Street and Broadway)

Official Information Kiosk at Macy's Herald Square
151 W. 34th St. between Seventh
Avenue and Broadway

REGIONAL TOURIST INFORMATION
FOR NEW YORK CITY (CONTINUED)

Saks Fifth Avenue Ambassador Desk
Fifth Avenue and 50th Street
(212) 940–4686
nyc-arts.org/organizations/443/
saks-fifth-avenue

34th Street Partnership Information Booth
231 West 30th St.
(between Eighth and Ninth Avenues)
(212) 868–0521
34thstreet.org

Village Alliance Information Booths
(seasonal)
Sixth Avenue and 8th Street
Astor Place Triangle in the East Village at Fourth Avenue and Astor Place
(212) 777–2173
greenwichvillage.nyc/blog/categories/
village-alliance/

TRANSPORTATION
Long Island Railroad
(718) 217–5477
http://mta.info/lirr

Metro-North Railroad
(800) METRO–INFO or
(212) 532–4900
mta.info/mnr

New York Waterway
(800) 533–3779
nywaterway.com

Port Authority of New York and New Jersey
panynj.gov

Staten Island Ferry
(718) 815–BOAT
siferry.com

Long Island

Just as New York is simply "The City," Long Island is "The Island," home to hundreds of thousands of commuters at the end of a ride on the bustling Long Island Railroad or, worse, the congested Long Island Expressway. But Long Island is much more than traffic jams and mega-malls. Venture out along Route 25A and enter the Great Gatsby era, when the families of fortune—the Vanderbilts, the Chryslers, the Woolworths, the Phippses, the Guggenheims—built astounding mansions sprawling over hundreds of acres, earning this part of the North Shore the nickname "Gold Coast."

Further east, of course, the magnificent beaches of the Hamptons beckon, with equally magnificent prices for anything from gas to meals and hotel rooms. Visit Montauk Point when the weather is blustery, when the wind turns the sea a menacing white-capped green-gray, and feel for the fishermen and farmers who still make a living from this sea and this land. Long Island's natural beauty has also attracted a number of artists—light reflects off both the sea and Long Island Sound to make these eastern reaches glow with a golden sheen, especially in the "magic hour" before sunset.

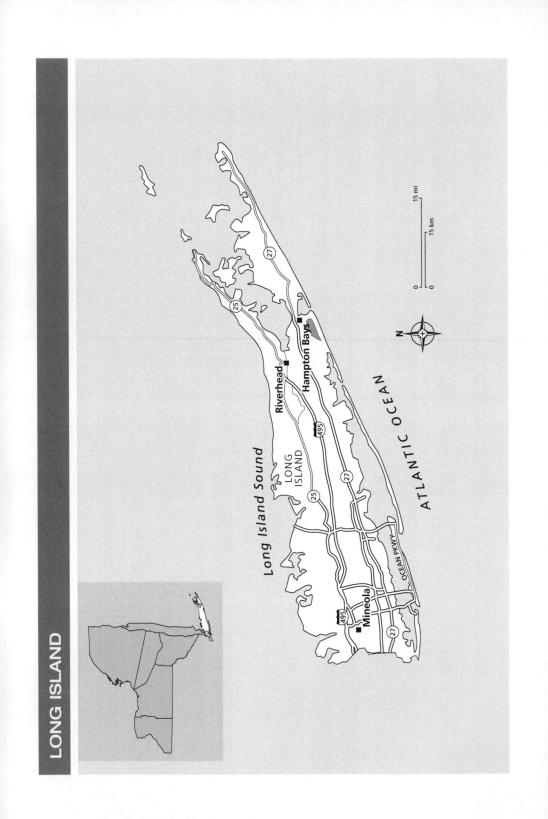

LONG ISLAND

North Shore

Who builds a 50,000-foot mansion for his own personal use? Howard Gould, the son of railroad mogul Jay Gould, commissioned **Hempstead House** in 1912 and lived here with his wife, Katherine Clemmons, after she rejected the first home he built for her, a 100,000-square-foot castle called Castle Gould. The castle remains on the property today; the family used it as a stable, a carriage house, and servants' quarters, and today it serves as the visitor center for **Sands Point Preserve**.

Designed by architects Hunt & Hunt, the 226-foot-long, 128-foot-wide Hempstead House features a foyer that extends 60 feet upward, which in turn houses a recently restored Wurlitzer Opus 445 theater organ. The furnishings used by the Goulds—and the Guggenheims, who purchased the home in 1917—were removed after Daniel Guggenheim died in 1930, but visitors can still see the library with its walnut paneling copied from the palace of King James I of England and its ceiling adorned with plaster-relief portraits of literary figures. A visit to the summer living room reveals stone gargoyles around the ceiling, and other rooms bring in natural light through tall Gothic windows.

While Florence Guggenheim had the mansion sealed when she moved out after Daniel's death, Hempstead House reopened in 1940 to provide a home to seventy-five British refugee children during World War II. Two years later, Mrs. Guggenheim donated the manor to the Institute of Aeronautical Sciences, and in 1946 it became the property of the US Navy, which used it as a training center. Nassau County acquired it for use as a park in 1967, along with 128 acres of the property, receiving the remaining 80 acres as a bequest in the will of Harry Guggenheim, the son of Daniel and Florence. Today this property is maintained by the Friends of Sands Point Preserve.

Two other mansions on the property are not as opulent as Hempstead House, but they are more than noteworthy. Florence Guggenheim had Mille Fleurs built for her after Daniel's passing, downsizing her space and belongings

AUTHOR'S FAVORITES ON LONG ISLAND

Bedell Cellars	Lobster Roll Restaurant
Big Duck	Montauk Point Light
Fire Island National Seashore	Orient Beach State Park
Jones Beach	Sands Point Preserve

for her later years. (Mille Fleurs is a private residence and is not open for tours.) Falaise, the mansion on the beach built in 1923 for Harry Guggenheim and his wife, Caroline Morton, resembles a thirteenth-century Norman manor house and is still furnished with antiques from the sixteenth and seventeenth centuries. You can tour Falaise for a per-person fee in addition to the parking fee.

Sands Point Preserve is located at 127 Middleneck Road, Sands Point, Long Island (516–571–7900 or 516–571–7901; sandspointpreserveconservancy.org). Nature trails are open Wed through Sun from 11 a.m. to 6 p.m. A gate fee of $15 is collected on weekends. Falaise is open for tours from early May through late Oct, Wed through Sun hourly between 11 a.m. and 6 p.m. Hempstead House is open weekends from early May through late Oct, 12:30 to 4 p.m.

Planting Fields Arboretum (1395 Planting Fields Rd., Oyster Bay, Long Island; 516–922–8684; plantingfields.org) has just the one sixty-five-room Tudor-style mansion, Coe Hall, former home of insurance magnate William Robertson Coe and his wife, Mai Rogers Coe, née Standard Oil heiress. The house and the magnificent 409-acre gardens remain much as the wealthy couple enjoyed them in the 1920s, with formal gardens, nature trails, and greenhouses filled with William Coe's favorite collections, including imported camellias. Coe also set up a working dairy and kept pigs and chickens, donating much of the milk and produce to the needy during the Great Depression.

Trees and shrubs commanded most of Coe's attention, and they were the subject of some of his greatest extravagances. He ordered the copper beech on the north lawn moved here from Massachusetts by barge and a team of seventy-two horses when the tree was already sixty feet high. Working with master landscape gardeners A. Robeson Sargent and James Dawson of Olmsted Brothers, Coe created grand allées of trees designed to frame the views from the house, and he established rambling azalea walks. As late as the 1950s, in the last years of his life, Coe planted the rhododendron park, which remains one of the outstanding features of Planting Fields.

From Apr through Sept (except on Labor Day and July 4), visitors can tour Coe Hall Tues through Sun, 10 a.m. to 4 p.m. The fee is $10 for adults, $9 for seniors, $5 for children ages 12 to 17, and free for those under 12. There are fees for parking as well, paid at self-serve pay stations.

Of course, it's not all champagne and caviar, even on the Gold Coast. The *Holocaust Memorial & Tolerance Center* of Nassau County, on the 204-acre Welwyn Preserve, works to teach the history of the Holocaust, the dangers of anti-Semitism and all forms of racism, and the consequences of intolerance. The center hosts ongoing exhibits and has a 1,850-volume library. It's at 100 Crescent Beach Rd. in Glen Cove, Long Island (516–571–8040; hmtcli.org/

museum/), and is open Mon through Fri, 10 a.m. to 4:30 p.m., and Sat, Sun, and holidays noon to 4 p.m. Adults $10, seniors $5, students $4.

Few people still remember whale-oil lamps or whalebone corsets, but whaling was once an important industry on Long Island, with ships setting out from Sag Harbor and Cold Spring Harbor. Today the **Whaling Museum & Education Center** celebrates the skills and adventures of the town's own whalers, as well as those of others who set out to sea in treacherous conditions from Colonial times through the nineteenth century.

The Whaling Museum houses a large collection of the implements used in whale "fishery," as it was known: harpoons, lances, and the tools used in separating blubber from whale carcasses. A permanent exhibit, "Thar She Blows: Whaling History on Long Island," details the impact of whaling on the locality, and how the industry fostered a conservation movement. The museum features the state's only fully equipped nineteenth-century whaleboat, with its original gear, an extensive collection of the whaler's art of scrimshaw, and "If I Were a Whaler," an immersive gallery designed to fascinate children as well as adults.

The Whaling Museum (301 Main St., Cold Spring Harbor, Long Island; 631–367–3418; cshwhalingmuseum.org) is open daily from Memorial Day through Labor Day, 11 a.m. to 5 p.m.; and Sat and Sun, 11 a.m. to 5 p.m. all other times of the year. Admission is $6 for adults, $5 for seniors 62+ and students 4 to 18, and free to children 3 and under.

The **Dolan DNA Learning Center**, the educational arm of Cold Spring Harbor Laboratory, is the world's first science center devoted to public genetics education. Nearly two thousand feet of exhibition galleries present two- and three-dimensional displays, computer multimedia, videos, and other elements to teach visitors about the human genome and what it makes possible. The DNALC (334 Main St., Cold Spring Harbor, Long Island; 516–367–5170; dnalc .cshl.edu) is open to the public Mon through Fri, 10 a.m. to 4 p.m. Admission is free.

Be sure to stop by **St. James General Store**, a landmark listed on the National Register of Historic Places (516 Moriches Rd., St. James, Long Island; 631–854–3740; suffolkcountyny.gov/Departments/Parks/Parks-History/ St-James-General-Store). In business since 1857, it's the oldest continuously operating general store in the country, and it looks just as it did from 1890 to 1910. The shelves are stocked with more than four thousand items, many of which are reproductions of nineteenth-century goods, including handmade quilts, salt-glaze pottery, hand-carved decoys, penny candy, exotic teas, and bonnets. The store is open daily (except Mon) from 10 a.m. to 5 p.m.

The village of Stony Brook on Long Island Sound has it all: a scenic location, a fascinating history, great food and lodgings, museums, and terrific

Hail Suburbia

Built by Levitt and Sons, Levittown, the country's first mass-produced suburb, sprang up in 1947 when the company erected 17,400 nearly identical freestanding houses. William Levitt bought up potato and onion fields on Long Island and built this suburb for returning World War II GIs and their growing families.

shopping. It owes its present-day success primarily to one man: Ward Melville, whose vision helped the rural village successfully transform into a suburban center while retaining its historic integrity. His plan, unveiled to the community in 1939, called for relocating businesses and homes to open the view to the harbor. The shops were moved to a shopping center at the head of the village green, and today *Stony Brook Village Center* houses more than forty of the trendiest shops on Long Island. Up the road, the Three Village Garden Club Exchange features two floors of antiques and collectibles.

Within walking distance of the inn, at 1200 Route 25A, is the *Long Island Museum of American Art, History, and Carriages*. This museum complex houses the Margaret Melville Blackwell History Museum, featuring American decor in miniature in a gallery of fifteen period rooms and one of the country's finest collections of antique decoys; the Dorothy and Ward Melville Carriage House, with its world-renowned collection of more than one hundred horse-drawn carriages; and the Art Museum, with changing exhibitions of American art from the eighteenth century to the present. It also features a 1794 barn, an 1867 carriage shed, an 1875 blacksmith shop, an 1877 one-room schoolhouse, a twenty-ton Beaux Arts fountain, and a Colonial burying ground. The museums are open daily in July and Aug; the rest of the year they're open Fri through Sun, noon to 5 p.m. Closed New Year's, Thanksgiving, Christmas Eve, and Christmas Day. Admission is $10 for adults, $7 for seniors, $5 for ages 6 to 17, and free for children under 6. Admission covers everything on the nine-acre grounds. For information call (631) 751–0066 or go to longislandmuseum.org.

Don't leave town without seeing the working *Stony Brook Grist Mill* (631–751–2244; stonybrookvillage.com/what-to-do-attractions/stony-brook-grist-mill-circa-1751/) at 100 Harbor Rd., built circa 1751 and renovated through the efforts of Ward Melville in 1947. The mill is open in May and June and Sept through Dec on weekends, noon to 4:30 p.m.; in July and Aug it's open Sat and Sun, noon to 4:30 p.m. Admission is $2 for adults and $1 for children under 12.

The Ward Melville Heritage Association, which operates the mill, also offers *Discovery Wetlands Cruises*, an opportunity to tour the eighty-eight-acre wetland in Stony Brook Harbor with a naturalist and see what lives among

Island Items

The largest island adjoining the continental United States, Long Island is approximately 118 miles long and 20 miles at its widest.

Long Island has more than 150 beaches; the largest is 2,400-acre Jones Beach.

King Kullen, the country's first supermarket, opened on Long Island in 1930.

the reeds. Call (631) 751–2244, or reserve online at wmho.org/education-programs/discovery-wetlands-cruise-2/; tickets reserved in advance are $28 for adults, $25 for seniors and students, and $18 for children under 6 (prices are significantly higher for walk-ons, and are cash-only in person).

Central Nassau, the South Shore, then Heading East

The city of Hempstead is home to the *African American Museum of Nassau County*, where visitors can learn about Black culture through education, interpretation, exhibitions, and collections that emphasize the Long Island population. In addition to local lore and history, the museum includes interpretive exhibits of traditional and contemporary native African culture. It also houses a genealogical society that provides workshops for the community, to help individuals learn more about their own heritage and ancestry. The museum provides displays of photographs, artifacts, lectures, workshops, fine arts exhibitions, and music and theater performances to reveal hidden or forgotten history and both past and present-day culture.

The African American Museum of Nassau County (110 North Franklin St., Hempstead, Long Island; 516–572–0730; theaamuseum.org) is open Wed through Sat, 10 a.m. to 5 p.m.; closed on federal and state holidays. Admission is $5 for anyone over 5 years old; $8 for a guided tour and $10 for the tour and video.

Not really in Hempstead but in the south-shore village of Lawrence, *Rock Hall Museum*, a 1767 mansion built by Tory merchant Josiah Martin, represents the high-water mark of late Georgian architecture in this part of the country. The paneling and mantels, as well as much of the eighteenth- and early nineteenth-century furniture and the replica of a Colonial kitchen (the original kitchen was in an outbuilding), came down virtually unchanged to our own time. Josiah Martin's family came through the revolution none the worse for being on the wrong side, and he lived in this comfortable home until 1823. The following year, Thomas Hewlett bought Rock Hall; his family lived in the mansion for more than a century after his death in 1841. In 1948 the Hewletts gave the place to the town of Hempstead—presumably then a larger municipal entity—for use as a museum.

Rock Hall Museum (199 Brdwy., Lawrence, Long Island; 516–239–1157; friendsofrockhall.org) is open year-round, Wed through Sat, 10 a.m. to 4 p.m., and Sun noon to 4 p.m. Admission is free; donations are encouraged.

With 8½ miles of waterfront, Freeport calls itself the "Boating and Fishing Capital of the East." Woodcleft Avenue, informally known as Nautical Mile, developed a reputation as a haven for bootleggers, pirates, and other scoundrels, but today sightseers and seafood lovers crowd the avenue to enjoy its

ANNUAL EVENTS ON LONG ISLAND

JANUARY

Long Island Winterfest
(through Mar)
longislandwinterfest.com

FEBRUARY

Long Island Boat Show
Uniondale
(631) 691–7050
nyboatshows.com/nassau/

MARCH

East End Restaurant Week
eastendrestaurantweek.com

Saint Patrick's Day Parade
Montauk
(631) 668–1578
lisaintpatricksparades.com/
st-patricks-day-parade-listings/

Shakespeare Festival
Hofstra University
(516) 463–6644
hofstra.edu/academics/colleges/hclas/
dd/dd-shakespearefestival.html

MAY

Dutch Festival
Hofstra University
(516) 463–6582
hofstra.edu/community/fest/

JUNE

Belmont Stakes
Elmont
(516) 488–6000
belmontstakes.com

JULY

July 4th at Jones Beach
Wantagh
(516) 785–1600 or
(516) 221–1000
jonesbeach.com

Mercedes-Benz Polo Challenge
Bridgehampton
polohamptons.com

AUGUST

Hampton Classic Horse Show
Bridgehampton
(631) 537–3177
hamptonclassic.com

restaurants, pubs, fish markets, and gift shops. One of the island's largest charter/sport-fishing fleets sails out of the harbor daily in season.

Not far from Bellmore is the **Bideawee Pet Memorial Park** in Wantagh, where Richard Nixon's beloved cocker spaniel, Checkers, rests in peace. More than sixty-five thousand other deceased pets lie in repose here. The cemetery, at 3300 Beltagh Ave. opposite Wantagh High School, is open daily for visitors, 8:30 a.m. to 5 p.m. (866–262–8133; bideawee.org/programs/pet-memorial-parks/).

On Long Island's south shore in Seaford, the eighty-acre **Tackapausha Museum and Preserve** provides an introduction to the ecology and natural history of the Northeast's coastal woodlands. Named after a sachem (chief) of Long Island's Massapequa people, this refuge commemorates a leader who

Hamptons Food & Wine Festival
East Hampton
thfwf.com

SEPTEMBER

Sag Harborfest
Sag Harbor
sagharborchamber.com/events/harborfest/

Shinnecock Powwow
Shinnecock Reservation
(631) 283–6143
shinnecockindianpowwow.com

OCTOBER

Hamptons International Film Festival
East Hampton and other locations
(631) 324–4600
hamptonsfilmfest.org

Long Island Fall Festival
Huntington
(631) 423–6100
lifallfestival.com

The Oyster Festival
Oyster Bay
theoysterfestival.org

NOVEMBER

Long Island Festival of Trees
Uniondale
(516) 378–2000
cpnassau.org/event/30th-annual-long-island-festival-of-trees/

DECEMBER

Charles Dickens Festival
Port Jefferson
(631) 473–4724
portjeff.com/dickens

Holiday Lights Spectacular
Wantagh
(516) 221–1000
jonesbeach.com

A Whale of a Deal

The first pastor of East Hampton's "Old Church," which was built in 1717, received a very generous package for his salary: ". . . forty-five pounds annually, lands rate free, grain to be first ground at the mill every Monday and one-fourth of the whales stranded on the beach."

lived on this land in harmony with its wildlife, its plant communities, and the balance of natural forces.

The Tackapausha Museum highlights the preserve's plants and animal life with exhibits that explain the relationship between habitat groups, the differences between diurnal and nocturnal animals, and the changes in life patterns brought about by the different seasons. A small collection of native animals, housed in as natural a setting as possible, provides an opportunity to see creatures usually hidden from view in their accustomed habitats. The preserve itself incorporates a variety of ecosystems, with a self-guiding trail that takes visitors through the different environments. Pick up the interpretive map at the museum.

The Tackapausha Museum and Preserve (2225 Washington Ave., Seaford, Long Island; 516–571–7443, nassaucountyny.gov/2951/Tackapausha-Museum-and-Preserve) is open Thurs through Sun, 11 a.m. to 4 p.m. Admission is $5 for adults, $3 for children, and free for children under 5.

From the unspoiled wilderness, step forward to **Old Bethpage Village Restoration** (1303 Round Swamp Rd., Old Bethpage; 516–572–8401; obvr nassau.com), a re-creation of a Long Island village, long before there was a Levittown or Long Island Expressway. Starting in the mid-1960s, officials moved threatened structures dating from 1660 to 1875 to this site. Now thirty-six buildings represent the typical domestic, commercial, and agricultural structures of times gone by. Historically attired guides and craftspeople ply their ancient trades, including a local militia. Old Bethpage is open Fri through Sun, 10 a.m. to 3:30 p.m. in summer and early fall; check the website for specific days. Admission is $15 for adults, $12 for children 5 to 12 and seniors 60+; free for children 4 and under.

Like Planting Fields in Oyster Bay, the south shore's **Bayard Cutting Arboretum State Park** opens another rich family's estate whose gracious gardens and majestic trees can now be enjoyed by all. William Bayard Cutting (1850–1912) was one of New York City's ablest financiers, as well as a lawyer, railroad director and president, insurance executive, and philanthropist noted for having built the first block of Manhattan tenements to feature indoor plumbing.

In his leisure time (whenever that might have been), Cutting enjoyed improving his scenic Long Island retreat, located right near what is now the state-managed Connetquot River State Park Preserve. Cutting did not believe in cutting corners, and when he built his sixty-eight-room Tudor mansion in 1886, he had his friend Louis Comfort Tiffany add a few decorative touches. When it came to landscaping, Cutting placed a good deal of trust in another friend, the great Harvard botanist and silviculturist Charles Sprague Sargent. Working with landscape architect Frederick Law Olmsted, who laid out Central Park, Sargent beautified the estate with a variety of trees and flowering plants; azaleas and rhododendrons grow here in profusion. The streams and ponds, with their ducks and geese and graceful little footbridges, are reason enough to spend an afternoon at the park.

The Bayard Cutting Arboretum State Park (440 Montauk Hwy., Great River, Long Island; 631–581–1002; bayardcuttingarboretum.com) is open Apr to Oct, Tues through Sun, 9 a.m. to 5 p.m.; Nov through Mar, Tues through Sun, 9 a.m. to 4 p.m. Admission is $8 per car.

Within a few miles of the Bayard Cutting Arboretum, the village of West Sayville presents its **Long Island Maritime Museum**. The whalers of Cold Spring Harbor were by no means the only brave Long Islanders to go down to the sea to pursue their quarry; here in West Sayville, fishing boats went out into dangerous waters to harvest the more commonplace but nonetheless important oyster. The maritime museum, in fact, includes a restored vintage 1907 oyster house, and has among its holdings the largest collection of small craft on Long Island. A restored boatbuilder's shop illustrates the skill and care that went into the building of these essential commercial vessels. Displays of yachting and racing memorabilia, model boats, and artifacts related to the US Life-Saving Service of the nineteenth century round out the museum's collection, as well as duck and other shorebird decoys, an integral part of American folk art in shoreline communities well into the twentieth century.

Long Island Maritime Museum (86 West Ave., West Sayville, Long Island; 631–HIS–TORY; limaritime.org) is open Mon through Sat, 10 a.m. to 4 p.m., and Sun noon to 4 p.m. Admission is $8 for adults, $6 for seniors and children.

A narrow barrier island off Long Island's southern shore, **Fire Island National Seashore** stretches for thirty-two miles from Robert Moses State Park in the west to Smith Point Park in the east. Designated a wilderness area by the National Park Service, the seashore can be a birding paradise, especially during the spring warbler migration—but any time you visit from spring to fall, you may find herring gulls, yellow warblers, gray catbirds, eastern towhees, song sparrows, and at least four species of swallows. Boardwalks take visitors across vast expanses of fragile sand dunes, giving you up-close looks at unusual plant

Hop Aboard

Two companies offer year-round ferry service across the Long Island Sound to and from Connecticut. *Cross Sound Ferry, Inc.* (631–323–2525; longislandferry.com), operates between New London and Orient Point; *Bridgeport and Port Jefferson Ferry Co.* (631–473–0286, 888–44–FERRY; 88844ferry.com) runs between Bridgeport and Port Jefferson. Both rides take approximately seventy-five minutes each way.

species as well as many birds. Be alert for deer ticks, carriers of Lyme disease, when you're in high grass.

Don't miss the uncommonly pleasant mile-long walk to *Fire Island Lighthouse* (631–687–4750; nps.gov/fiis) on a sturdy boardwalk to see the light from the inside—including its huge, original Fresnel lens in the lighthouse museum. Parking fees (at Robert Moses Park, where the boardwalk begins) may be charged in season; there's also a fee to climb to the top of the lighthouse.

If your poodle has always wanted to sleep in the same bed that Jack Nicholson did, we've got a great place for you: the *Southampton Inn*. (Columbia Films rented the entire inn during the 2003 filming of *Something's Gotta Give*.) The ninety-room Tudor-style hotel offers elegant accommodations, fine dining, conference facilities, a heated swimming pool, all-weather tennis, a fitness room, a game room, and beach access. The Southampton Inn (91 Hill St., Southampton, Long Island; 631–283–6559; southamptoninn.com) is open year-round. Rates for a double start at $250.

In 1954 abstract expressionist painter Jackson Pollock moved with his wife, artist Lee Krasner, to a two-story 1879 shingled house overlooking Accabonac Creek. He lived there until his death in 1956, painting some of his most famous pieces in the studio he converted from a barn.

Travel Light

No cars are allowed on Fire Island. Take a ferry to reach the seventeen communities there: *Sayville Ferry Service* (631–589–0810; sayvilleferry.com/about-haven .php) services Fire Island Pines and Cherry Grove, Apr to Nov; *Davis Park Ferry Co.* (631–475–1665; davisparkferry.com) goes from Patchogue to Davis Park, Watch Hill, and Fire Island Seashore from Mar to Sept; *Fire Island Ferries* (631–665–3600; fireislandferries.com) leaves from Bay Shore for Saltaire, Ocean Beach, Atlantique, Kismet, Dunewood, Fair Harbor, Seaview, and Ocean Bay Park year-round.

Today, at the ***Pollock-Krasner House and Study Center***, visitors can tour the artists' studio and their home, filled with the couple's furniture and belongings, and their library, including Pollock's extensive collection of jazz albums. Also on view is a documentary photo essay chronicling Pollock's artistic development and detailing his working methods.

The Study Center, established to promote scholarship in twentieth-century American art, houses a growing art reference library built around the personal papers of those who witnessed the birth of abstract expressionism.

The Pollock-Krasner House and Study Center (830 Springs-Fireplace Rd., East Hampton; 631–324–4929; stonybrook.edu/commcms/pkhouse/) is open June through Oct, Thurs through Sat, for guided tours at noon, 2 p.m., and 4 p.m.; Sun tours are at noon and 2 p.m.; call for appointments the rest of the year. Tours are given every hour on the hour. Admission is $15 for adults, $10 for children under 12; free for infants. SUNY and CUNY students, faculty, and staff are also admitted free.

Who ya gonna call if you come across a stranded sea creature? The ***New York Marine Rescue Center***, of course. The foundation takes charge of rescuing any whale, porpoise, dolphin, seal, or sea turtle stranded anywhere in New York. Established in 1980, the organization has responded to more than 4,200 incidents of stranded animals, with more than 1,000 successful rehabilitations. You can visit the sea turtles, seals, and other animals currently in rehab at the Long Island Aquarium (467 East Main St., Riverhead, Long Island; 631–369–9840; longislandaquarium.com/riverhead-foundation-rescue-center/), 10 a.m. to 4 p.m. daily. Tickets to the aquarium are $35 for adults, $26 for seniors 62+, $23 for children 3 to 12, and free for children 2 and under. The twenty-four-hour stranding hotline is (631) 369–9829.

Why is there a giant duck on the side of the road just outside the town of Flanders? Built in 1931 by Martin Maurer, the proprietor of a local duck farm, the thirty-foot-long, twenty-foot-high white duck launched an architectural and advertising trend that spread around the world. Maurer wanted to bring

Not Where, but When

The streets in the Hamptons may see as much Manolo-shod foot traffic as anyplace on the French Riviera; for travelers seeking the serenity these seaside villages once offered, avoid the summer season. In spring and fall, prices, crowds, and traffic are all far gentler, and the weather can be sublime. You'll find the traffic all but disappears in winter, though many businesses shut down altogether in the cold season, especially closer to the east end of the island.

attention to his daily harvest of duck eggs and his white Pekin duck breeding business, so he hired a team of Broadway set designers and built this enduring, if bizarre, tribute to the Long Island duck. Today the term "duck architecture" applies to any structure that represents a product literally, from ice-cream shops housed in giant soft-serve cones to a coffee shop that looks like a huge paper cup.

The Big Duck (655 Flanders Rd., Flanders, Long Island; 631–852–8292; bigduck.org) houses a shop run by Friends for Long Island's Heritage, a great place to stock up on duck collectibles and souvenirs. It's open year-round, Mon through Fri and Sun, 10 a.m. to 5 p.m.; Sat 10 a.m. to 3 p.m., with a break for the volunteers to have lunch.

At *Slo Jack's Miniature Golf*, Long Island's oldest, the windmill has turned since 1960. It's the mini-golf course of our dreams, complete with a wishing well, paddle wheels, and a 1960s restaurant that serves up hamburgers, hot dogs, soft-serve ice cream, Mexican food, and local seafood. Official season at Slo Jack's Miniature Golf (212 West Montauk Hwy., Hampton Bays, Long Island; 631–728–9601; slojacksdrivein.com) is Memorial Day to Labor Day, but the restaurant is open Mar through Christmas, and unofficially the course is also open during that period. Both are open daily, 11 a.m. to 8 p.m.

America's oldest cattle ranch isn't out west—it's on the South Fork of Long Island in Montauk. Established in 1658, *Deep Hollow Ranch* puts a different spin on Long Island beach life: a ninety-minute guided trail ride along a lovely stretch of beach designated for horseback riding. Sprawling across four thousand acres, the ranch offers horses for all levels of riding skill, along with English and Western saddle lessons. Pony rides and a petting farm stocked with baby animals delight the youngest visitors. In summer Deep Hollow offers nightly chuck-wagon rides and barbecues, as well as a dinner theater. Teddy

Give or Take a Few Decades . . .

In 1796, on the recommendation of President George Washington, New York State built **Montauk Point Light**, the state's first lighthouse and the first public works project undertaken by the new United States. Washington calculated that it would stand for two hundred years on its location, some three hundred feet from the sea's edge. He could not have foreseen the acceleration in the forces of erosion, however, and today, the 110½-foot tower—the fourth-oldest in the United States—is only 100 feet from the water, which nibbles steadily at the tip of Long Island. Anti-erosion efforts have been implemented to protect the historic structure, which has already outlasted Washington's estimate. The Department of the Interior designated Montauk Light a National Historic Landmark in 2012.

Location, Location, Location

East Hampton's earliest white settlers were Puritans from Maidstone, Kent, who first landed in Salem, Massachusetts, and then went on to found the Long Island town in 1649. In 1660 they acquired from the native Montauk people "all the neck of land called Montauk, with all and every part and parcel thereof from sea to sea, from the utmost end of the land eastward to the sea-side, unto the other end of the said land westward, adjoining to the bounds of East Hampton . . . with meadow, wood, stone, creeks, ponds, and whatsoever doth or may grow upon or issue from the same, with all the profits and commodities, by sea or land, unto the aforesaid inhabitants of East Hampton, their heirs and assigns, forever."

The price: £30 4s. 8d. sterling; in today's currency, approximately $1,000.

Roosevelt camped here with his Rough Riders after the Spanish-American War. You'll find the ranch three miles east of Montauk Village on Route 27, in Suffolk County Park (631–668–2744; deephollowranch.com).

You might suspect that it's the celebrity clientele, such as Billy Joel and Paul Simon, that gets the homey **Lobster Roll Restaurant** (1980 Montauk Hwy., Amagansett, Long Island; 631–267–3740; facebook.com/LunchLobster Roll/) so much ink in major publications like *Gourmet* magazine and the *New York Times*. But this place that many locals simply call "Lunch" (for the outsized sign on the roof) is an institution that gets consistently high marks for its fresh seafood, including salmon burgers and, of course, the wonderfully unpretentious sandwich of fresh lobster meat, chopped celery, and mayo served on a hot-dog bun. The Lobster Roll serves lunch and dinner daily in summer, from 11:30 a.m. to 8 p.m.

If you're looking for peace and quiet, beautiful beaches, or simply a taste of island life, take a short ferry ride to **Shelter Island**, cradled between the North and South forks of Long Island. The car ferries leave from Greenport on the North Fork and North Haven on the South Shore. The Nature Conservancy owns nearly one-third of the eight-thousand-acre island, ensuring that this portion, at least, will remain unspoiled. Find information for the North Ferry at northferry.com, and for the South Ferry at southferry.com.

In 1871 a small group of Methodist clergy and laymen from Brooklyn purchased land on a bluff overlooking Shelter Island Sound. American landscape architect Robert Morris Copeland laid out plans for a camp meeting place, and four years later the Union Church, intended by Copeland to be the camp's visual and social center, came to fruition in a natural amphitheater that served as an open-air preacher's stand. Over the years, residents built 141 buildings in a variety of styles, from steep-gabled, delicately trimmed cottages to Stick, Queen Anne, and Colonial Revival homes. The *Shelter Island Heights Historic District* retains the original character of the property, while maintaining a sensitivity to the nineteenth-century American ideal of respect for the natural landscape.

Four trails on the Nature Conservancy's *Mashomack Preserve* lead into the wilderness for nature study and birding, varying in length from 1½ to 11 miles. A barrier-free braille trail for the visually impaired creates an unusual hiking opportunity here. Visit nature.org/en-us/get-involved/how-to-help/places-we-protect/long-island-mashomack/ for a trail map and other information.

In Shelter Island Heights, you can rent bicycles at *Piccozzi's Bike Shop* (631–749–0045; jwpiccozzi.com), grab a bite at *The Dory Restaurant* (185 N. Ferry Rd.; 631–749–8300; facebook.com/thedorysi/), have a lovely meal at the *Chequit Inn* (23 Grand Ave.; 631–749–0018), or stop in at one of the other restaurants. The Chequit Inn also has guest rooms, as do a number of other places, including the *Beech Tree House* (1 South Ferry Rd.; 631–749–4252), which has suites with full kitchens, and *Sunset Beach Hotel* (35 Shore Rd.; 631–749–2001; sunsetbeachli.com), overlooking Shelter Island Sound. For more information contact the Shelter Island Chamber of Commerce (877–893–2290; shelterislandchamber.org).

The North Fork

Far less crowded than the South Fork and loaded with farm markets, wineries, and lovely scenery, Long Island's North Fork offers a completely different experience from the southern edge of the island and its high-flown residents and guests.

Cutchogue's Village Green on Route 25 is home to numerous historic buildings, including the beautifully preserved *1649 Old House*, a National Historic Landmark and the oldest structure on Long Island. Among the outstanding features of this English-style dwelling: the pilastered top chimney and the three-part casement window frames.

Take time to wander through the nearby *Old Burying Ground*, where many of the tombstones date back to the early 1700s and provide fascinating insight into the area's rich history. Among the stones:

REV. THOMAS PAYNE

B. 1723 / D. 10–15–1766

AH CRUEL DEATH WHY DIDST THOU STRIKE SO QUICK

THAT GUIDE THE SOULS AND HEALER OF THE SICK

THEM BY TO PRIZE SUCH USEFUL DEATH DOTH TEACH.

The Old House is owned and maintained by the Old House Society, Inc., and managed by the Cutchogue–New Suffolk Historical Council (631–734–6977; cutchoguenewsuffolkhistory.org/timeline/the-old-house-2/).

If you're a wine enthusiast, the North Fork becomes a playground, with many tasty vintages that beg to be sampled. Once you pass through Cutchogue, you'll see fields of grapes and one winery after another: *Bedell Cellars* (36225 Main Rd., Cutchogue; 631–734–7537; bedellcellars.com) may be a familiar name as the grand master of Long Island wines, with a long history and the highest-scoring red blend of any eastern American wine (its famous Musée). *Castello di Borghese* (17150 Rte. 48, Cutchogue; 631–734–5111; castellodi borghese.com), Long Island's first vineyard, makes the most of the climate's similarity to Bordeaux in France and grows French grape varietals; *Jamesport Vineyards* (631–722–5256; jamesportwines.com) features a restaurant serving light fare, including wood-fired pizzas to pair with their wines; and *Lenz Winery* in Peconic (631–734–6010; lenzwine.com) is so confident in its wines that it invites professional critics to its tasting room annually to blind-taste their wines alongside fine French vintages. Lenz wines always receive high marks, so chances are you will find one you like here as well.

If you abhor spitting out a good wine (and would prefer to sip Long Island's splendid wines), safety would dictate that you leave your car at home and travel from vineyard to vineyard on the *North Fork Trolley* (631–369–3031; northforktrolley.com) or take advantage of the services of *Vintage Tours* (631–765–4689; vintagetour1.com). Proprietor Jo-Ann Perry is a font of knowledge about both wine and local lore. The basic tour begins at 11:30 a.m. (in her air-conditioned van), and tours last from four to five hours, taking you to three wineries and even providing a picnic lunch.

Since 1976, folks have stopped by the unprepossessing *Hellenic Snack Bar and Restaurant* (631–477–0138; thehellenic.com), at 5145 Main Road (Route 25) in East Marion, for some of the best Greek food on Long Island. Among the house specialties: dolmades (stuffed grape leaves), spanakopita (spinach pie), moussaka, and fried calamari. The desserts are all homemade, and fresh lamb, chicken, and pork are prepared on the outdoor rotisserie. The Hellenic is open for three meals daily.

Many more wineries await along the road to Orient Point at the end of the island. Your last stop must be *Orient Beach State Park*—not only because of the vanishing-point view from here as you look out over the Atlantic Ocean, but because this is where Long Island's North Fork ends. Orient Beach borders a maritime forest full of aromatic red cedar, so breathe deep and stop to scan the saltwater marsh for great egret, black-crowned night heron, and osprey before you head back down the island for your night's rest.

REGIONAL TOURIST INFORMATION ON LONG ISLAND

Discover Long Island
330 Motor Pkwy.
Hauppauge
(631) 951–3900
discoverlongisland.com

East Hampton Chamber of Commerce
58B Park Pl.
East Hampton
(631) 324–0362
easthamptonchamber.com

Greater Westhampton Chamber of Commerce
7 Glovers Ln.
Westhampton Beach
(631) 288–3337
westhamptonchamber.org

Montauk Chamber of Commerce
742 Montauk Hwy.
Montauk
(631) 668–2428
montaukchamber.com

Sag Harbor Chamber of Commerce
8 Wharf St.
Sag Harbor
(631) 725–0011
sagharborchamber.com

Shelter Island Chamber of Commerce
47 W. Neck Rd.
Shelter Island
(631) 749–0399
shelterislandchamber.org

Southampton Chamber of Commerce
76 Main St.
Southampton
(631) 283–0402
southamptonchamber.com

Places to Stay on Long Island

EAST HAMPTON

Huntting Inn
94 Main St.
(631) 324–0410
thepalm.com/huntting-inn/

EAST MARION

Arbor View House Bed and Breakfast
8900 Main Rd.
(631) 477–8440
arborviewhouse.com

MONTAUK

Gurney's Montauk Resort & Seawater Spa
290 Old Montauk Hwy.
(631) 668–2345
gurneysresorts.com

QUOGUE

Quogue Club at Hallock House
47 Quogue St.
(631) 653–0100
quogueclub.com

SHELTER ISLAND

The Pridwin
81 Shore Rd.
(631) 749–0476
pridwin.com

Ram's Head Inn
108 Ram Island Dr.
(631) 749–0811
theramsheadinn.com

Sunset Beach
35 Shore Rd.
(631) 749–2001
sunsetbeachli.com

SOUTHAMPTON

1708 House
128 Main St.
(631) 287–1708
1708house.com

Southampton Inn
91 Hill St.
(631) 283–6500
southamptoninn.com

OTHER ATTRACTIONS WORTH SEEING ON LONG ISLAND

American Merchant Marine Museum
300 Steamboat Rd.
Kings Point
(516) 726–6047
usmma.edu/museum

Belmont Park Race Track
2150 Hempstead Tpke.
Belmont
(844) 697–2238
nyra.com/belmont/

Hofstra University Museum
112 Hofstra University
Hempstead
(516) 463–5672
hofstra.edu/community/museum/

Long Island Children's Museum
11 Davis Ave.
Garden City
(516) 224–5800
licm.org

Montauk Point Lighthouse and Museum
Montauk Point State Park
2000 Montauk Point Hwy.
(631) 668–2544
montauklighthouse.com

Nassau County Museum of Art
One Museum Dr.
Roslyn Harbor
(516) 484–9338
nassaumuseum.org

Old Westbury Gardens
71 Old Westbury Rd.
Old Westbury
(516) 333–0048
oldwestburygardens.org

Sagamore Hill National Historic Site
20 Sagamore Hill Rd.
Oyster Bay
(516) 922–4788
nps.gov/sahi

Vanderbilt Museum, Mansion, and Planetarium
180 Little Neck Rd.
Centerport
(631) 854–5579
vanderbiltmuseum.org

Walt Whitman Birthplace State Historic Site
246 Old Walt Whitman Rd.
Huntington Station
(631) 427–5247
waltwhitman.org

Places to Eat on Long Island

BRIDGEHAMPTON

Bobby Van's Steakhouse
2393 Montauk Hwy.
(631) 537–0590
bobbyvansbridgehampton
.com

EAST HAMPTON

The Palm
94 Main St., Ste. 1800
(631) 324–0411
thepalm.com

EASTPORT

Trumpets on the Bay
58 South Bay Ave.
(631) 325–2900
trumpetsonthebay.com

MONTAUK

The Dock Bar & Grill
482 West Lake Dr.
(631) 668–9778
thedockmontauk.com

Harvest on Fort Pond
11 South Emery St.
(631) 668–5574
harvestfortpond.com

Surfside Inn
Old Montauk Hwy.
(631) 668–5958
surfsideinnmontauk.com

SAG HARBOR

The American Hotel
45 Main St. #3012
(631) 725–3535
theamericanhotel.com

SHELTER ISLAND

Ram's Head Inn
108 Ram Island Dr.
(631) 749–0811
theramsheadinn.com

SOUTHAMPTON

Le Chef
75 Jobs Ln.
(631) 283–8581
lechefbistro.com

Southampton Publick House
62 Jobs Ln.
(631) 283–2800
publick.com

WESTHAMPTON BEACH

The Claddagh Restaurant & Tap Room
141 Montauk Hwy.
(631) 998–0609
thecladdaghwhb.com

Starr Boggs
6 Parlato Dr.
(631) 288–3500
starrboggs.com

Index